Gui

George Lennoty
8461216

ISBN	AUTHOR	TITLE
0-07-056578-3	Sherman	*The CD-ROM Handbook*
0-07-039006-1	Lusardi	*Database Experts' Guide to SQL*
	(hardcover)	
0-07-039002-9	(softcover)	
0-07-016609-6	DeVita	*Database Experts' Guide to FOCUS*
	(hardcover)	
0-07-016604-8	(softcover)	
0-07-036488-5	Larson	*Database Experts' Guide to Database 2*
	(hardcover)	
0-07-023267-9	(softcover)	
0-07-048550-X	Parsons	*Database Experts' Guide to IDEAL*
0-07-008207-3	Brown	*Database Experts' Guide to SAS/DB2*
0-07-065120-5	Tran	*Introduction to DB2 Programming*
0-07-000474-9	Adrian	*The Workstation Data Link*
0-07-057336-0	Simpson, Casey	*Developing Effective User Documentation*
0-07-007248-5	Brathwaite	*Analysis, Design, and Implementation of Data Dictionaries*
0-07-035119-8	Knightson	*Standards for Open Systems Interconnection*
0-07-044938-4	McClain	*VM and Departmental Computing*
	(hardcover)	
0-07-044939-2	(softcover)	
0-07-046302-6	Nemzow	*Keeping the Link*
0-07-038006-6	Lipton	*User Guide to FOCUS™*
0-07-057296-8	Simon	*How to Be a Successful Computer Consultant*
0-07-016188-7	Dayton	*Integrating Digital Services*
	(Ranade, Ed.)	
0-07-002673-4	Azevedo	*ISPF: The Strategic Dialog Manager*
	(Ranade Series)	
0-07-050054-1	Piggott	*CICS: A Practical Guide to System Fine Tuning*
	(Ranade Series)	
0-07-043152-3	Morgan, McGilton	*Introducing UNIX™ System V*
0-07-050686-8	Prasad	*IBM Mainframes*
	(Ranade Series)	
0-07-065087-X	Towner	*IDMS/R Cookbook*
	(Ranade Series)	
0-07-062879-3	Tare (hardcover)	*UNIX™ Utilities*
0-07-062884-X	(softcover)	
0-07-045001-3	McGilton, Morgan	*Introducing the UNIX™ System*
0-07-062295-7	Su	*Database Computers*
0-07-041920-5	Milenkovic	*Operating Systems Concepts and Design*
0-07-010829-3	Ceri/Pelagatti	*Distributed Databases*

Guide to DB2 and SQL/DS

Fritz Wipper
IMI Systems Inc.

McGraw-Hill Publishing Company

New York St. Louis San Francisco Auckland Bogotá
Caracas Hamburg Lisbon London Madrid Mexico
Milan Montreal New Delhi Oklahoma City
Paris San Juan São Paulo Singapore
Sydney Tokyo Toronto

Library of Congress Cataloging-in-Publication Data

Wipper, Fritz.
  Guide to DB2 & SQL/DS.

  Bibliography: p.
  Includes index.
  1. Data base management.   2. IBM Database 2
(Computer system)   3. SQL/DS (Computer program)
I. Title.   II. Title: DB2 and SQL/DS.
QA76.9.D3W585 1989   005.74   89-2644
ISBN 0-07-055170-7

IBM is a registered trademark of the International Business
Machines Corporation.

SQL/DS and DB2 are trademarks of the International Business
Machines Corporation.

LOTUS is a trademark of the Lotus Development Corporation.

ORACLE is a trademark of the Oracle Corporation.

SAS is a trademark of the SAS Institute.

INGRES is a trademark of the Relational Technologies
Corporation.

1234567890   DOC/DOC   8965432109

ISBN 0-07-055170-7

*The editors for this book were Theron Shreve and Kay Magome,
and the production supervisor was Richard A. Ausburn.*

Printed and bound by R. R. Donnelley & Sons Company.

*For more information about other McGraw-Hill materials,
call 1-800-2-MCGRAW in the United States. In other
countries, call your nearest McGraw-Hill office.*

For Eleonora and Verena

Contents

Foreword xi

Preface xiii

Introduction   1

    From System R to DB2 and SQL/DS   1

Chapter 1. Evolution and Philosophy   5

    Introduction   5
    Process Centered Data Management   5
    Data Centered Data Management   11

Chapter 2. Data Models   15

    Introduction   15
    The Hierarchical Model   17
    The Network Model   20
    The Relational Model   23

Chapter 3. Relational Data Model   27

    Introduction   27
    Relational Operators   27
    UNION   28
    INTERSECTION   29
    DIFFERENCE   31
    Cartesian Product   33
    PROJECTION   34
    SELECT   36
    JOIN   37
    Referential Integrity   39
    Normalization   41
    General Considerations   49

Chapter 4. System Components - Overview   51

    Introduction   51
    SQL/DS Objects   50
    DB2 Objects   54
    Catalog Tables   58

Chapter 5. Data Definition   59

Introduction   59
REFERENTIAL INTEGRITY   59
Table   65
Delete Rules   74
Creating Tables   74
View   84

Chapter 6. SQL/DS Data Definition   93

Introduction   93
DBSPACE   93
Storage Pools   103
Utilities   108

Chapter 7. DB2 Data Definition Language   113

Introduction   113
Table   113
Storage Group   116
Database   117
Buffer Pool   118
Table Space   118
Simple Table Space   119
Table Space Creation   126
Index Space   131
Index   131
Monitoring Indexes   136
Utilities   138

Chapter 8. Data Retrieval-Simple Query Structures   145

Introduction   145
SELECT Statement   146
SELECT Clause   146
FROM Clause   150
WHERE Clause   154
Ordering Rows of a Result Table - ORDER BY   158
Summary - SELECT Statement - General Format   161

Chapter 9. Data Retrieval - Advanced Query Structures   163

Introduction   163
Special Comparison Operators   164
JOIN Operations   174
UNION   177
Subqueries   182
EXISTS Keyword   189
Correlated Subqueries   190
SQL Expressions   192

Built-in Column Functions   196
Built-in Scalar Functions for Data Manipulation   199
Built-in Scalar Functions for Date/Time Operations   205
The GROUP BY Clause   214
The HAVING Clause   216
Summary - SELECT Statement   217
Representation of Manipulation Schemes Using SQL   218

Chapter 10. SQL Data Manipulation Language   225

Introduction   225
INSERT Statement   226
Copying Data from Other Tables   230
INSERT Statement   231
UPDATE Statement   233
UPDATE Statement -General Format   236
DELETE Statement   238
DELETE Statement - General Format   240

Chapter 11. SQL Language Elements for Security   241

Introduction   241
Accessing the SQL/DS Databases   242
RESOURCE Authority Under SQL/DS   243
Accessing DB2   244
Privileges Held by the Creators of Objects   245
The GRANT Statement   245
The GRANT Statement - General Format   249
Querying Catalog Tables   249

Appendix: DB2-SQL/DS Comparison   251

Bibliography   261

Index   263

Foreword

As a major project-oriented computer consulting and systems integration company, IMI Systems has a long-standing involvement in relational database systems. This book is an outgrowth of that experience.

This manuscript was written by Fritz Wipper, one of IMI's senior consultants for data systems. His expertise is based on more than a decade of theoretical study and the practical development of relational database systems during his career with IMI as well as with major multinational firms in Germany, Italy and the United States. He has contributed significantly to the design and implementation of numerous application systems utilizing DB2 and SQL/DS. For several years Fritz served on the Data Base Administration committee of IBM's European Guide Group. Fritz currently resides in the United States and is responsible for the development of an integrated marketing decision support system.

This book was initially prepared by Mr. Wipper as training material in support of an SQL/DS-DB2 course presented by IMI. It has been expanded and rewritten as an introduction to data bases, in general, and relational data base products, in particular. We believe that both novices and experienced database users can benefit from this book. Subsequent editions will be prepared to keep the information current with future IBM releases.

We would like to thank Richard Schasberger and Alison Chandler for their role in bringing forth this book and Bill Goldschein for editing the manuscript as well as preparing and producing the book for publication. We are especially grateful to Fritz Wipper, who has done superior work both as a consultant and as an author.

Robert S. Forman
President
IMI Systems, Inc.

Preface

My first contact with relational database systems was in mid-1970 at the University of Köln. I was asked to prepare a paper on security features of hierarchical network and relational database systems. Because of the overall lack of documentation available to the public for the first relational prototypes, this task was presented to me at that time with an almost impossible challenge. Today, more than a decade later, many relational products for the mainframe and personal computer environments are available and the bookshelves are filled with literature on various aspects of relational systems. So why add another book on relational databases? My experience has shown that many users are simply overwhelmed by the amount of detailed information available in the literature and especially in IBM manuals.

My intention is to give the user a comprehensive view of relational systems, in general, and IBM's relational database systems DB2 and SQL/DS in particular.

The primary audience for this book is end-users and programmers in support of Information Centers and Decision Support Systems who are required to extract information for reporting and analytical purposes out of centralized strategic relational databases. However, their managers will find knowledge of the data storage and query issues involved equally valuable.

There are many people who deserve credit for helping to bring about this book. I am particularly indebted to Bill Goldschein who showed a lot of patience with me and the skill to make the manuscript look like a book. Special thanks also to Alan Cole for the time he contributed to read and critique the manuscript. Their comments helped make the text more readable.

Fritz Wipper

Introduction

From System R to DB2 and SQL/DS

The work of E. R. Codd, starting in 1970, laid the foundations of the relational model. Based on this work, IBM developed a number of relational systems and corresponding query languages. More than a decade later, in 1982, SQL/DS, the first relational IBM product, was released. SQL/DS was followed only a year later by DB2, a similar product for the MVS operating environment.

Both relational products are characterized by the availability of the SQL (Structured Query Language) interface and the presence of all functions required for a true database management system which provide the following:

- Support for concurrent access to the data by several users;
- System integrity -- i.e. complete recovery of lost and destroyed data during a system failure;
- Logical security to protect the data from unauthorized access and update.

Although both systems derived from a common predecessor, the same relational prototype System R, they present a number of differences in the structure of data storage due to the different operating environments and in the syntax of certain elements of the SQL interface.

To better understand these systems, we will start by examining the user interface -- i.e., the SQL language. SQL is designed to create, manipulate and query data within a relational database. It is not a complete programming language for database environments. For this reason SQL is frequently embedded within third-generation programming languages -- such as COBOL or PL1 -- or called from other high-level interfaces that provide a procedural language to perform data validation or more complex functions such as statistical calculations.

SQL provides the user with several major benefits. Since data manipulation statements are completely independent from the underlying physical data structure, it is possible to easily migrate from one computer environment to another without losing the programming skills previously acquired. It also provides the basis for a true database connectivity solution. For example, the information stored within one database on a mainframe can be accessed and used in conjunction with data maintained in other database systems -- on a PC within a Local Area Network. This is true as long as all involved systems support a common set of SQL commands. Because of its simplicity and the fact that it gives the end-user or programmer the capacity to retrieve and manipulate the required data -- without having to know how the data is physically stored or how to navigate along access paths -- SQL improves the programmer's productivity in developing database applications.

Because of these advantages and the resulting popularity among end-users and programmers the SQL language has become a standard for man-machine interfaces within database environments, in general, not just for IBM products.

Since SQL is a true application system, it is capable of executing not only ad hoc queries but also repetitive standard queries, repeated hundreds or thousands of times during a day. The system efficiently manages both situations using different strategies according to the nature of the query.

To execute any SQL statement, the system performs the following steps:

- **Parsing:** The Database Management System controls the syntax of the SQL statement and translates it into a tree structure;
- **Optimization:** Based on the tree structure and the information in the catalog tables, the optimizer determines the optimum access strategy (access path) to retrieve the requested information. In this step, SQL also controls whether or not the user has the necessary authority to perform the indicated operations for the required data.

To perform this optimization, SQL subdivides the query into more elementary tasks, so called query blocks. Each query block corresponds to a single SQL statement. Queries containing only a single SQL statement represent the majority of queries within a relational environment. In our discussion of the SQL language later on in this book you will learn how to build more complex queries including two or more nested SQL statements.

Based on the characteristics of each single query block -- such as accessed tables and types of operations -- the optimizer determines the cost and access path for each query block as well as the ideal sequence of execution for the whole query.

Finally, the last step that has to be performed is the generation of required access routines:

- **Code generation:** Based on the access path calculated by the optimizer, SQL creates executable routines.

These operations -- parsing, optimization and code generation -- must be performed before the query can be executed and produce the required result table. In case of an ad hoc query, interactively entered by the user from one of the available interfaces, -- QMF (*Query Management Facility*), SPUFI (*User Friendly Interface*), ISQL (*Interactive SQL*) -- these tasks are executed dynamically at run-time -- i.e., as soon as the user enters the RUN command. For standard applications this would result in an undesirable overhead and a decrease in performance. For these repetitive queries SQL creates the executable routines during the precompilation and BIND steps of the corresponding program, e.g., written in COBOL or PL1, and stores them internally. Whenever the program requests the execution of the query, SQL simply loads the corresponding routines and runs them. In this way, the time consuming operations required for the query preparation are ideally performed only once, although the query itself may be executed thousands or millions of times.

In our discussion of the optimizer, we have seen that the system determines internally which way is the best to reach the desired data or perform the required operation, based on the user specified selection criteria. In contrast to languages of other Database Management Systems, in SQL you only specify what you want done, rather than how to do it. The separation between the logical user view of the data and the navigation within the physical structure automatically performed by the optimizer is certainly one of the most important aspects of the SQL language interface.

Due to this approach, it is possible to completely change the characteristics of the physical storage without having to change the corresponding programs or interactive queries. Every time the validity of predefined access paths is affected by changes in the database structure -- for example, by deleting an index -- SQL automatically invalidates all plans or executable routines based on these objects. The first time the program tries to execute an invalidated plan SQL generates a new access path according to the new structure and replaces the invalidated plan with its new version. Unfortunately, SQL does not automatically recognize other changes that do not affect the validity of plans -- for example, the creation of a new index. SQL does not invalidate any existing plan, since the calculated access paths are still valid, although they may no longer be optimal and it is left to the user or programmer to rebind the corresponding plans.

The concept of logical independence from the physical data structure can be extended further within SQL with the definition of VIEWs. A VIEW may be described as a window through which the user can see data that is stored in one or more tables. VIEWs are defined to reduce the complexity of a database by presenting a smaller and simpler version of the base tables or by anticipating the combination of multiple tables (VIEWs defined based on join-operations). Furthermore, VIEWs are used to prevent unauthorized users or application programs from having access to sensitive data. Since VIEWs allow the user to assign new column names, combine multiple tables, include 'virtual' columns as a result of calculations or built-in functions, etc., they offer the user an opportunity to build a personal vision of the database not only independent from the physical data structures but also from predefined logical subschemes.

1

Evolution and Philosophy

Introduction

Originally the data processing center was an organizational unit of the department that was its primary user. Today, MIS (Management Information Systems) functions are independent units on the staff of upper management.

Process Centered Data Management

In the beginning, automatic procedures performed their tasks similarly to procedures formerly used, the only difference being that they were faster. Each procedure was developed to stand alone with few, if any, connections to the surrounding environment.

During this phase, neither the overall structure of the existing information system nor the information flow between organizational untis were significantly changed with the introduction of electronic data processing. The data processing center was considered a powerful server producing reports or performing tedious administrative tasks -- such as payroll processing -- for a limited number of users. For this reason, the data processing center was organizationally located under the department that was its primary user -- such as the accounting or personnel department.

From the technical point of view the situation was characterized by a nearly complete lack of *system software*. (The term system software is used for those programs where the end user may be a programmer or an application program and which do not produce any directly usable results for the user.) The programmer not only had to solve application related problems but those caused by the hardware structure as well.

The application programs directly accessed the stored data *(see* **Figure 1.1**) and the data description had to be completely embedded in these application programs. The possible choices of data representation were dependent on the capacities of the storage devices available -- such as tapes, disks or cards. A major programming objective was to maximize the efficiency of the use of this hardware. This required the programmer to have a knowledge of the physical characteristics of each storage device.

Because most of the available storage devices -- i.e., tapes and cards -- only allowed a sequential access to data, the programmer was responsible for more sophisticated access, as required. With the introduction of new storage techniques, the programs and related data had to be changed and converted to take advantage of the expanding hardware capabilities. In addition to these difficulties, the ability to expand data -- such as adding new fields to existing files or increasing the length of a field -- was costly and tedious.

Considering data as a user's or program's private resource changed rapidly for the following reasons:

- A change of market structure and competition from national to international. To adapt to these ever changing situations, companies needed better and more accurate information.
- Introduction of new organizational models using team structures, matrix organization, etc. These models were no longer based on a strict hierarchical structure and required integrated information. They represented the organizational answer to the diversification of markets.

These changes necessitated better and more accurate information on the company as well as on the market in which the company was operating. Data processing was no longer considered the private domain of individual departments but became one of the company's major resources comparable to human and financial resources.

This new understanding of data caused an organizational change in most companies. Because the data processing center was now designed to serve the whole company, its location within a single department could no longer be justified. In many organizations, the data processing center became an independent unit on the staff of top management.

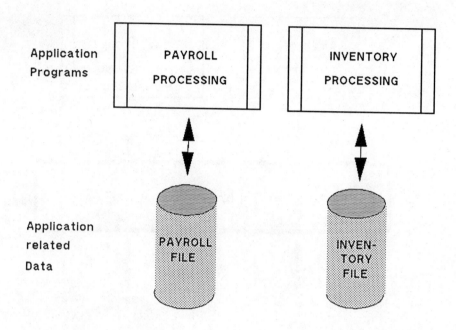

Figure 1.1 Application programs directly access the physically stored data.

The introduction of *operating systems* was an important factor in allowing the Electronic Data Processing *(EDP)* department to fulfill many of the new tasks derived from these organizational changes. An operating system is a collection of generalized routines needed in most application programs. Routines include access methods or loaders to load application programs into the central memory for execution. Access methods such as Basic Sequential Access Method *(BSAM)* and Queued Sequential Access Method *(QSAM)* contain the program modules necessary to transfer data between peripheral devices and computer storage.

Although the generalized access methods improved programming activities, many limitations still existed, including:

- Application programs were written to take full advantage of specific access methods, such as indexed access. As new and improved techniques became available, upward compatibility was limited and the application programs often had to be rewritten.

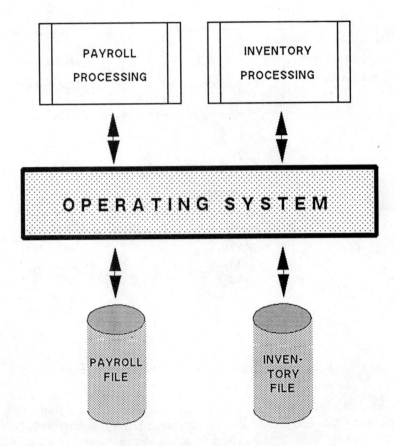

Figure 1.2   Introduction of operating systems

- The description of the physical file had to be included in the application program. Each time a file was changed -- e.g., to add a new field -- all programs that included this file had to be changed in order to make the record area large enough to hold all the information.
- As the access methods did not allow concurrent access to a single file for multiple users, the data was reproduced in another file when the same data was required elsewhere (*see* **Figure 1.3**). Multiple copies of the same file caused problems maintaining data integrity during update.

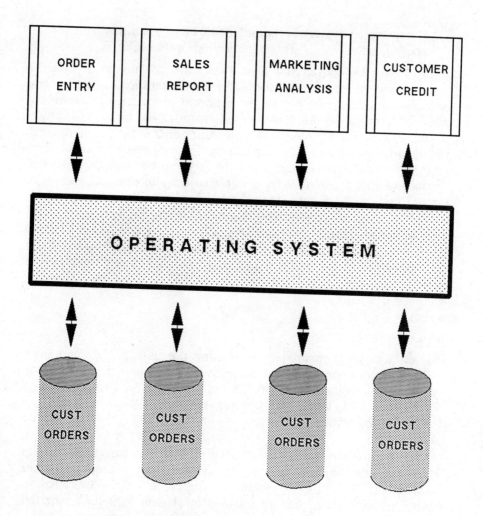

Figure 1.3   Multiple copies of the CUSTOMER ORDER FILE required for different applications.

- During file design, the programmer had to establish the sequence in which data was accessed. In order to provide a different access path, the file had to be duplicated and redefined or sorted corresponding to the new sequence.

- In designing files with fixed record length, the programmer had to limit the number of occurrences of repeated data fields or data groups -- such as multiple addresses of the customer, multiple information on articles in the order file, etc. When this limit was exceeded, extensive program modifications were required.

As we have seen above, EDP at that time was not able to provide the company with the required integrated information through the integration of data. The only way to give different procedures access to the same information was to store data redundantly. But multiple copies of the same file caused problems in maintaining data integrity and reduced the already insufficient human resources for programming tasks. Programmers spent most of their time writing routines to copy files, synchronizing update activities on multiple copies and changing their programs to reflect the changes in the underlying base files.

With increased levels of integration within the information systems and the introduction of online systems allowing users to access information from a remote terminal, the problem of data security and system reliability arose. The problem had to be approached at three different levels:

■ Physical security
■ System reliability
■ Logical security

Physical security is assured by protecting the data processing center against intruders and external destructive events like fire, water, etc. System reliability includes all procedures for system recovery and restart -- copies of files, logging of updates, updates in parallel -- and the duplication of critical resources -- communication networks, crucial files.

All the necessary measures to ensure physical security and system reliability were implemented almost immediately, a major problem remained in attempting to guarantee *Logical security*. Measures to ensure logical security are aimed to protect data from unauthorized access or use.

To protect data logically against access by unauthorized individuals, the following must be implemented:

■ Identification of the user and/or the terminal -- for example, using passwords and terminal-IDs;
■ Identification of application programs;
■ Identification of sensitive data and the limits on access levels for single users or programs -- read, update, delete, etc.;
■ Specification of control level -- file, record or field level.

Unfortunately, the available system software at that time did not provide the necessary functions for logical security.

Data Centered Data Management

To overcome the above problems caused by data redundancy, the physical characteristics of data storage had to be completely separated from the logical use of the same data by an application. Establishing data independence was the major objective of the first Database Management Systems (DBMS). We may define a database as an integrated collection of all data needed for different applications or users and the relationships between the data. Another definition describes a database as "a collection of interrelated data stored together with controlled redundancy according to a schema to serve one or more application" (*Dictionary of Computing*, IBM 1986).

The DBMS is interposed between the operating system and the various applications and becomes the only owner of the physical files it manages. The description of the logical data structure and the relationships between data are defined in a unique logical scheme. We will discuss these relationships between data and their representation in the logical scheme in the next chapter.

A single application is completely independent from the physical characteristics of the files. It accesses data by using "personalized" logical data structure subschemes. The definitions of these subschemes are based on the general scheme and may include data from a single physical file or from multiple files.

The benefits derived from a database management system can be summarized as follows:

- *Making data a shared resource*
  Information systems in a database environment share data by means of a database to increase consistency. Process centered data management employed application dedicated files; to allow multiple access to the same data both redundancy and inconsistency of data occurred. The shared use of data in a database and the ability to build integrated information systems are characteristic of a database environment.
- *Eliminating application vulnerability to hardware and software changes*
  Because the single application program only uses its own personalized subscheme to access data, all software and hardware changes can be incorporated into the DBMS, completely transparent to the application program.
- *Providing application independence from changes in the physical files*
  When adding new fields to an existing file only the subschemes of those applications which are actually using the new information have to be changed .

- *Reducing data redundancy*
  The DBMS normally maintains only one copy of the physical file. In case of concurrent access to the same data by multiple users, the DBMS guarantees data integrity and synchronization of updates.
- *Providing logical security*
  The DBMS maintains an authorization scheme to control user access to certain activities and protects sensitive data against unauthorized access or update.
- *Providing system integrity functions*
  Data manipulation activities performed by the DBMS and the changes in data they caused are registered in LOG files. These LOG files allow the DBMS to recover lost or destroyed data during a system failure.

The introduction of DBMSs had a positive affect on data security and control. It also increased the productivity of application programmers by eliminating the problems caused by hardware and software dependencies. But this increase in productivity remained far below expectations. As we will see in our discussion of data models in the following chapter, the first DBMS based on the hierarchical and network models did not free the application programmer from navigation problems through the database structure.

In a time of continuously growing demand from end users, especially among middle and top management for new applications, the EDP department was not able to develop and implement the corresponding programs. It was not possible to reduce the number of required applications simply by putting end users into direct contact with the stored data. The problem of navigating through the database, along access paths to reach the needed information, presented non-technical users with a major obstacle.

The development of relational DBMSs improved both the productivity of application programmers and the capabilities of end users to solve many of these problems on their own.

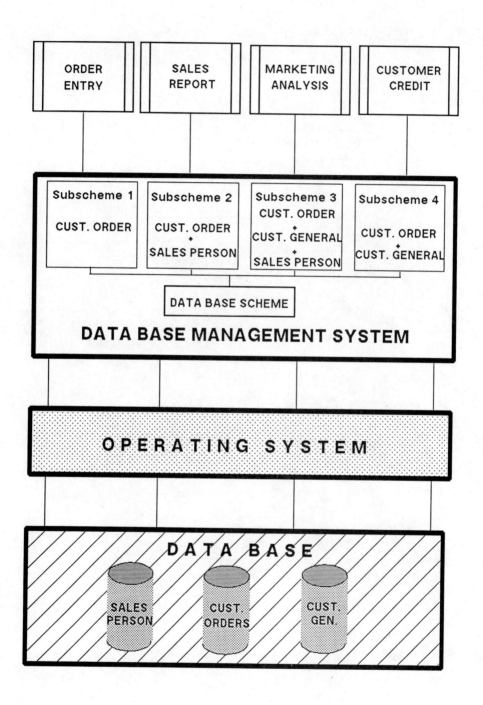

Figure 1.4   Use of subschemes for file access with DBMS

Chapter

2

Data Models

Introduction

A Database Management System is a tool used to organize and retrieve data that allows application programs and users to access and manipulate a shared collection of data. A *data model* is a method used to structure and retrieve or modify data. It includes a collection of general integrity rules sometimes expressed as insert-update-delete rules (Codd, E. F., *Relational Database: A Practical Foundation for Productivity.* Communications for the ACM, February, 1982, Vol. 25, Number 2). There are three different database models:

- Hierarchical
- Network
- Relational

Example

The use of a specific data model in a DBMS provides certain benefits and disadvantages in terms of efficiency of data access and capacity to represent reality. To discuss the different base models, we begin with an example.

Suppose we want to store information about the following objects:

- Department
- Employee
- Product

Analyzing the situation, we observe the following:

Each employee always has an employee number, a name, and a location. The employee number is unique and can be used to identify a single employee.

Each employee works in one department and produces several products. Each department has a department number and a name. Similarly, each product has just one product number and one name. Both department numbers and product numbers are unique in the corresponding collection of data and can be used to identify departments and products respectively.

Each department employs several people. The production of a product usually requires several people.

Our observations of the situation could be described graphically as follows:

DEPARTMENT	DEPT#	NAME
	10	A
	20	B

EMPLOYEE	EMP#	NAME	LOCATION
	901	SMITH	NY
	902	BROWN	NJ
	903	WHITE	CA
	904	SMALL	NJ
	905	JONES	NY

PRODUCT	PROD#	NAME
	1	A
	2	B
	3	C

1 : M

M : M

Figure 2.1 Example of data structure

In the above example, two different types of relationships exist:

Department: Employee   **1**(one) : **M**(any)

Employee: Product   **M**(any) : **M**(any)

The above structure may include a third type of relationship -- the **1 : 1** (one to one) relationship. Suppose that each department has exactly one manager:

Department: Employee   (manager) **1 : 1**

The Hierarchical Model

Hierarchical diagrams are often used for data description and for other complex representations of reality -- such as organizational diagrams, parts lists, etc.

A hierarchical structure consists of a single entry point, called a *root*, found at the top of the structure. Under this root there may be any number of dependent subsets of data. Each of these subsets may branch into more elementary or detailed subsets.

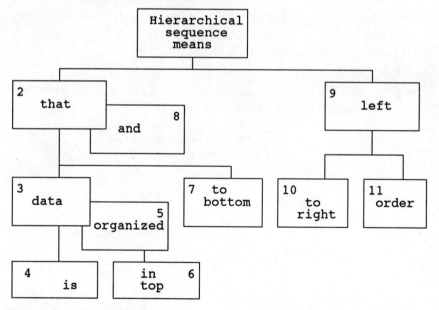

Figure 2.2   Hierarchical sequence

The root definition must contain a field to uniquely identify a single occurrence of an entity. For the purpose of this overview an entity is defined as an object, real or imaginary, represented in a database. A database normally contains some or all of the data elements needed to describe a single entity. Because each dependent may have only one parent, there is only one path from a dependent subset to the root. This path is called a *hierarchic path.*

Another aspect of DBMSs are that they are based on the hierarchical model in which the data are normally physically stored and accessed in *hierarchical sequence.* Hierarchical sequence means that the subsets of data (root and dependent) are organized in top-to-bottom and left-to-right sequence.

In order to query the database, the application program has to specify the hierarchical path along which the required data can be retrieved and provide a procedure to navigate the database. For example, if we want to know the names of all employees working in Department 20, the following procedure is required to retrieve this information:

1. Find department 20 in the root record;
2. Retrieve first dependent employee record and print employee name;
3. Retrieve next dependent employee record and print employee name;
4. Go to 3 until all employees are found;
5. End.

The following is a hierarchical structure -- of the example described above -- with three different subsets and three levels:

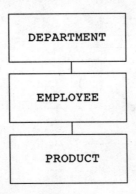

Figure 2.3 Hierarchical structure -- example

The complete database with the data applied to the structure would appear as fiollows:

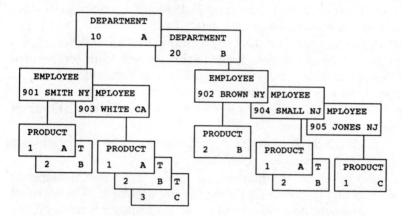

Figure 2.4 Hierarchical database -- example

In the above structure, the product data is stored as a dependent under the corresponding employee occurrence. Although this is an optimal structure to answer the question which products are produced by a single employee, it does present the following problems:

- The product information is redundantly stored under the employee occurrences. Besides the inefficient utilization of storage space, it means that if there is an update of the product data the entire database must be searched to locate each occurrence of that specific product.

- Moreover, the structure is inadequate to answer the question -- *Who produces a certain product?* This information can only be obtained by searching the entire database. (In this chapter we will not attempt to discuss other possibilities of data access such as secondary indexes and their related problems.)

To solve the above problems caused by the existence of a many-to-many relationship, for example, we can use pointer structures (logical segments) or indexes. However, these more sophisticated elements very often cause more problems than they help to solve.

Summarizing the characteristics of the hierarchical model, we may state the following:

- The user or application must know and specify the access path to retrieve or manipulate the desired data.

- The implementations of the hierarchical model are inflexible in regard to structural changes. Since the access path must be specified in the application programs, changes in the hierarchical structure cause re-programming of the corresponding applications.

- The model is adequate for the representation of 1:M relationships (Department - Employee).

- The model is inefficient for representation of M:M relationships (Employee - Product).

- DBMSs, based on the hierarchical model, provide statements to handle multiple records along the hierarchical path. For all other situations where multiple record retrieval or update is required, the application program must contain routines that are executed iteratively (loops) to treat sets of records.

- The model provides very fast and efficient access for queries following the hierarchical sequence -- for example; *List all employees in department 20. What products are produced by WHITE in department 10?*

- The model provides low efficiency to locate a specific occurrence at a lower level of hierarchy -- for example; *List all information on* WHITE *without specifying in which department he is working or if the structure is entered at a level different from the root. (Who produces product 2?)*

Because of the these problems, a hierarchical databases are often designed to match the needs of a specific application and not to store data in a generally usable form which would be required by an integrated information system.

The Network Model

The data in a network model is stored in independent files based on a simple file structure (flat files). To represent the relationships between data in the network system we have to define access paths, in so called *links*. A link is a named collection of *pointers* between two files. A pointer relates a single occurrence in the first file to one or more elements in the second file. For example, the department - employee link connects the department file and the employee file. Links are directional -- i.e., to represent the **M:M** relationship between product and employee we need two links (the employee-product link and the product-employee link).

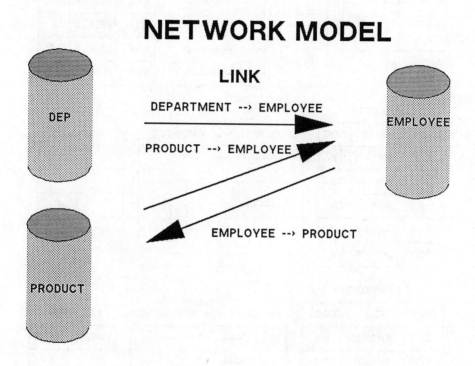

Figure 2.5   Data Links in a network structure

To query the database, the user or application program has to specify the links needed for navigation through the model to obtain the required information. For example, if we want to know what products are produced by the employees working in a specific department, we first have to find all the employees of the specified department by using the department - employee link. In a second step, using the employee - product link, we retrieve the products each employee produces. This procedural description required for navigation through the database is similar to the procedural approach needed in the hierarchical model.

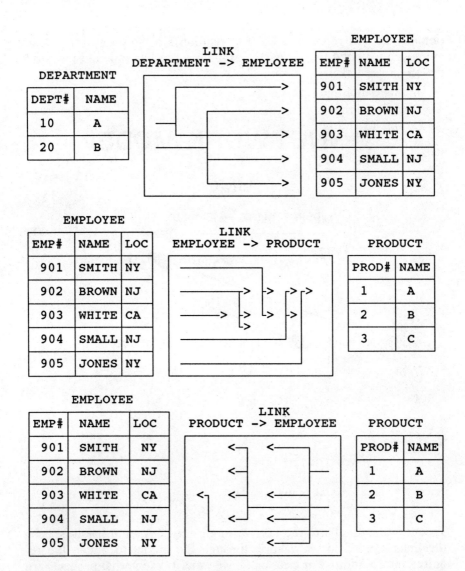

Figure 2.6   Example of a network structure

In comparison to the hierarchical model, the network structure is certainly more flexible and better suited to store the data required by an integrated information system. However, it still presents the following disadvantages:

■   The user or application must know and specify the access path (link) to retrieve or manipulate the desired data.

- No statements are provided to handle multiple records at a time (set processing). The application program must contain sets of instructions that are executed iteratively (loops) in order to retrieve or manipulate multiple records.
- Because of the tight connections between single files, the implementations of the network model are inflexible in regard to structure changes. Furthermore, since the access path must be specified in the application programs, changes in the network structure result in re-programming of the corresponding applications.

The Relational Model

The Relational Datastructure

The relational data model deals with logical and physical objects about which we want to store information and the existing relationships between them. Objects are also called *entities* or *entity-types*. Examples of physical objects are customers or employees, while logical objects are orders and accounts.

Each entity has attributes that describe its characteristics. For example, attributes of the entity *customer* are name, address and customer name.

```
CUSTOMER [NAME, ADDRESS, #CUSTOMER]
```

One characteristic of an entity is that each occurrence within the entity is different from all others -- i.e., duplications are not allowed. This means if each occurrence is different from all others, there is at least one attribute or group of attributes that uniquely identifies each single occurrence. An attribute or group of attributes that uniquely identifies each single occurrence is called a key. If there is more than one attribute or group of attributes with key properties, they are called *candidate keys*. For example, a single employee in the EMPLOYEE table (*see* **Figure 2.8**) is uniquely identified by his employee number, social security number or the combination of last name, first name and date of birth. The attribute that is finally chosen as the principal element to identify a single row is called a *primary key* -- normally, the candidate key with the smallest number of characters. The relational model requires that all values of the primary key have to be defined; no NULL values are allowed for a column defined as a primary key.

All information in a relational model is represented by values in *tables* consisting of *rows* (horizontal) and *columns* (vertical). Ideally, each table contains information concerning one and only one entity. Columns represent the attributes that describe various aspects of an entity. A row describes a single occurrence of the entity. Rows are also called *tuples*.

That each table has a key does not mean that the rows are ordered in logical key sequence. Table rows are not required to have any inherent order. Information is addressed by its value and not by its position along an access path.

Table rows are the smallest unit of insertion and deletion. An insert operation adds one or more rows to a table, while a delete operation removes one or more rows. The intersection of a column and a row is called a *field value* or *column value*.

C O L U M N S

	COL_1	COL_2	COL_3	COL_4	COL_5
R					
O					
W			field val.		
S					

Figure 2.7   Table structure

The following is a relational structure for the example with three tables. Note that the department number has been introduced into the employee table. Since there are no physical links between tables in the relational model, tables are combined by the values contained in matching columns. The DEPT# column in the EMPLOYEE table is needed to represent the department-employee relationship.

DEPARTMENT

DEPT#	NAME
10	A
20	B

EMPLOYEE

EMP#	NAME	LOC	DEPT#
901	SMITH	NY	10
902	BROWN	NJ	20
903	WHITE	CA	10
904	SMALL	NJ	20
905	JONES	NY	20

PRODUCT

PROD#	NAME
1	A
2	B
3	C

Figure 2.8   Relational structure

There are no matching columns between the EMPLOYEE and the PRODUCT tables. To introduce the M:M relation between employee and product we have to define a new table. This table contains all valid combinations of employee and product occurrences.

EMPLOYEE_PRODUCT

EMP#	PROD#
901	1
901	2
903	1
903	2
903	3
902	2
904	1
904	2
905	1

Figure 2.9   Representation of the EMPLOYEE – PRODUCT relation

Relational Operators

Besides the method used to store and manage data within the database, another important element of the relational model is the availability of simple but powerful relational operators. These relational operators allow the performance of basic set processing on tables (relations). The following operators are supported within the relational model: UNION, INTERSECTION, DIFFERENCE, PROJECTION and JOIN. The first three may only be used for tables with identical structure. This restriction does not apply for the PROJECTION and JOIN operations.

Note: Relational operators are discussed in greater detail in Chapter 3 -- Relational Data Model.

In summary, the characteristics of the relational model may be described in the following terms:

- The relational model provides language elements that allow you to easily perform set operations -- such as union, intersection, difference, projection and join -- on multiple rows or records.
- The relational database together with a powerful query interface provide the end-user or programmer a nearly complete operational flexibility and the capacity to retrieve and manipulate the required data without having to know how the data is physically stored or how to navigate along predefined access paths.

Relational Data Model

Introduction

In our discussion of data models we provided a brief introduction of the relational data structure. This chapter provides an overview of two other aspects of data the relational model is concerned with, including:

- operators handling multiple records at a time -- set processing;
- data integrity.

A section on normalization has been included in this chapter in order to introduce minimal rules to be considered during data design.

Relational Operators

A relational database is characterized by its simplicity of data management, independence of logical user views from the physical data storage structure and the availability of simple but powerful relational operators. Relational operators allow the user to perform set operations on one or more tables. The following operators are supported within the relational model: UNION, INTERSECTION, DIFFERENCE, PROJECTION, SELECT and JOIN. While UNION, INTERSECTION and DIFFERENCE may only be used for tables with identical structure, this restriction does not apply to the projection, select and join operations.

UNION

The UNION operator combines two tables (relations) with analogous structure -- i.e., both tables must have the same number of columns and corresponding columns must be of the same type. The result of a UNION operation is a new table with the same structure as the original tables. Each row in the new result table is also part of at least one of the original tables. When a row occurs in both tables, it is reported only once in the result table. If the initial tables are completely different, the number of rows in the result table equals the sum of the rows in the original tables.

UNION

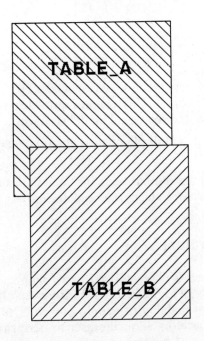

Figure 3.1   UNION operator

Suppose we have the following two tables:

INDOOR_FURNITURE

DESC	PROD #	PROD COST	COLOR WEIGHT
DESK	200	75	1.2
CHAIR	100	35	0.5
WARDROBE	300	95	1.8

OUTDOOR_FURNITURE

DESC	PROD #	PROD COST	COLOR WEIGHT
BENCH	400	150	1.4
DESK	200	75	1.2
GARD CHAIR	500	15	0.6

Combining the two tables with the UNION operator results in a new table -- TOTAL_FURNITURE.

TOTAL_FURNITURE

DESC	PROD #	PROD COST	COLOR WEIGHT
DESK	200	75	1.2
CHAIR	100	35	0.5
WARDROBE	300	95	1.8
BENCH	400	150	1.4
GARD_CHAIR	500	15	0.6

Figure 3.2 UNION operator -- example

Since the information on the article DESK is contained in each of the initial tables, the duplicate is eliminated.

INTERSECTION

The INTERSECTION operation combines two tables that must satisfy the same limitations as those discussed for the UNION operator. (Tables that correspond to the above limitations are also called *union-compatible*.) The result of an intersection is a new table containing all rows that belong to both tables. This means that if the two initial tables are completely different, the result table created by an intersection is empty.

INTERSECTION

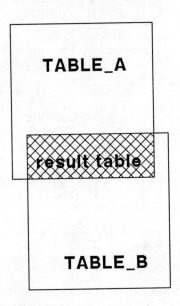

Figure 3.3   INTERSECTION operation -- example 1

Applying the INTERSECTION operation to the two furniture tables, we obtain a result table with exactly one row, since only desks are sold both as indoor and outdoor furniture:

INDOOR_OUTDOOR_FURNITURE

DESC	PROD #	PROD COST	COLOR WEIGHT
DESK	200	75	1.2

Figure 3.4   INTERSECTION operation -- example 2

DIFFERENCE

With the UNION and INTERSECTION operations, the order of the combined tables was of no importance. We would have obtained the same result tables even inverting the order of processing of the two original tables. But when we use the DIFFERENCE operation the order of tables becomes important. We can say that the DIFFERENCE between two tables is a result table containing all rows that belong to the first table but not to the second.

DIFFERENCE

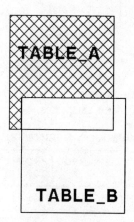

Result table containing
rows that belong to
the first table but not
to the second

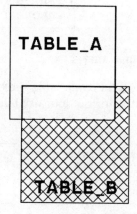

Result table containing
rows that belong to the
second table but not to
the first

Figure 3.5 DIFFERENCE operator

In our example, we will create two different result tables. The first result table -- ONLY_INDOOR -- contains all furniture that is intended for indoor use but not sold as outdoor furniture.

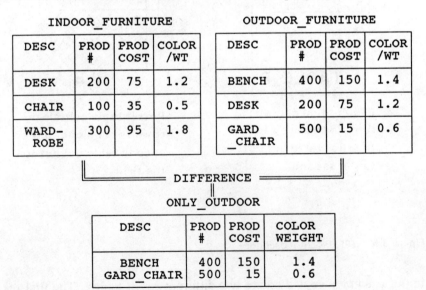

INDOOR_FURNITURE

DESC	PROD #	PROD COST	COLOR /WT
DESK	200	75	1.2
CHAIR	100	35	0.5
WARD-ROBE	300	95	1.8

OUTDOOR_FURNITURE

DESC	PROD #	PROD COST	COLOR /WT
BENCH	400	150	1.4
DESK	200	75	1.2
GARD CHAIR	500	15	0.6

DIFFERENCE

ONLY_INDOOR

DESC	PROD #	PROD COST	COLOR WEIGHT
CHAIR	100	35	0.5
WARDROBE	300	95	1.8

Figure 3.6   DIFFERENCE operation -- example 1

The second result table -- ONLY_OUTDOOR -- contains all furniture that is intended for outdoor use but not sold for indoor purposes.

INDOOR_FURNITURE

DESC	PROD #	PROD COST	COLOR /WT
DESK	200	75	1.2
CHAIR	100	35	0.5
WARD-ROBE	300	95	1.8

OUTDOOR_FURNITURE

DESC	PROD #	PROD COST	COLOR /WT
BENCH	400	150	1.4
DESK	200	75	1.2
GARD _CHAIR	500	15	0.6

DIFFERENCE

ONLY_OUTDOOR

DESC	PROD #	PROD COST	COLOR WEIGHT
BENCH	400	150	1.4
GARD_CHAIR	500	15	0.6

Figure 3.7   DIFFERENCE operation -- example 2

CARTESIAN PRODUCT

The CARTESIAN PRODUCT of two tables is the concatenation of each row from the first table to each row from the second table. The length of the result table is the number of rows in the first table multiplied by the number of rows in the second table.

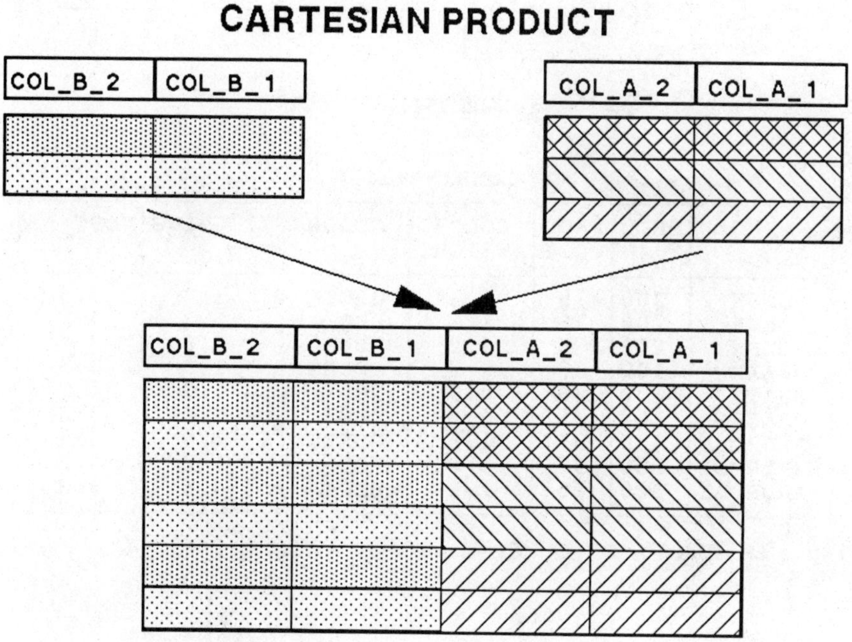

CARTESIAN PRODUCT

Figure 3.8 CARTESIAN PRODUCT

Let's suppose that our small factory uses three different colors to paint the indoor furniture. Let's also suppose that each piece of furniture is available in all three colors. The result table, COMBINATIONS, is the Cartesian Product of the COLOR and the INDOOR_FURNITURE tables. Note that the order of the original tables is not important. By inverting the sequence of the input tables, the order of rows within the result table and the order of columns within each row change. In the relational model, where neither the order of rows nor the sequence of columns is considered, the two result tables are equivalent.

INDOOR_FURNITURE   COLOR

DESC	PROD #	PROD COST	COLOR /WT
DESK	200	75	1.2
CHAIR	100	35	0.5
WARD-ROBE	300	95	1.8

COLOR	YIELDING	COST_LB
GREEN	1	3.5
RED	1.2	4.2
BLUE	0.8	3.3

CARTESIAN PRODUCT

COMBINATIONS

DESC	PROD #	PROD COST	COLOR WEIGHT	COLOR	YIELDING	COST_LB
DESK	200	75	1.2	GREEN	1.0	3.5
DESK	200	75	1.2	RED	1.2	4.2
DESK	200	75	1.2	BLUE	0.8	3.3
CHAIR	100	35	0.5	GREEN	1.0	3.5
CHAIR	100	35	0.5	RED	1.2	4.2
CHAIR	100	35	0.5	BLUE	0.8	3.3
WARDROBE	300	95	1.8	GREEN	1.0	3.5
WARDROBE	300	95	1.8	RED	1.2	4.2
WARDROBE	300	95	1.8	BLUE	0.8	3.3

Figure 3.9   CARTESIAN PRODUCT -- example

PROJECTION

To generate a report or to create a simpler view of a table, you want to select only certain columns from a table. The operation used to achieve this objective is called PROJECTION. The PROJECTION operator generates a vertical subset of a table. Since this subset of columns may not always include the key attributes of the table, a PROJECTION may yield duplicate rows. We distinguish between two types of projection, i.e., general projection including possible duplicate rows and a projection with the DISTINCT option which generates only unique rows. The projection may also be combined with a SELECT operation to further limit the included rows to those that satisfy the required selection criteria.

PROJECTION

TABLE_A

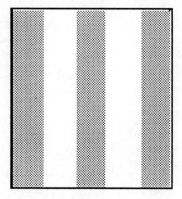

Figure 3.10 PROJECTION operator

Now, let's suppose we have the following table, SALES, containing information about which merchandise certain salespersons (EMP_NO)
have sold within a company store (STORE) during certain weeks (WEEK).
If we want to display the information on the assignment of salespersons
to stores, we have to apply the projection function to the SALES table
selecting only the columns STORE and EMP_NO. Depending on whether
or not the DISTINCT option applies, we obtain two different result tables,
as illustrated in **Figure 3.11.**

SALES

WEEK	STORE	EMP_NO	MKT_CDE	NET_SALE
8708	75	612666	U	110.22
8708	80	1474050	I	45.29
8708	84	4174690	G	1147.47
8709	75	866520	R	144.89
8709	77	1621720	R	55.83
8709	80	1474050	I	32.17
8709	84	4174690	G	264.35

PROJECTION

without DISTINCT

STORE	EMP_NO
75	612666
80	1474050
84	4174690
75	866520
77	1621720
80	1474050
84	4174690

with DISTINCT Option

STORE	EMP_NO
75	612666
80	1474050
84	4174690
75	866520
77	1621720

Figure 3.11   PROJECTION -- example

SELECT

The SELECT operation identifies the occurrences or rows within a table that satisfy a specified condition or set of conditions. Different from the PROJECTION operator that created a vertical subset, the SELECT operator yields a horizontal subset of a table, as illustrated in **Figure 3.12**.

SELECT

TABLE_A

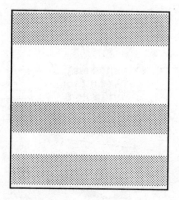

Figure 3.12 SELECT operation

Let's now suppose we want to identify in the above PARTICIPATION table all representatives that have sold more than $100 during campaign 8709. Applying this SELECT operation to the table we obtain the following result table:

RESULT TABLE

WEEK	STORE	EMP_NO	MKT_CDE	NET_SALE
8709	75	866520	R	144.89
8709	84	4174690	G	264.35

Figure 3.13 SELECT operation -- example

JOIN

In our discussion of the CARTESIAN PRODUCT, we have seen that the product of two tables is the concatenation of each row from the first table to each row from the second table. The number of rows in the result table is the product of the number of rows of each combined table, since each combination of rows is considered valid.

The JOIN operation is, instead, controlled by a *join-condition* which compares the values from specified columns. Only if the condition is satisfied is the corresponding combination of rows from the two tables considered valid. There are several types of join-conditions, but the most frequently used is the *equi-join*. An equi-join requires that the values from specified columns have to be equal.

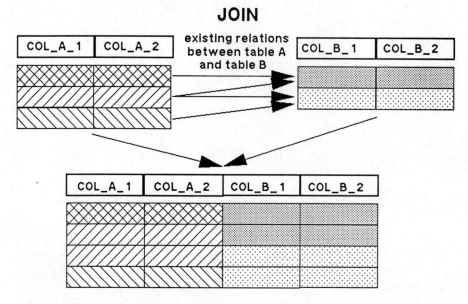

The JOIN operation selects the rows that have to be combined via
a join-condition

Figure 3.14   JOIN operation

Let us return to our factory and assume that the indoor furniture is only painted with certain colors. This assumption would result in a modified INDOOR_FURNITURE table. To combine this table with the COLOR table, we would look for a match of the values in the COLOR columns. The COLOR column in both of the following tables represent the joining column and the join condition would appear as illustrated in **Figure 3.15**.

COLOR from INDOOR_FURNITURE = COLOR from COLOR

INDOOR_FURNITURE

DESC	PROD #	PROD COST	COLOR WEIGHT	COLOR
DESK	200	75	1.2	GREEN
DESK	200	75	1.2	BLUE
CHAIR	100	35	0.5	GREEN
CHAIR	100	35	0.5	RED
CHAIR	100	35	0.5	BLUE
WARDROBE	300	95	1.8	BLUE

COLOR

COLOR	YIELDING	COST_LB
GREEN	1	3.5
RED	1.2	4.2
BLUE	0.8	3.3

COMBINATIONS

DESC	PROD #	PROD COST	COLOR WEIGHT	COLOR	YIELDING	COST_LB
DESK	200	75	1.2	GREEN	1	3.5
DESK	200	75	1.2	BLUE	0.8	3.3
CHAIR	100	35	0.5	GREEN	1	3.5
CHAIR	100	35	0.5	RED	1.2	4.2
CHAIR	100	35	0.5	BLUE	0.8	3.3
WARDROBE	300	95	1.8	BLUE	0.8	3.3

Figure 3.15   JOIN operation - example

Referential Integrity

The problem of referential integrity has been extensively examined in the literature concerning relational database systems. The major objective of this section is to make the reader familiar with the concept of referential integrity. For a more detailed discussion of the term see Date and Codd (C.J. Date, *Relational Database: Selected Writings*, Addison-Wesley, 1986 and E. F. Codd, *Extending the Database Relational Model to Capture More Meaning*, ACM TODS, No.4.)

As we have already seen in our discussion of database management systems, the reduction of data redundancy leads to an increase of data

integrity. Unfortunately, it is not possible to completely eliminate redundant storage of information. The process of normalization, as described below, reduces redundancies within a single subset of data.
However, it causes multiple storage of key columns in related relations:

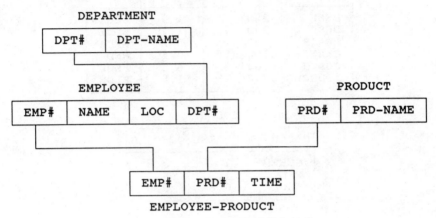

Figure 3.16   Multiple storage of key columns in related relations

The column DPT# in the EMPLOYEE subset as well as the columns EMP#
and PRD# in the EMPLOYEE-PRODUCT subset are necessary to recon-
struct the relationships between the single subsets:

- An employee works in a department.
- An employee produces many products.
- A single product may be produced by several employees.

The DPT# field in EMPLOYEE and the EMP# and PRD# columns in
EMPLOYEE-PRODUCT are also called foreign keys. A foreign key is a
column in relation A that is at the same time a primary key of relation
B. In our example, the column DPT# in the EMPLOYEE subset represents a foreign key since the same column appears as the primary key of
the DEPARTMENT subset. We previously defined a primary key as a column or group of columns in a relation or subset that uniquely identifies
each single tuple or row of the relation. No duplicate or NULL values
are allowed in the primary key column. A foreign key may correspond
to a non-key field (DPT# in the EMPLOYEE relation) or may itself be part
of a new complex primary key (EMP# and PRD# in the EMPLOYEE-
PRODUCT relation).

Referential integrity deals with the relationships between primary
keys and foreign keys as a special case of overall data integrity. We may
roughly define data integrity as the rule requiring that each value in the

record with DPT# = 30 if the value 30 does not occur in the DPT# of the DEPARTMENT relation.

The new releases of DB2 Version 2 and SQL/DS Version 2 Release 2 introduce system functions that allow you to define referential constraints that exist between two tables. Based on these user definitions, DB2 and SQL/DS automatically maintain referential integrity during data manipulation operations. Without these rules violations may occur during INSERT and UPDATE operations -- i.e., inserting or updating an employee record with a non-existing department number as well as by deleting or updating primary key values. For example, if we delete the second row in the department table which contains all information on Department 20, the employee records with EMP# 902, 904, and 905 would violate referential integrity rules since the indicated department number is no longer valid.

Normalization

Normalization rules defined in the relational data model represent guidelines for data design. These guidelines are useful for relational database systems as well as for any logical data model.

Normalization is a decomposition process where an initial set of unnormalized relations is substituted in various steps by other relations with a simpler and more regular structure. It is important that the decomposition of the unnormalized relations into elementary and normalized relations occurs without loss of information. In other words, it must be possible to rebuild the original relations based on the new elementary relations.

The normalization technique has been studied extensively. As a result of these studies the following advantages and disadvantages have emerged:

- The normalization process allows for better understanding of the nature and content of information.
- Normalization rules are designed to reduce data redundancies and to eliminate update anomalies and data inconsistencies.
- Normalization (especially if it is taken to the level of the fourth and fifth normal form) may lead to a decomposition of the initial relations into many very elementary subsets of data, each having only a few attributes. This causes a trade off in performance during data retrieval and manipulation operations, since the required information may have to be selected from several records in a fully normalized form.

Unnormalized Relations

To introduce the normalization rules we recall the example already used for the discussion of data models:

An employee always has an employee number, a name and a location. The employee number is unique and can therefore be used to identify a single employee.

Each employee works in one department and produces several products. The production time required for a single product depends on the employee. Each department has a department number and a name. Similarly, each product has just one product number and one name. Both department numbers and product numbers are unique in the corresponding collection of data and can therefore be used to identify departments and products respectively.

Each department employs several persons. The production of a product usually requires several persons.

These observations may be presented in the following unnormalized relation as illustrated in **Figure 3.17**. Each row is identified by EMP#.

EMP#	NAME	LOC	DPT#	DPT-NAME	PRD#	PRD-NAME	TIME
901	SMITH	NY	10	A	1,2	A, B	10,45
902	BROWN	NJ	20	B	2	B	34
903	WHITE	CA	10	A	1,2,3	A, B, C	15,40,25
904	SMALL	NJ	20	B	1,2	A, B	12,40
905	JONES	NY	20	B	1	A	10

Figure 3.17   Example of an unnormalized relation

Unnormalized relations present the following disadvantages and anomalies:

- Since the number of elements or fields may vary from tuple to tuple, it is very difficult to determine the correct record length to store a variable number of occurrences of repeated data fields or data groups (such as multiple product information or production times).
- The department and product information is repeated in the corresponding employee records. If, for example, the product information changes, every employee record that contains information on this product has to be updated.

■ Because of the above redundancies, data manipulation operations may lead to anomalies:

● **INSERT anomalies**

Suppose we want to insert a new employee:

EMP#	NAME	LOC	DPT#	DPT NAME	PRD#	PRD NAME	TIME
906	GREEN	NY	10	C	1,2	A, B	10,45

Figure 3.18 Insert anomalies

Since the key 906 does not exist, the new record is inserted although the department name is different from the name declared for the same department in other records. Validation would assume the existence of a relation which lists the correct name for each department number.

Furthermore, we cannot insert a new department or a new product without assigning it to at least one employee. To store information on a new department or product without assigning it to an existing employee we have to define a dummy employee record.

● **DELETE anomalies**

Suppose WHITE leaves the company and we delete the corresponding employee record. Since WHITE is the only employee to produce product 3, we would lose all available information on that product when deleting the employee record.

● **UPDATE anomalies**

During update operations you may encounter the same problems as those described for inserts.

Relations in the First Normal Form

The first normal form requires that all repeated data fields or data groups have to be eliminated. This restriction is derived directly from the relational data model since this form of organization does not support a variable number of fields in a data record.

To satisfy the first normal form the initial relation may be altered in either of the following ways:

■ By combining the initial primary key (EMP#) with the key of the repeated group (PRD#).

EMP#	NAME	LOC	DPT#	DPT-NAME	PRD#	PRD-NAME	TIME
901	SMITH	NY	10	A	1	A	10
901	SMITH	NY	10	A	2	B	45
902	BROWN	NJ	20	B	2	B	34
903	WHITE	CA	10	A	1	A	15
903	WHITE	CA	10	A	2	B	40
903	WHITE	CA	10	A	3	C	25
904	SMALL	NJ	20	B	1	A	12
904	SMALL	NJ	20	B	2	B	40
905	JONES	NY	20	B	1	A	10

Figure 3.19   Relation in first normalized form -- alternative 1

■ By splitting up the repeated group from the unnormalized relation. Since the key of the repeated group (PRD#) is not sufficient to identify each occurrence of the new relation, we have to combine it with the primary key of the original relation.

EMPLOYEE

EMP#	NAME	LOC	DPT#	DPT-NAME
901	SMITH	NY	10	A
902	BROWN	NJ	20	B
903	WHITE	CA	10	A
904	SMALL	NJ	20	B
905	JONES	NY	20	B

Figure 3.20a   Relation in the first normalized form -- alternative 2

EMPLOYEE-PRODUCT

EMP#	PRD#	PRD-NAME	TIME
901	1	A	10
901	2	B	45
902	2	B	34
903	1	A	15
903	2	B	40
903	3	C	25
904	1	A	12
904	2	B	40
905	1	A	10

Figure 3.20b Relation in the first normalized form -- alternative 2

Relations in first normal form present the same problems as those described for unnormalized relations.

- The department and product information is repeated in the corresponding records. If, for example, the department information changes every employee record that contains information on this department has to be updated.
- Because of the above redundancies, data manipulation operations may lead to the same INSERT, DELETE and UPDATE anomalies described for unnormalized relations.

Relations in the Second Normal Form

The rules that define the second and third normal form are based on dependencies between key and non-key fields. Therefore, we will first discuss the term *dependency* or *functional dependency*.

An attribute or field B in a relation in first normal form is called dependent on another attribute A, if each value of A corresponds or identifies exactly one value of B. For example, since every employee number (EMP#) uniquely identifies one employee name, we say that the employee name is functionally dependent on EMP#. By definition, all non-key fields are functionally dependent on the key, since there cannot be two occurrences having the same key value.

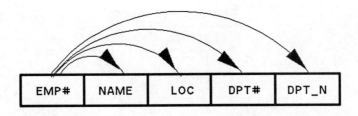

Figure 3.21 Functional dependencies between key and non-key fields in the EMPLOYEE
relation

The second normal form requires that the relations are in first normal
form and that all non-key attributes fully depend on the whole key and
not on any subset of the key. This normal form is only relevant when
the key is composite -- i.e., consists of several fields. Let us consider the
EMPLOYEE-PRODUCT relation, as illustrated in **Figure 3.22**.

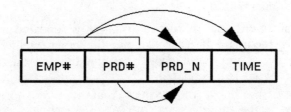

Figure 3.22 Functional dependencies between subsets of the key and non-key fields in
the EMPLOYEE-PRODUCT relation

The key here consists of the two fields EMP# and PRD# together but the
product name is only identified by the product number PRD#. To satisfy
the second normal form, the above relation has to be split into the following two subsets:

EMPLOYEE-PRODUCT

EMP#	PRD#	TIME

PRODUCT

PRD#	PRD-NAME

After the decomposition, the previous EMPLOYEE-PRODUCT relation would therefore look like this:

EMPLOYEE-PRODUCT

EMP#	PRD#	TIME
901	1	10
901	2	45
902	2	34
903	1	15
903	2	40
903	3	25
904	1	12
904	2	40
905	1	10

PRODUCT

PRD#	PRD-NAME
1	A
2	B
3	C

Figure 3.23   Second normal form of the EMPLOYEE-PRODUCT relation

The relations in the second normal form still present the following problems:

- The department information is repeated in the record of every employee who works in the department. In case of an update of a department's information, every employee record that contains information on this department has to be changed.
- Because of the above redundancies, data manipulation operations may lead to the same INSERT, DELETE and UPDATE anomalies described for unnormalized relations.

Relations in the Third Normal Form

The third normal form deals with dependencies between non-key fields. We may say that a relation is in third normal form if it is in second normal form and if there are no functional dependencies between non-key fields.

The third normal form is violated if a non-key field uniquely identifies values of another non-key field as in the following EMPLOYEE relation:

EMPLOYEE

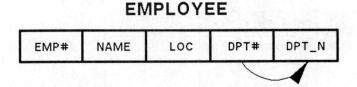

EMP#	NAME	LOC	DPT#	DPT_N

Figure 3.24 Functional dependencies between non-key fields in the employee relation

Since the EMP# is the key, the department name is, by definition, functionally dependent on EMP#. As each department has exactly one name, the department name is also uniquely identified by DPT#. The department name is functionally dependent on both the employee and the department number. To satisfy the third normal form, the EMPLOYEE relation has to be decomposed into the following two subsets:

EMPLOYEE

EMP#	NAME	LOC	DPT#

DEPARTMENT

DPT#	DPT-NAME

After the decomposition the EMPLOYEE relation looks like this:

EMPLOYEE

EMP#	NAME	LOC	DPT#
901	SMITH	NY	10
902	BROWN	NJ	20
903	WHITE	CA	10
904	SMALL	NJ	20
905	JONES	NY	20

DEPARTMENT

DPT#	DPT-NAME
10	A
20	B

Figure 3.25 Relations in third normal form

General Considerations

The database management systems, SQL/DS and DB2, do not require tables to be in a normalized form. As explained earlier, unnormalized tables might lead to data anomalies and loss of data integrity caused by data manipulation operations like INSERT, UPDATE and DELETE of table rows. On the other hand, the process of normalization results in a larger number of small tables, many of which have to be combined again for the selection of table data (using JOIN operations). JOIN operations cause a decrease in performance of database operations and, therefore, longer response times are required to produce the desired result.

Because of these performance problems, there are no overall valid criteria to determine the optimal degree of normalization. Since the process of normalization helps you to better understand the existing relationships within your data, you should always begin by normalizing your tables. If you anticipate performance problems with the resulting design, denormalize as far as necessary.

4

System Components - Overview

Introduction

The term *system components* refers to anything you can define or manipulate using SQL/Data Definition Language. System components are also called *objects*.

This chapter provides you with a brief description of each object within the SQL/DS and DB2 database structure. Normally, users of SQL deal only with tables, views and, occasionally, indexes. In general, they are not concerned with the physical characteristics of these objects. However, you should have some familiarity with these system components and insight into their internal relationships.

SQL/DS Objects

Physical Objects

SQL/DS operations under VM/SP are serviced by one or more SQL/DS *database machines*. An SQL/DS database machine is a virtual machine in which the SQL/DS system code runs.

You may define multiple database machines that have access to multiple databases. Each database is *owned* by only one database machine. This is usually the virtual machine that is the primary user of the database. For every user of the SQL/DS system you must define an SQL/DS *virtual user machine*.

SQL/DS data is stored on CMS minidisks. A minidisk is a portion of a DASD volume (such as a 3380 device) that is defined under VM/SP by adding an MDISK control statement to the VM/SP directory of the database machine. There are three types of minidisks required for a database machine:

- SQL/DS DIRECTORY minidisk
- SQL/DS LOG minidisks
- SQL/DS DBEXTENT minidisks

While the first two types of minidisks support the operational functions of SQL/DS, DBEXTENTS are used to store the data from tables and indexes. Each DBEXTENT is a CMS minidisk. SQL/DS supports up to 999 DBEXTENTS defined for a single database. DBEXTENTS are grouped together to form storage pools. A storage pool is subdivided into 4K blocks, called slots. Each time SQL/DS wants to store a new DBSPACE page, it looks for a free slot in the corresponding storage pool. Storage pools are units of physical storage as well as objects for logging and recovery.

SQL/DS distinguishes between two types of storage pools:

- recoverable storage pools
- nonrecoverable storage pools

For recoverable storage pools, SQL/DS provides complete logging of data manipulation activities on the data stored in the corresponding storage pool and therefore assures full recovery in case of system failures or errors. For those DBSPACES assigned to a nonrecoverable storage pool, SQL/DS provides only reduced recovery functions. It is left to the user to create backup copies of the data to restore a consistent situation in case of system failure or abend.

Logical Objects

Data under SQL/DS is stored in tables consisting of rows (horizontal) and columns (vertical). Columns are identified by their name, while rows are identified by column values contained within the individual rows. Table rows are not only objects of data retrieval and manipulation operations, they are also the smallest unit of *data locking*. Data locking means that a certain data portion (such as one or more rows, a page, etc.) is exclusively reserved for a single user for the duration of a required data manipulation operation. Locking reduces the possibility of concurrent access to data and ensures data consistency.

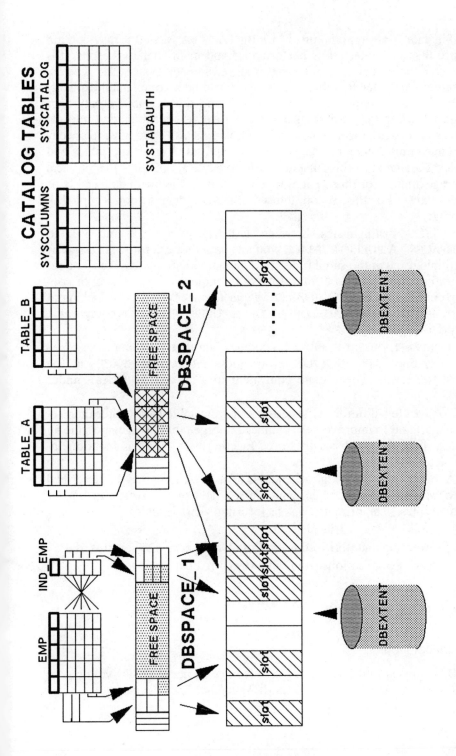

Figure 4.1 Overview of SQL/DS system components

Table data is always contained in a DBSPACE. A DBSPACE may contain more than one table. For performance and maintenance reasons, it is recommended that only one table is stored in each DBSPACE. The assignment of a specific table to a DBSPACE can be accomplished explicitly with the user supplying the DBSPACE name during table creation or SQL/DS using the default DBSPACE. A DBSPACE is subdivided into 4K pages for data storage. When you define a DBSPACE, you have to specify the maximum number of pages that is required to store the tables and indexes assigned to this DBSPACE. However, SQL/DS allocates physical storage on disk for those pages that are actually filled with data (table or index data). For this reason, unused DBSPACE pages do not occupy disk storage.

SQL/DS distinguishes between PRIVATE DBSPACES and PUBLIC DBSPACES. A PUBLIC DBSPACE contains data that has to be accessed by multiple users at the same time, for data manipulation as well as data retrieval operations. As PUBLIC DBSPACES require a higher level of concurrent data access, SQL/DS allows you to specify DBSPACE locking at various levels (ROW, PAGE, DBSPACE). A PUBLIC DBSPACE is comparable to a DB2 Table Space.

A PRIVATE DBSPACE, instead, contains data that is normally accessed by only one user. SQL/DS always locks PRIVATE DBSPACES at the DBSPACE level. There is no equivalent to a PRIVATE DBSPACE under DB2.

To provide a different type of access to your table data (other than sequential) and to improve performance on large tables, you can define an *index*. Indexes are physically stored together with the corresponding table data in the same DBSPACE.

Another important logical object is a *view*. A view may be described as a window through which you can see data that is stored in one or more tables. The primary reasons for using views include:

- simplified data retrieval;
- preventing unauthorized users from having access to sensitive data;
- isolating applications from table structure changes.

DB2 Objects

Physical Objects

DB2 data is stored on *Direct Access Storage Device* (DASD) volumes or disks. Some typical disk types are IBM 3350 or 3380 devices.

DB2 does not deal directly with single disks, but with storage groups. We can define a storage group as a collection of single DASD devices. There are certain things you should know about storage groups.

- All volumes in a storage group must be of the same device type. This means, for example, that you cannot mix up IBM 3350 and 3380 devices.

- Storage groups may be overlapping, which means you can use the same volume in more than one storage group.

Another important physical storage unit utilized by DB2 is a *table space*. A table space corresponds to a VSAM/ESDS (*Virtual Sequential Access Method/Entry Sequenced Data Set*) dataset or, in case of a partitioned tablespace, to as many single VSAM/ESDS datasets as there are defined partitions. Each table space is physically divided into pages. Pages contained in a table space are all of the same size. DB2 allows two different sizes: 4K and 32K pages. Every time DB2 accesses data to execute your query, it does not read the data row by row, but reads the data into memory one page at a time.

In order to let DB2 retrieve your data more efficiently, you may define an *index*. For each index DB2 allocates an *index space*. The index data is stored in 4K index pages within the index space.

DB2 is not allowed to access the data directly on the disk; it must request the data through the operating system. The routines of the operating system physically access the data and move a *copy* into a virtual storage area, called a *buffer*, which can be manipulated by DB2. If DB2 alters the contents of the page contained in the buffer -- for example, by inserting or updating the data -- it requests the operating system to rewrite the page to the physical storage device. You can compare the process of physically accessing data to the administration of safe deposit boxes in a bank. You are not allowed direct access to the safe deposit room. You must request that the clerk provide you with your box in a customer booth (buffer), where you can look at (read) or alter the contents of the box.

The constant travel of data between the two storage areas (physical and virtual storage) consumes most of the processing time required for data retrieval. Consequently, you should instruct DB2 to read only that data you need and to provide all the information DB2 requires in order to locate your data efficiently. This includes defining indexes and using query structures with redundant search criteria.

Logical Objects

In DB2, all data is stored in *tables* consisting of *rows* (horizontal) and *columns* (vertical). A table normally stores data about objects that are important for the company. Columns typically describe various aspects of these objects. Columns are identified by their name and not by their order within the table. A row describes a single occurrence of an entity. Table rows are the smallest unit of insertion and deletion. An insert operation adds one or more rows to a table, while a delete operation removes one or more rows. Users have the ability to retrieve rows and columns in any order that they need on individual requests.

A table is always contained in a *table space*. From the logical point of view we may distinguish between simple, segmented and partitioned table spaces.

A *simple table space* contains one or more tables. Each page (physical structure) holds one or more rows of a table. If there is more than one table in the table space, each page may contain rows from different tables. Simple table spaces with multiple tables in previous releases of DB2 have presented the user with various problems such as table space locking and I/O overhead. *(The above problems will be discussed in detail in the corresponding chapter.)* In DB2 Version 2, these concerns have been addressed with the introduction of segmented table spaces. A *segmented table space* is divided into equal sized sets of pages called *segments*. While the segmented table space may hold multiple tables, each segment contains rows of only one table.

A group of table spaces that are related to each other by referential constraints, is called a table space set. All table spaces that belong to a table space set must be recovered when all of their data is consistent, i.e., no referential constraints are violated.

A *partitioned table space* holds exactly one table. The table space is divided, based on partitioning key values, into partitions.

Another logical object of DB2 is a *view*. A view is derived from one or more base tables and represents an alternate way of seeing table data. Views may also be derived from other views or a combination of views and tables.

To provide a different type of access to your data other than sequential, you may define an *index*. In DB2, indexes logically reorder data (clustering indexes also reorder data physically) so that DB2 can locate data without a lengthy sequential search. Indexes are based on one or more columns of a table.

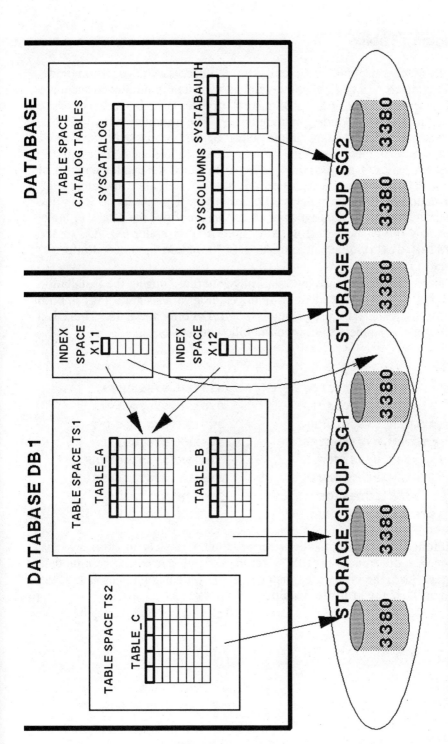

Figure 4.2 Overview of DB2 system components

Catalog Tables

Both systems use catalog tables to store all necessary information on defined objects. Each time you create, alter or delete an object, such as a table or view, DB2 or SQL/DS inserts, updates or deletes one or more rows in the corresponding catalog tables. The execution of utilities like RUNSTATS or STOSPACE under DB2 or UPDATE STATISTICS under SQL/DS also modify certain catalog tables to reflect changes in the characteristics of the examined objects. Because the catalog consists of normal tables, you can use the SQL SELECT statement to retrieve information on specific objects. For example, if you want to know the column names and data types of all columns defined for a certain table, you may query the SYSTEM.SYSCOLUMNS table under SQL/DS or the SYSIBM.SYSCOLUMNS table under DB2 to obtain the needed information.

The catalog tables are automatically generated during the installation process. The number of tables in the catalog varies significantly in both systems. While DB2 uses 30 tables, SQL/DS only needs 15. There is a direct correspondence between the following tables:

SQL/DS	DB2
SYSTEM.SYSCATALOG	SYSIBM.SYSTABLES
SYSTEM.SYSCOLAUTH	SYSIBM.SYSCOLAUTH
SYSTEM.SYSCOLUMNS	SYSIBM.SYSCOLUMNS
SYSTEM.SYSINDEXES	SYSIBM.SYSINDEXES
SYSTEM.SYSSYNONYMS	SYSIBM.SYSSYNONYMS
SYSTEM.SYSTABAUTH	SYSIBM.SYSTABAUTH
SYSTEM.SYSUSAGE	SYSIBM.SYSUSAGE
SYSTEM.SYSVIEWS	SYSIBM.SYSVIEWS

Although the above tables describe similar objects in both systems, there are differences in table structure, column names and column data types. Also, the prefix used under SQL/DS for catalog tables is SYSTEM. Under DB2 the prefix for catalog tables is SYSIBM.

5

Data Definition

Introduction

In this chapter we will discuss the SQL data definition statements required to manipulate the objects that are of interest to all users; tables and views. Both objects are treated similarly in SQL/DS and DB2. Owing to differences in the utilities used within SQL/DS and DB2 for loading data into tables and updating information stored in the catalog tables, it is necessary to examine the corresponding chapters that discuss the data definition language in SQL/DS and DB2. In addition to tables and views, we also introduce the concept of referential integrity under DB2 Version 2 and SQL/DS Version 2 Release 2.

REFERENTIAL INTEGRITY under DB2 Version 2 and SQL/DS Version 2 Release 2

The new releases of DB2 Version 2 and SQL/DS Version 2 Release 2 introduce system functions that allow you to define referential constraints that exist between two tables. Based on these user definitions DB2 and SQL/DS automatically maintain referential integrity during data manipulation operations. The following section is an overview of the system functions that have been implemented in these releases.

Changes to data definition language elements such as CREATE TABLE or ALTER TABLE are explained in the corresponding sections.

Primary and Foreign Keys

As we have already seen in our discussion of the relational data model, referential integrity deals with the relationship between primary and foreign keys. A primary key is a column or group of columns in a table that uniquely identifies each single row of the table. At most, there may be only one primary key per table. The following restrictions apply for primary key values:

- it must be unique -- i.e., no duplicate values are allowed;
- it cannot be NULL.

To verify these restrictions, DB2 and SQL/DS require the existence of a unique index on the column or columns that compose the primary key of a table. While SQL/DS automatically generates the required index for the primary key, DB2 leaves the user responsible for the index creation with the CREATE INDEX statement. The automatically generated index under SQL/DS has a name starting with PKEY and ending with a timestamp.

A foreign key is a column or group of columns in a table that is at the same time a primary key in another table. Each table may have one or more foreign keys. The foreign key in a table may correspond to a non-key field or may itself be part of a new complex primary key. The data values allowed in a foreign key are limited the following manner:

- Every foreign key value must correspond to a primary key value, i.e., the data values contained in the foreign key column at any given point of time must be a subset of the list of actual data values in the primary key column. This rule also applies to a composite primary key where each component of the foreign key must match the corresponding portion of the primary key. The foreign key is considered NULL if any component contains the value NULL. DB2 Version 2 and SQL/DS Version 2 Release 2 utilize the unique index built on the primary key to verify the correspondence between foreign and primary keys.
- A foreign key may be null. NULL values in a foreign key column should only be allowed in certain circumstances and normally only for a limited period of time. For example, an employee may not be assigned to a specific department during the orientation period.
- A primary key may match none, one or many foreign key values. The foreign key may contain duplicate values and not all of the primary key values may be present in the table containing the foreign key. For example, one department normally has many employees and there may be some new departments with no employees assigned to them.

Besides the above limitations for data values, it is also important that the column definition is equal for data type and size for primary and foreign key columns.

Application of referential constraints in data manipulation operations

Referential constraints consist of a set of rules to assure referential integrity that apply to a specific pairing of primary and foreign keys. Some of these rules are fixed within DB2 and SQL/DS, while for others (see delete operations) the user may chose from several options. The application of rules assuring referential integrity has no impact on SELECT operations, but apply during data manipulation activities.

Insert of a new primary key

To insert a new primary key, DB2 and SQL/DS verify that the supplied value is not NULL and that it is not a duplicate of an existing primary key. This validation is performed using the unique index defined on the primary key column. If the supplied value is incorrect, the insert operation is rejected.

Update of an existing primary key

DB2 and SQL/DS perform the update of a primary key if the following two conditions are met:

- The new primary key value corresponds to the general restriction, i.e., it may not be NULL and not a duplicate of another existing value;
- The old primary key value that you want to replace, does not exist in the foreign key column. To facilitate the validation of this restriction, you should always create an index on the foreign key column(s). The update of the primary key is rejected, if there are any dependent rows in the table containing the foreign key column.

If the update operation affects multiple rows, the above conditions must be met for each row that has to be updated. DB2 and SQL/DS do not allow even any temporary violations of referential integrity rules.

Deletion of an existing primary key

As we have seen during update and insert operations of primary keys, the dependent table(s) control whether or not the operation may be executed. These tables are not directly affected by any changes in the primary key column.   Delete operations, instead, may lead to the deletion or update of rows in dependent tables.

To control the effect of the deletion of a primary key on the dependent tables, DB2 and SQL/DS offer the following three different delete rules:

SET NULL-   Delete primary key and set foreign key values to NULL in all rows in the dependent table(s) that contain the deleted primary key value in the foreign key column.

RESTRICT-   Delete primary key only if the value is not used as a foreign key in any of the dependent table(s). This rule is also the <u>default delete rule</u>.

CASCADE -   Delete primary key and delete all rows in the dependent table(s) that contain the deleted primary key value in the foreign key column.   If multilevel dependencies exist under DB2 Version 2, the deletion of rows in the dependent table(s) also causes changes (according to the defined delete rule) in the descendent tables.   **Multilevel dependencies are not supported under SQL/DS Version 2 Release 2.**

The delete rule that you want to apply to a specific dependent table must be chosen during the definition of the foreign key column with the CREATE TABLE statement.   For multiple dependent tables you may choose a different delete rule for each of these tables.

If you use a subquery in the DELETE statement, you have to assure the table referenced by the subquery is not changed by the delete operation. When the table in the subquery is in the delete path of the primary table (i.e., the table you delete from), the delete path must be defined as 'RESTRICT'.

Under DB2, the deletion of a primary key may not only involve the table itself and all of its dependent tables but all descendant tables under CASCADE dependents.   The following example demonstrates the impact on dependent and descendent tables.

Suppose our environment may be described using the following four tables:

DEPARTMENT   The department table stores the department number (DEPT_NO primary key) and name for each department.

EMPLOYEE   The employee table contains the employee number (EMP_NO primary key), the name and salary, as well as the department number (DEPT_NO foreign key) of the department to which the employee is assigned. The delete rule between the department and the employee table is the CASCADE rule -- i.e., if a department is deleted the corresponding employee records are deleted, too.

INVENTORY   The inventory table contains the inventory number (INV_NO primary key), the item description and the department number (DEPT_NO foreign key) of the department where the item is actually located. The delete rule between the department and the inventory table is the SET NULL rule, i.e., inventory items are temporarily unassigned when the corresponding department is deleted.

RELATIONS   The RELATIONS table contains the internal identification (REL_NO   primary key), the employee number (EMP_NO foreign key), and a description of the type of relation with the employee. Records in the RELATIONS table are automatically deleted if the corresponding employee record is deleted (CASCADE rule).

The initial situation is described in **Figure 5.1**. If we delete the Finance department (20), this would not only impact the DEPARTMENT table but also its direct dependents, i.e. the INVENTORY and the EMPLOYEE table. Since the INVENTORY table is connected to the DEPARTMENT table via the 'SET NULL' delete rule, the DEPT_NO for inventory items 001017 and 001020 is automatically set to NULL. This means that these items are temporarily unassigned. The delete rule between the DEPARTMENT and the EMPLOYEE tables, instead, is the 'CASCADE' rule, i.e. in case a department is dissolved all its employees are laid off. The effect of the 'CASCADE' rule on our tables is that the records containing information on BROWN and BLAKE are automatically deleted. Since SQL/DS 2.2 does not support multi-level CASCADE operations, there would be no further adjustments to the data bases in that environment. Under DB2 Version 2 the RELATIONS table is also updated deleting all descendent rows that contain the employee numbers 10002 and 10020 in the foreign key column. The final result of the deletion of the Finance department under DB2 Version 2 is represented in **Figure 5.2**.

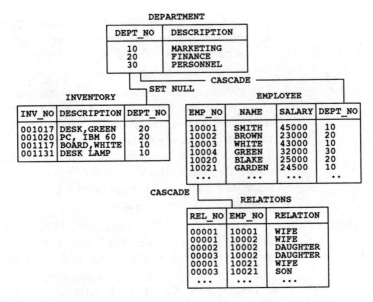

Figure 5.1 Referential integrity under DB2 V2 and SQL/DS 2.2 - Example

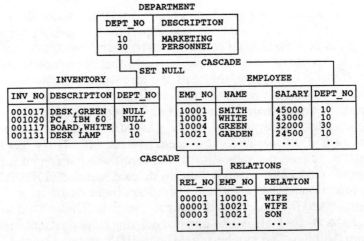

Figure 5.2 Referential integrity under DB2 V2 - Application of the multilevel CASCADE rule

If the descendent table under DB2 Version 2 is connected to the primary table through multiple delete paths, each path must have the same effect on the descendent table, i.e., the delete rules must be all restricted or all CASCADE. Let's assume that the RELATIONS table also contains the department number as a foreign key and that the table is connected to the DEPARTMENT table via the CASCADE delete rule (*see* **Figure 5.3**).

The deletion of a department would impact the RELATIONS table directly through the CASCADE path to the DEPARTMENT table as well as indirectly through the path connecting the table to the EMPLOYEE table. Since both paths are of the same type, there is no conflict and DB2 deletes the involved rows in all three tables.

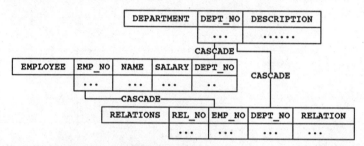

Figure 5.3   Referential integrity under DB2 V2 -- Multilevel delete paths

Data manipulation operations on foreign keys

Data manipulation activities on foreign keys such as INSERT, UPDATE and DELETE, only impact the dependent table and not the parent tables. DB2 and SQL/DS execute UPDATE and INSERT operations only if the new foreign key is considered valid, i.e.:

- NULL values for foreign keys or portions of foreign keys are valid if the corresponding column definitions do not exclude NULL values.
- If the foreign key value is not NULL, it must match an existing value in the primary key column. Duplicate foreign key values are allowed.

DELETE operations are always carried out by DB2 and SQL/DS.

Table

In both SQL/DS and DB2, all data is presented as tables consisting of rows (horizontal) and columns (vertical).

Columns typically describe various aspects or attributes of these objects. The order of columns for an entity is not important from a conceptional point of view, since columns are identified by their name and not by the column order (sequence number). In considering performance aspects, the order may assume greater importance. *(We will discuss the importance of column order when a table contains VARCHAR columns later on in this section.)* All values in a column have the same characteristics, ensured by the data type definition.

A row describes a single occurrence of an entity. Table rows are the smallest unit of insertion and deletion. An insert adds one or more rows to a table, while a delete operation removes one or more rows. Rows normally have no inherent order but SQL/DS and DB2 provide facilities (indexes) that ensure logical or physical order and may enforce uniqueness of the rows.

The intersection of a column and a row is called a *field value or column value*.

TABLENAME

C   O   L   U   M   N   S

	COL1	COL2	COL3	COL4	COL5
R					
O					
W			field val.		
S					

Figure 5.4 Table structure

Number of Tables

One of the critical design decisions that can affect performance is the number of tables that have to be joined. The tradeoff is between SQL performance and the anomalies that result in tables which have not been designed to be in their 'technically correct' form.

To design your tables, you must first identify the information elements you need in terms of entities and their attributes. Entities may correspond in reality to logical objects (like service orders) or to physical objects (like customers, employees, etc.)

The second step is to determine the key attributes that uniquely identify a single occurrence of an entity -- for example, customer numbers used to identify individual customers. Next, you may list all the other elements or attributes that further describe the entities -- for example, name, address and social security number.

The result of this design approach is a list of attributes for each base entity. Typically, this list of attributes is not normalized. Attribute lists that are not normalized may contain redundant data, repeating groups of attributes (such as multiple addresses for each customer) or dependencies between attributes, that are not key attributes.

SQL/DS and DB2 do not require tables to be in a normalized form. As we have discussed previously, unnormalized tables may lead to data anomalies and loss of data integrity caused by data manipulation operations like INSERT, UPDATE, and DELETE of table rows. Taken to its ultimate conclusion, the process results in a large number of small tables, many of which have to be combined (joined) again for the selection of table data.   JOIN operations cause a decrease in performance of SQL/DS or DB2 operations and longer response times are required to produce a desired result.

Because of these performance problems, there are no overall valid criteria used to determine the optimum degree of normalization. You should avoid both the use of completely unnormalized tables and the application of normalization rules to their final level.   The use of *code* tables should especially be minimized where very little is gained from their use, accepting the requirement for additional storage and the potential update anomalies resulting from redundant data.

Size of Table Rows

SQL/DS and DB2 store data in 4K pages. (DB2 also allows 32K pages.) If table rows are defined with a maximum length greater than 4K, you should consider the possibility of splitting the table by separating less frequently used columns into a separate table. SQL/DS and DB2 store table rows with a length exceeding 4K inefficiently and need larger buffering areas and longer response times to retrieve the required data.

Data Types

The following data types are supported as field values:

INTEGER or INT

Fullword 31-bit signed binary values (the maximum range of numbers that can be stored is from -2,147,483,648 to +2,147,483,647).   In earlier releases of SQL/DS a value of -2,147,483,648 cannot be assigned to an INTEGER column.

SMALLINT

Halfword 15-bit signed binary values (the maximum range of numbers that can be stored is from -32,768 to +32,767). In earlier releases of SQL/DS a value of -32,768 cannot be assigned to an INTEGER column.

FLOAT or FLOAT[p]

Double word long floating point values.   The range of magnitudes is approximately 5.4E-78 to 7.2E+75. The FLOAT[p] datatype specifies floating point values of either single or double precision depending on p:

P < 22   single precision

P > 21   double precision

If P is omitted, the default value FLOAT defines a double precision floating point value.

REAL

The REAL data type corresponds to the definition of a single precision data type FLOAT[p] with $0 < P < 22$

DOUBLE PRECISION

The DOUBLE PRECISION data type is supported only within DB2 and corresponds to the definition of a double precision data type FLOAT[p] with $21 < P < 53$.

DECIMAL(p[,q])
or DEC(p[,q])

Packed decimal values of 'p' (1 to 15) digits and 'q' (0 to 'p') number of decimals to the right of the implied decimal point may be specified. **The value for 'q' should be odd** -- e.g., DECIMAL (7,2) instead of DECIMAL (6,2). If you specify an even number for 'q', SQL/DS changes it automatically to the next higher odd precision. If there is no value indicated for 'q', SQL/DS uses a precision of 5. You should use INTEGER or SMALLINT data types instead of decimal numbers with a precision of 0.

Under DB2, if you have defined a column with even precision and with a scale greater than 0 -- for example, DECIMAL(8,4) -- DB2 does not use an index created for that column. If the scale is zero, DB2 may use the index in ORDER BY operations, but not in COMPARE operations. A definition with odd precision may result in the use of the index.

CHARACTER(n)
or CHAR(n)

A fixed length character value of up to 'n' (1 to 254) alphanumeric characters.

VARCHAR(n)

Variable length character value of up to 'n' alphanumeric characters. (Under SQL/DS n must be less than 255 whereas DB2 supports up to 32,674 characters with this data definition.) Unused positions of a VARCHAR column do not occupy physical storage.

If the length of the VARCHAR column under SQL/DS exceeds 254 characters, the column datatype is automatically changed to LONG VARCHAR. In this case, ISQL no longer allows INSERT, UPDATE or DELETE operations for this table.

Under DB2, the actual maximum length is dependent on physical storage characteristics and is 4K or 32K (depending on the page size chosen for the table).

LONG VARCHAR   Variable length character value of up to 32,767 characters. Note that ISQL does not allow INSERT, UPDATE or DELETE operations on tables containing columns defined as LONG VARCHAR.

Under DB2, this specification is equivalent to VARCHAR with a system calculated maximum and is supported for compatibility with SQL/DS.

GRAPHIC(n)   Fixed length DBCS (Double-Byte Character Set) value of up to 127 characters. Each DBCS characters occupies 2 bytes of storage.

VARGRAPHIC(n)   Variable length DBCS (Double-Byte Character Set) value of 'n' characters. Each DBCS characters occupies 2 bytes of storage. Under SQL/DS, if the length of the VARGRAPHIC column exceeds 127 characters the column datatype is automatically changed to LONG VARGRAPHIC.

LONG VARGRAPHIC   Variable length DBCS (Double-Byte Character Set) value of up to 16,383 characters. Each DBCS characters occupies 2 bytes of storage. Note that under SQL/DS ISQL does not allow INSERT, UPDATE or DELETE operations on tables containing columns defined as LONG VARGRAPHIC.

Under DB2, this specification is equivalent to VARGRAPHIC with a system calculated maximum and is supported for compatibility with SQL/DS.

With the introduction of SQL/DS Version 2, Release 1 and DB2 Release 3, the following three new data types are available:

DATE   The DATE data type identifies a column containing legal date values (composed of year, month, day) stored internally as a 4 byte string. The date values within a column defined as DATE may be displayed in the following standard formats:

YYYY-MM-DD	(Intl. Standards Org.)
MM/DD/YYYY	(US Standard)
DD.MM.YYYY	(European)
YYYY-MM-DD	(Japanese Ind. Standard)
LOCAL	User defined format specified at installation time.

where;

YYYY   -   Year with a valid range from 0001 to 9999

MM   -   Month with a valid range from 01 to 12

DD   -   Day with a valid range from 01 to 31

TIME   The TIME data type identifies a column containing legal time values (composed of hour, minute, second) stored internally as a 3 byte string. Time may be displayed in the following standard formats:

HH.MM.SS	(Intl. Standards Org.)
HH.MM.SS	(European)
HH:MM AM/PM	(USA) Hours vary from 01 to 12
HH:MM:SS	(Japanese Industrial Standard)
LOCAL	User defined format specified at installation time.

where;

HH   -   Hour with a valid range from 00 to 23

MM   -   Minute with a valid range from 0 to 59

SS   -   Second with a valid range from 0 to 59

TIMESTAMP   TIMESTAMP is a single seven-part value occupying 10 bytes, which represent date and time by year, month, day, hour, minute, second, and microsecond. The timestamp is only provided in the following format:

`YYYY-MM-DD-HH-MM-SS-XXXXXX`

where;

`XXXXXX`   corresponds to microseconds

When a query is run, the current date, time, and timestamp are available. You may define columns for any table to store the current date, time or timestamp during insertion of new rows. If you use the date/time data type under DB2 with the option NOT NULL WITH DEFAULT, the default is current.

Matching Column Data Types and Length

The data type of a column should be determined on the basis of the use of the column values in applications. For most columns, the choice between numeric and character representation is obvious. There are some cases where it is not, for example telephone numbers, customer-IDs, etc. may be stored as numeric data or as alphanumeric data. They should be stored in a numeric format if you want to perform arithmetic operations on the data -- for example, totals for control purposes. If the data is used only in character format then it should be stored as character data.

Another important point to consider in specifying the data type of a column is its use in conditions. The data types of columns which may be used in a WHERE clause must be compatible; only number to number and character string to character string comparisons are allowed. Data types of INTEGER, SMALLINT, DECIMAL, and FLOAT are compatible. Also CHAR, VARCHAR and LONG VARCHAR are compatible.

In the following cases DB2 does not consider using an index:

- If two character type columns of different lengths are compared (character type columns used in the WHERE clause should be of the same length).

- If you compare a character type column with a literal that is longer than the column length. If the literals are shorter than the column length, DB2 and SQL/DS pad the literals with blanks and attempt to use any available index on the column.

- If the literal in a numeric comparison has greater precision than the data type of the column. Besides, if the numeric data types are different, DB2 and SQL/DS have to do a conversion between data types.

Besides the considerations concerning the use of an index, you should be aware of the following:

- If you compare a column value to a constant in the WHERE clause the required data type of the constant depends upon the data type of the column it is compared to. If the column is numeric the literal must contain only numeric data   (0-9, . , - , +). In DB2 and SQL/DS Version 2 Release 2 any leading and trailing zeroes of decimal constants are used in determining the precision and scale of the number. In the previous releases of SQL/DS, instead, leading and trailing zeroes are ignored for determining the precision and scale.

- If the column data type is alphanumeric (CHAR, VARCHAR or LONG VARCHAR) the constant value has to be enclosed in apostrophes. The compared literal does not have to be of the same length as the column value because DB2 and SQL/DS always perform the comparison of two strings of unequal length using a copy of the shorter string, which has been extended on the right with blanks, so that it has the same length as the other string.

- When comparing two columns you should consider if both columns are defined as variable in length, SQL/DS does not pad the shorter column or column value with blanks. This means, that only the first *n* pairs of characters are compared, where *n* is the length of the shorter string. Even if the first *n* pairs of characters are equal and the rest of the longer string is blank, the two strings are not recognized as equal. **Thus, two variable length strings of different length cannot be equal in SQL/DS.**

- When you compare two numeric columns with different data types, i.e., SMALLINT and DECIMAL, DB2 and SQL/DS must convert the data to a common format *(see also the previous discussion of compatible data types)*. Since data conversion has a negative impact on performance, you should only compare numeric columns with the same data type.

Variable Length Columns

In general, you should avoid the use of variable length columns unless there is a anticipated average saving of at least 20 bytes per column. To optimize for a given table, all fixed length columns should precede the variable length columns. (There is additional cost in CPU time for locating all columns that follow a variable length column.)

Keep in mind the following considerations on variable length columns:

- A 2-byte overhead is required to store the effective length of a variable length column.

- Additional CPU time is needed to locate a variable length column with a row.

- If a variable length column contains seldom used information (such as comments or verbal descriptions) it should be stored in a separate table. In this way, the rows of the table containing the frequently used part of the information is shorter. Therefore, more rows fit into one page of physical storage. The result is a shorter response time because of a reduced number of I/O operations used to serve a single query.

- If a variable length row is increased in length during update and SQL/DS or DB2 cannot find space for the updated row on the same page, the row is stored on another page and a pointer is placed on the original page. Subsequent retrieval of the updated row requires at least two I/O operations.

- Within SQL/DS, index entries based on VARCHAR columns are always extended by 25% when stored as part of a key in a cluster. Furthermore, SQL/DS adds one byte to the field to store its actual length. Under DB2, if you define an index on long variable length columns, index entries are automatically padded to the maximum length of the column.

- Under SQL/DS, LONG VARCHAR columns should only be used when the maximum column length may exceed 254 characters.

- Under SQL/DS, if a table includes columns defined as LONG VARCHAR or LONG VARGRAPHIC or as VARCHAR and VARGRAPHIC with a column length exceeding 254 characters, ISQL does not allow any INSERT, UPDATE or DELETE operations on this table.

- If the length of the column causes the row size to be near the maximum page size it prevents you from adding new columns to the table.

Null Columns

Any field value in a table, regardless of its data type, may have the special value NULL. A NULL value may be thought of as an empty space or a space reserved for later insertion of data. NULL values can be prohibited by specifying NOT NULL (Not Null with default under DB2) for the desired columns during table creation.

Each nullable column requires one extra byte of DASD storage, extra processing time and adds to the complexity of application programming. This extra byte contains X'FF' if the field value is NULL; otherwise it contains X'00'.

Delete Rules

As we have seen in our discussion of referential constraints in data manipulation operations, the dependent tables during update and delete operations control whether the deletion of rows in the primary table may be carried out or not. Delete operations may directly impact dependent tables, i.e., dependent rows can be updated or even deleted according to the delete rule specified by the user in the CREATE TABLE statement. The following delete rules are available under DB2 Version 2 and SQL/DS Version 2 Release 2:

RESTRICT-   The RESTRICT rule is the <u>default rule</u>. The rule signifies that the primary key is only deleted, if there is no foreign key with the same value in any dependent table. For example, a department may be deleted if there are no employees working for it.

SET NULL-   With the SET NULL rule, DB2 and SQL/DS delete the primary key row and update the descending tables setting the foreign key values to null in all rows in the dependent table(s) that contain the deleted primary key value in the foreign key column. For example, when a department is deleted all employees, who had been previously working for the department are automatically considered unassigned.

CASCADE-   The CASCADE rule is the most powerful of all delete rules and should be used with extreme caution. The rule causes the deletion of the row containing the primary key as well as the deletion of all dependent rows having the primary key value in the corresponding foreign key column. For multilevel dependencies under DB2 Version 2, the deletion of the primary key may also impact the descendent tables, i.e., tables that are connected via referential rules to dependent tables. **Multilevel dependencies are not supported under SQL/DS Version 2 Release 2.**

Creating Tables

Tables are created using the CREATE TABLE statement. Since the CREATE TABLE statement under DB2 uses several more options (such as EDITPROC, VALIDPROC, Default assignments) we will discuss these options in the corresponding chapter on DB2 data definition statements.

```
CREATE TABLE  [creator-prefix.] tablename
(column-name   data-type   [NOT NULL],
.........     ......    ..........,
.........          ..........,
[PRIMARY KEY (column-name1[,column-name2,...]),]

[ FOREIGN KEY (column-name3[,column-name4,...])
                REFERENCES tablename-2

          ON DELETE [ RESTRICT
                      CASCADE
                      SET NULL  ]

                                                ]
[IN [owner_id.]dbspace_name]   only SQL/DS   )
[      tablespace-name]        only DB2
```

where;

creator_prefix   The creator_prefix defaults to the userid of the user that executes the CREATE TABLE statement. You only have to specify the creator_prefix if you define a table for another user. *(DBA authority is needed to define a table for other users.)*

tablename   The tablename may be up to 18 characters long. The first character must be alphabetic (A-Z, @, #, $) and the rest either alphabetic, '_', or numeric. The fully qualified name for tables is formed by qualification with the creator-prefix (creator-prefix.tablename).

Column-name   The column-name may be up to 18 characters long. The first character must be alphabetic (A-Z, @, #, $) and the rest either alphabetic, '_', or numeric. The column-name must be unique within a table.

data-type   *For valid data types, see Data Types - pp. 67 ff.*

column-name1,[column-name2] Column (or group of columns for a composite key) that forms the primary key of the table. The primary key column(s) must be defined as NOT NULL or under DB2 also as NOT NULL WITH DEFAULT if it is assured that the default values are unique. (This is only possible with the use of data type TIMESTAMP) A unique index must be created on the primary key column(s).

column-name3,[column-name4]   Column (or group of columns for a composite key) that forms the foreign key of the table. It is recommended to create an index on the foreign key column(s).

tablename-2   Name of the table that contains the primary key column(s).

If you do not specify a DBSPACE name, SQL/DS attempts to create the table in a PRIVATE DBSPACE that is owned by the user executing the CREATE TABLE statement. If the user does not own any PRIVATE DBSPACE, SQL/DS returns an error message.

If you only specify the DBSPACE name, omitting the owner ID, SQL/DS looks for a PRIVATE DBSPACE owned by the user executing the CREATE TABLE command. If there is no such DBSPACE, SQL/DS searches for a PUBLIC DBSPACE with the indicated name. The following actions may be taken by SQL/DS:

■   If a PUBLIC DBSPACE with this name exists and the user has RESOURCE or DBA authority, SQL/DS creates the table in the specified PUBLIC DBSPACE.

■   If a PUBLIC DBSPACE with this name exists, but the user has neither RESOURCE nor DBA authority, the table creation fails and SQL/DS returns an error message.

■   If there is no such PUBLIC DBSPACE, the table creation fails and SQL/DS returns an error message.

Under DB2, it is recommended that you always provide the tablespace name in the CREATE TABLE statement. If you omit the tablespace name, DB2 may read every page of the table space catalog table to check if you are creating a table in a non-existent table space. Then, DB2 automatically creates a table space with the same name as the table itself (implicitly created table space).

The following CREATE TABLE statement creates the table EMP. SQL/DS automatically creates the table in a PRIVATE DBSPACE owned by the user executing the CREATE TABLE command. Under DB2, a new table space with the same name as the table is created implicitly.

```
CREATE TABLE    EMP
                (EMP_NO          CHAR(5),
                NAME             CHAR(20),
                DEPT_NO          CHAR(3),
                MGR_NO           CHAR(5),
                SALARY           DECIMAL(11,2));
```

The CREATE TABLE statement alters the contents of the following catalog tables:

SQL/DS	DB2
SYSTEM.SYSCATALOG	SYSIBM.SYSTABLES
SYSTEM.SYSCOLUMNS	SYSIBM.SYSCOLUMNS
SYSTEM.SYSTABAUTH	SYSIBM.SYSTABAUTH

Altering the Table Structure

SQL/DS and DB2 allow only limited variations in the structure of an existing table without recreating it. You can use the ALTER TABLE statement only to add a new column or to add and delete referential constraints.

Note: DB2 Version 2 also allows changing the validation routine by using the ALTER TABLE command.

For all other changes, such as modifying the length or data type of an existing column or to delete a column, you have to drop the existing table and completely recreate it.

Adding a New Column

SQL/DS and DB2 allow you to add one or more new columns to an existing table with the following statement:

```
ALTER TABLE   tablename
ADD (column-name1 datatype[,column-name2 datatype,..])
```

where;

column-name	The column-name may be up to 18 characters long. The first character must be alphabetic (A-z, @, #, $) and the rest either alphabetic, '_' or numeric. The column-name must be unique within a table.
data-type	*For valid data types see Data Types p. 67 ff.*

When you issue the ALTER TABLE command, SQL automatically changes the information related to the table in the following catalog tables:

SQL/DS	DB2
SYSTEM.SYSCATALOG	SYSIBM.SYSTABLES
SYSTEM.SYSCOLUMNS	SYSIBM.SYSCOLUMNS
SYSTEM.SYSTABAUTH	SYSIBM.SYSTABAUTH

If you add a new column under SQL/DS it can only be defined as NULL; **you may not define a column as** NOT NULL. If you add a new column within DB2, you may define it as NULL or NOT NULL WITH DEFAULT. In the latter case, when you retrieve a row from the table, the value for the new column is the default value. **You may not define a column as** NOT NULL.

SQL/DS or DB2 adds the new column in the table structure to the right of the right most column of the table. This means that if you retrieve the rows by using the SELECT * statement, the new column is displayed as the last column on the right. However, no changes of the physical record are made until you update the table rows by inserting values in the new column.

When adding a new column to an existing table you should consider the following:

- If you insert values into a new column, DB2 or SQL/DS may not find enough space on the actual page to store the up-dated row. The row is forced to another page and a pointer placed in the original page to point to its new location. Subsequent retrieval of the updated row requires at least two I/O operations, resulting in decreased performance.

- If the new column is preceded by variable length columns, DB2 and SQL/DS have to recalculate its actual position within the row each time you want to retrieve values from that column. This added CPU time for finding the column causes a decrease in performance.

- In DB2, a column cannot be added to a table that has an edit routine or a column defined as LONG VARCHAR.

Adding a new referential constraint

To add a referential constraint to your existing data environment, you must follow the steps described below in the indicated sequence. *(The described procedure implies that neither the primary nor the foreign keys exist. If the primary key has been already defined skip the first two steps.)*

- DB2 and SQL/DS require a unique index created on the primary key column(s) (see CREATE INDEX statement). If an index already exists on the column(s) that forms the primary key, query the SYSTEM.SYSINDEXES catalog table to assure the uniqueness of the index.

■ Add the primary key to the existing table with the following statement:

```
ALTER TABLE   tablename
   PRIMARY KEY (column-name1 [,column-name2,....])
```

where;

tablename   Name of the table that contains the primary key column(s).

column-name1,[column-name2] Column (or group of columns for a composite key) that forms the primary key of the table. The primary key column(s) must have been previously defined as NOT NULL or as NOT NULL WITH DEFAULT (under DB2) if the default values are unique (This is only possible with the use of the data type TIMESTAMP).

■ Create the foreign key in the dependent table:

```
ALTER TABLE   tablename
FOREIGN KEY [const-name] (col-name1[,col-name2,...])
           REFERENCES tablename-2

           ON DELETE ⎡ RESTRICT ⎤
                     ⎢ CASCADE  ⎥
                     ⎣ SET NULL ⎦
```

where;

tablename   Name of the table that contains the foreign key column(s).

col-name1,[col-name2] Column (or group of columns for a composite key) that forms the foreign key of the table. It is recommended that you create an index on the foreign key column(s) (*see* CREATE INDEX *statement*).

const-name   The constraint name identifies internally the new referential constraint. If you omit the name, it is automatically generated by DB2 or SQL/DS. The constraint name is utilized in error messages and to delete an existing constraint.

`tablename-2`   Name of the table that contains the primary key column(s).

If the table containing the foreign key had been already loaded, it is automatically marked by DB2 and SQL/DS as 'CHECK PENDING' until it is scanned for violations of the referential constraint -- i.e. all foreign keys must correspond to an existing primary key.

Deleting a referential constraint

A referential constraint is deleted for the following reasons:
- if the independent or dependent table is dropped;
- if the primary key of the independent table is dropped using the following statement:

```
ALTER TABLE   tablename
  DROP PRIMARY KEY
```

where;

`tablename`   Name of the table that contains the primary key column(s).

- if the referential constraint is removed using the following statement:

```
ALTER TABLE   tablename
  DROP FOREIGN KEY constraint-name
```

where;

`tablename`   Name of the table that contains the foreign key column(s).

`constraint-name`   Internal or user assigned name of the referential constraint.

Performing Other Changes

If you want to modify the length or data type of an existing column or if you want to delete an unused column, you must drop the existing table and recreate it corresponding to the new structure. Before dropping a table, you should consider the following:
- all indexes created for the table are also dropped;
- all synonyms based on the table are also dropped;

- all authorizations to access the table are dropped;
- all application plans using the table are invalidated;
- all defined referential constraints involving the table are also dropped.

If you want to increase the length of an alphanumeric column or the precision of a numeric column, you must recreate the table. To recreate the table, you should perform the following tasks:

- Create a temporary table identical to the table that has to be changed. You can query the catalog tables to determine the definition of the old table.
- Copy the data from the old table to the temporary table by using the INSERT statement.
- Drop the old table.
- Recreate the table with the new column definitions.
- Copy the data from the temporary table to the new created table by using the INSERT statement.
- Drop the temporary table.
- Inform the other users that the table definition has changed and that they must recreate views or synonyms previously defined for the table.

To delete a column, you must perform the same tasks except that you have to specify which columns you want to copy when executing the INSERT statement to create the temporary table.

If you want to change the data type from alphanumeric to numeric or vice versa, use an application program to copy the data and convert it, as needed.

Dropping Tables

Before dropping a table, consider the following:

- all indexes created for the table are also dropped;
- all synonyms based on the table are also dropped (only SQL/DS);
- all authorizations to access the table are dropped;
- all application plans using the table are invalidated;
- the drop operation must be committed before you can create a table with the same name.
- All defined referential constraints involving the table are also dropped.
- Under DB2, if the table has a partitioning index, you must drop the table space and not the table. If a simple table space contains more than one table, space held by a dropped table cannot be reused until

the table space has been reorganized. *(This problem has been addressed with the introduction of segmented table spaces under DB2 Version 2)*

You should issue the following queries to verify whether there are any access modules or views based on the table or are any users with authority to access the table. **If these queries return any rows, you should make sure that the corresponding applications have been changed and that all the users have been notified, before dropping the table.**

Queries under SQL/DS:

```
SELECT  DNAME, DCREATOR, DTYPE
  FROM  SYSTEM.SYSUSAGE
 WHERE  BTYPE = 'R'
   AND  BNAME = 'table name'
   AND  BCREATOR = 'creatorprefix'
   AND  DTYPE = 'X'              (access modules)
    OR  DTYPE = 'V';            (Views)
```

```
SELECT  TTNAME, GRANTEE, GRANTEETYPE, TIMESTAMP
  FROM  SYSTEM.SYSTABAUTH
 WHERE  TTNAME = 'table name'
   AND  TCREATOR = 'creatorprefix'
   AND  GRANTEETYPE ¬= 'P'       (access module)
    OR  GRANTEETYPE ¬= ' ';     (user)
```

Queries under DB2:

```
SELECT  DNAME, DCREATOR, DTYPE
  FROM  SYSIBM.SYSUSAGE
 WHERE  BTYPE = 'T'
   AND  BNAME = 'table name'
   AND  BCREATOR = 'creator prefix'
   AND  DTYPE = 'P'              (Application plans)
    OR  DTYPE = 'V'             (Views)
```

```
SELECT   TTNAME, GRANTEE, DATEGRANTED
  FROM   SYSIBM.SYSTABAUTH
 WHERE   GRANTEETYPE ¬= 'P'
   AND   TTNAME = 'table name'
   AND   TCREATOR = 'creator prefix'
```

The DROP statement for tables is the same for SQL/DS and DB2:

```
DROP   TABLE   [creatorprefix.] table-name
```

To drop a table space under DB2 you must execute the following statement:

```
DROP   TABLESPACE   [database-name.]tablespace-name
```

Defining Table Synonyms

Synonyms are alternate names for tables or views. Each user may individually assign a synonym to any table or view.

The user who creates a table is automatically considered its owner. If another user want to use the table, the owner must grant them the authority. Others may then access the table by referring to it with the creatorprefix followed by the name of the table.

If you are using a table owned by another user, it becomes bothersome to always refer to it by using the fully qualified name. To avoid this you may create a synonym.

A synonym is only effective for the user who created it. If many users want to use the same synonyms, they must each define it.

The syntax for the CREATE SYNONYM statement is as follows:

```
CREATE SYNONYM username FOR creatorprefix.tablename
```

To delete a defined synonym execute the following statement:

```
DROP SYNONYM user-name
```

In DB2, a synonym on a table or view is implicitly dropped when a table or view is dropped.

View

A view may be described as a window through which you can see data stored in one or more tables. Views can be defined based on the following table subsets:

■ A subset of the rows of one or more base tables. This subset is obtained using the WHERE clause of the subselect in the CREATE VIEW statement.

COL_1	COL_2	COL_3	COL_4	COL_5
0001				
0002				
0003				
0004				
0005				
0006				
0007				

Subset of rows

Figure 5.5   View definitions as a subset of rows

```
CREATE VIEW V1 AS SELECT * FROM  BASETABLE
       WHERE   COL-1 BETWEEN 0003 AND 0005;
```

■ A subset of the columns of one or more base table(s). Such subsets are formed by selecting only certain columns of the base table(s).

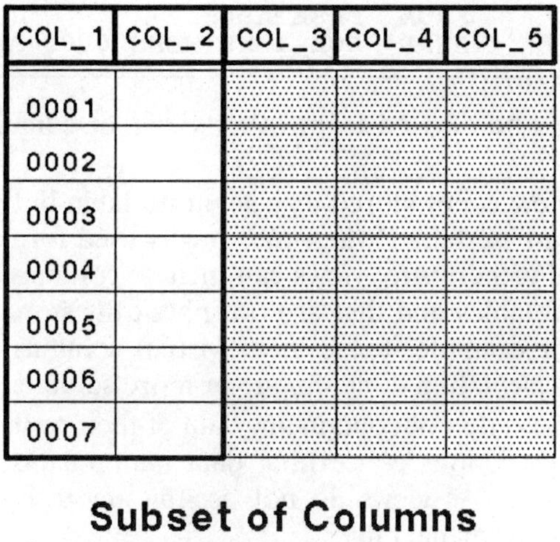

COL_1	COL_2	COL_3	COL_4	COL_5
0001				
0002				
0003				
0004				
0005				
0006				
0007				

Subset of Columns

Figure 5.6 View definitions as a subset of columns

```
CREATE VIEW   V2
        AS SELECT   COL1, COL2
           FROM   BASETABLE;
```

■ Row and column subset. Any combination of row selection and column selection.

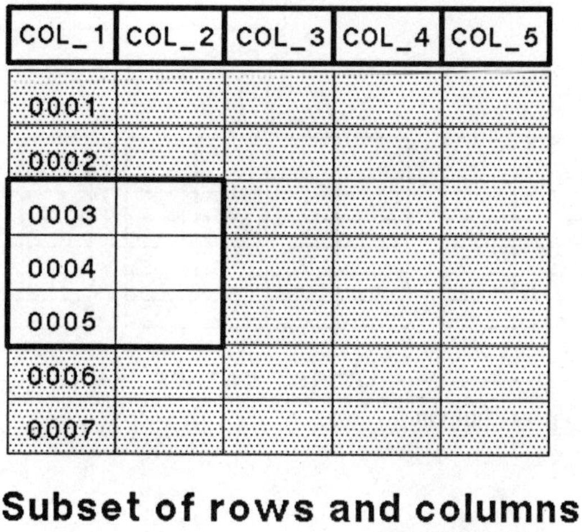

COL_1	COL_2	COL_3	COL_4	COL_5
0001				
0002				
0003				
0004				
0005				
0006				
0007				

Subset of rows and columns

Figure 5.7 View definitions as a combination of row and columns selection

```
CREATE VIEW   V1
         AS
         SELECT   COL-1, Col*
         FROM     BASETABLE
         WHERE    COL-1 BETWEEN 0003 AND 0005;
```

Views can also be derived from other views or combinations of views and tables.

Data in a view is not stored as a separate table but is retrieved from the underlying base tables when the view is used for data manipulation or retrieval. Furthermore, views can include columns that are not part of the original tables and that are not physically stored throughout the database. For example, these 'new' virtual columns may contain the result from a calculation done on one or more columns.

Although views do not contain any data of their own, they can be used (with some restrictions concerning data manipulation) just as if they were real tables. As views do not occupy any disk storage, they are sometimes called 'virtual tables'.

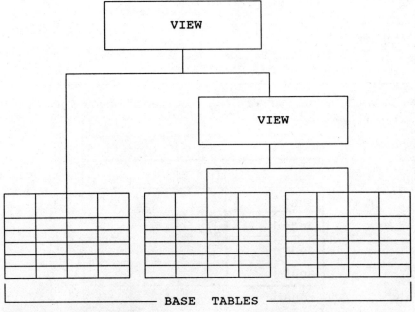

Figure 5.8   View definition

Views are used for the following reasons:

- *Simplify data retrieval.* Views can reduce complexity by presenting a smaller and simpler version of the table or tables upon which they are based.
- *To store efficient queries.* Views may be utilizied to store validated and efficient queries in an easily accessible form.
- *Prevent unauthorized users or application programs from having access to sensitive data.* Views can be defined so that each user of the table is permitted to access and manipulate only specific parts of the table.
- *Isolate the application from table structure changes.* Seen from the application point of view the most important use of views is to isolate the application from table structure changes (i.e., addition of new columns, etc.). Furthermore, by specifying part of the application logic in the subquery of the view definition, you can save time and decrease expenses for application development and maintenance.

Creating Views

As the execution of a query produces a new table (the result table) a query is used to define a virtual table or view. In other words, the table on which a view operates is nothing more than the result table of a SELECT statement.

A view is created using the following statement:

```
CREATE VIEW  [creatorprefix.] view-name
             [(column-name1, column-name2,....)]
        AS   subselect
             [WITH CHECK OPTION]            only DB2
```

where;

creatorprefix   The creatorprefix defaults to the userid of the user who is actually executing the CREATE VIEW statement.

`view-name`	The view name may be up to 18 characters long. The first character must be alphabetic (`A-z`, `@`, `#`, `$`) and the rest either alphabetic, '`_`' or numeric. The complete name for views is formed by qualification with the creator-prefix (`creator-prefix.view name`). The `view name` must be unique among all names for tables, views, and synonyms within the userid.
`column-name`	The column-name may be up to 18 characters long. The first character must be alphabetic (`A-z`, `@`, `#`, `$`) and the rest either alphabetic, '`_`' or numeric. The column-name must be unique within a view.

The WITH CHECK OPTION clause is available only under DB2. This clause assures that DB2 only allows inserts into the base tables through the view for the column and row subset defined in the view.

As you can see in the CREATE VIEW statement above, a view can have column-names that are different from the names of the corresponding columns in the underlying table(s). For these column-names apply the same naming rules described in the CREATE TABLE statement.

The data identified by a view can be queried and, with some restrictions, manipulated (update, delete and insert instructions) in the same manner as a real table.

To create a view on tables or views owned by other users, you need at least SELECT authority for the underlying objects (tables and views). If you want to update, insert or delete rows through the view, you need the corresponding privilege for the base objects. The creation of a view, although you introduce a new object that is exclusively owned by you, does not alter your privileges for the objects on which the view is defined.

Example:

```
CREATE VIEW    VTAB  (COL1,COL2,COL3)
          AS
               SELECT   TCOL1,TCOL2,TCOL3
               FROM    TAB;
```

Using Views in Queries

A view defines a subset of the data stored in the underlying tables. If you update, delete or insert rows into the base tables, those changes are visible through the views of those tables.

The base subset of data covered by the view can be further subdivided by adding a WHERE clause to your query of the view. The condition specified in the WHERE clause of the query is logically concatenated with the AND operator to the condition in the SELECT statement specified for the definition of the view.

If, for example, VIEW1 is defined as the following:

```
CREATE   VIEW VIEW1
     AS  SELECT  A,  B,  C
         FROM   TAB1
         WHERE   A > 1000;        condition for
                                  view creation
```

and if you execute the following query;

```
SELECT   *
  FROM   VIEW1
  WHERE  B BETWEEN 10 AND 20;     condition for
                                  view query
```

you obtain the same result table as if you would have used the query;

```
SELECT   A,  B,  C
  FROM   TAB1
  WHERE  A > 1000                 condition for
                                  view creation

     AND                          logical connection

       B  BETWEEN 10 AND 20;      condition for
                                  view query
```

Views Based on More Than One Table

A view can combine data from more than one table or view. You can do this by defining a view using a JOIN operation.

Although you may join together any number of tables or views, you should keep in mind that there is a degradation in performance when using JOIN operations.

Virtual Columns in Views

Views can include columns that are not part of the underlying tables, like the results of a built-in function or arithmetic calculations based on one or more columns. These expressions or functions appear to be the same as other columns of the view, even though they are not physically stored throughout the database. For this reason these columns are also called 'virtual columns' or 'virtual fields'.

When you use built-in functions or arithmetic expressions, you have to specify column-names for all columns in the view.

Deleting Views

In SQL/DS and DB2 a view is automatically dropped when its creator no longer holds any privileges on the view. Under DB2, a view is also automatically dropped when the SELECT privilege used to create the view is revoked (with the REVOKE statement).

To drop a view explicitly, you have to use the following statement:

```
DROP VIEW view-name
```

View Synonyms

Synonyms are alternate names for tables or views. Each user may individually assign a synonym to any table or view.

The person who created a view is automatically considered the owner of the view. If another user wants to use the view, the owner must first grant them the authority. Only then are other users allowed to access the view by referring to it with the creatorprefix followed by the name of the view.

If you are using a view owned by another user, it becomes bothersome to always refer to it by using the fully qualified name. To avoid this you can create a synonym.

A synonym is only effective for the user who created it. If many users want to use the same synonyms, they must each define it separately.

```
CREATE SYNONYM username FOR [creatorprefix.] view name
```

To delete a defined synonym execute the following statement:

```
DROP SYNONYM user-name
```

In SQL/DS, synonyms can only be explicitly dropped. The creation or deletion of synonyms using the CREATE and DROP SYNONYM statements are reflected in the SYSTEM.SYSSYNONYMS catalog table. In DB2, a synonym on a table or view is implicitly dropped when the table or view is dropped.

Limitations for the Use of Views

The following limitations apply for the use of views in UPDATE, INSERT and DELETE operations:

- If you use a JOIN operation to define a view (whether two or more tables/views are joined together or a table/view is joined to itself) the view's data can only be selected. **You cannot update, delete or insert data into a view that is based on a JOIN operation.**
- You cannot update, delete or insert data into a view that is defined by using the DISTINCT keyword.
- When inserting a row into a table using a view, the row must contain a value for each column of the base table that is defined as NOT NULL. SQL/DS or DB2 does not insert a row into a table via a view, if you do not explicitly provide a value for each column defined as NOT NULL.
- You cannot update a view's data if the view definition includes one of the following:
  - Built-in functions (AVG, MIN, MAX, SUM, COUNT)
  - GROUP BY clause

In these cases you can only select the data by using the view.
- If you use an arithmetic expression for a column in the definition of the view, you cannot update that column or insert rows to the base table, but you can select and delete rows or update the other columns.

Additional considerations when using views include:
- You cannot build an index based on a view. An index is defined only on a table.
- The definition of an existing view cannot be altered. **This also means that if you define a view using SELECT * (all columns of the underlying tables) and a new column is added to the base tables, the**

new column is not be visible through the view. To include the new
column, you have to drop the view and recreate it.

- The UNION keyword may not be used to create a view.
- Under SQL/DS the ORDER BY clause may not be used to create a view.
- A view definition may include no more than 16 different tables (in all clauses) and may not contain more than 140 columns.

6

SQL/DS Data Definition

Introduction

In the previous chapter, we discussed common elements of the data definition language and logical storage structure of DB2 and SQL/DS. In this chapter we will examine, in detail, specific elements of SQL/DS. In particular, we will discuss the following:

- DBSPACES
- STORAGE POOLS
- INDEXES

Since this book addresses end-users and application programmers, we will avoid detailed discussions of activities that require specific knowledge of system functions.

DBSPACE

Tables and indexes under SQL/DS are stored in DBSPACES. A DBSPACE can hold more than one table or index. The total number of tables and indexes for a single DBSPACE may not exceed 255. DBSPACES are divided into pages. Each page holds one or more rows of a table or index; the page size is always 4K. **Figure 6.1** illustrates the way SQL/DS stores information in a DBSPACE.

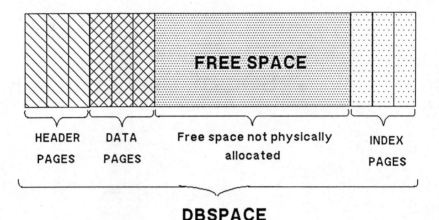

Figure 6.1   Structure of DBSPACE

The first pages (*header pages*) of each DBSPACE are used by SQL/DS to store control information on the tables and indexes contained in the DBSPACE. Following the header pages, are the table data pages. If there is more than one table in the DBSPACE, SQL/DS may store rows from different tables on the same data page. Index data is contained in index pages. During DBSPACE definition you have to reserve space (default 33%) for the insertion of index information. Index pages are always stored in the right-hand portion of the DBSPACE and unused pages are always logically found in the middle of a DBSPACE. Since a DBSPACE defines only a virtual allocation of space in a database, these unused pages do not occupy DASD storage and no physical storage is wasted.

During its acquisition, each DBSPACE is assigned to a specific storage pool. Storage pools are units of physical storage and are subdivided into 4K blocks. Each time you insert new rows into a table, SQL/DS attempts to store them on data pages that have already been used. If the rows do not fit, SQL/DS starts a new DBSPACE data page and searches for an available block (slot) in the corresponding storage pool to store the page.

When you create a DBSPACE, you first have to determine its characteristics in terms of the following considerations:

- number of tables and approximate size;
- use of the tables;
- required indexing.

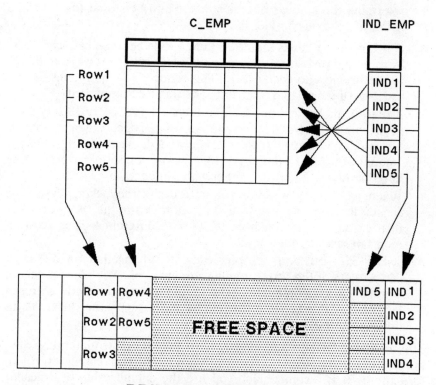

Figure 6.2 DBSPACE

Once the requirements are defined, the DBA adds the DBSPACE to the database by using the SQLADBSP EXEC command. To use the DBSPACE to create tables and to load data, the DBSPACE has to be acquired by issuing the ACQUIRE DBSPACE statement. With the ACQUIRE DBSPACE statement the user establishes the maximum size of the DBSPACE, the locking size, and the ownership. To control physical storage usage, DBSPACES are often acquired for the users by the DBA.

DBSPACE Size

The size of the DBSPACE depends on the number of tables and indexes contained in the DBSPACE as well as the number and size of rows stored for each table.

To determine the number of tables that are to be stored together in a DBSPACE, you should consider the following:

- If two or more tables are often joined together, you can load them by using the DATALOAD operation to place related rows from different tables close to each other. This reduces I/O operations for the retrieval of the related rows and performance is improved.

- If there is more than one table in the DBSPACE, SQL/DS may store rows from different tables on the same data page. When an index is not used, the entire DBSPACE is scanned, necessitating a larger amount of I/O operations. For this reason, you should avoid storing infrequently used tables together with frequently used ones.

- When acquiring a DBSPACE, you must define the locking level. The chosen locking level is effective for all tables in the DBSPACE. For this reason, you should store tables with different locking requirements in separate DBSPACES.

- Tables in a DBSPACE are physically stored together on the same DBEXTENTS of the corresponding storage pool. To reduce potential storage device contention, you should place frequently accessed large tables into separate DBSPACES and assign these DBSPACES to different storage pools.

The number of tables and indexes in a DBSPACE also determines the number of header pages necessary to store the corresponding control information. It is recommended you use the default value of 8 header pages (which is also the maximum value). You should reduce the number of header pages only if there are very few objects in the DBSPACE.

Once a DBSPACE has been acquired, you cannot allocate additional storage for it. Allow ample space when estimating the amount of space to be reserved for table growth. IBM recommends an allowance from 50% to 200% (1/2 to 2X the space estimated for table data). Although these values seem extremely high, you should remember that unused pages of a DBSPACE do not occupy physical storage. On the other hand, if your definition for the size of a DBSPACE is too small, you limit the possibilities of inserting and updating table rows or creating new tables. It is better to overestimate the required number of pages, rather than to underestimate the size of a DBSPACE. The DBSPACE size calculation is based on specific formulae. This task is typically performed by the DBA based of the number and type of required indexes, the estimated number of rows, etc., provided by the user.

DBSPACE Type

SQL/DS distinguishes between two types of DBSPACES: PUBLIC DBSPACES and PRIVATE DBSPACES.

Public DBSPACE

You should define a DBSPACE as public when its tables are to be accessed by multiple users at the same time using either data retrieval or data manipulation commands. Public DBSPACEs also allow you to choose the locking level. SQL/DS allows the locking of PUBLIC DBSPACEs at row, page and DBSPACE level. The default locksize is page. You should define row level locking, if the tables contained in the DBSPACE are small and frequently accessed. By specifying row level locking for table data pages, SQL/DS automatically locks the corresponding index pages at key level. Default index page locking is at page level. In order not to add unnecessary overhead for locking operations, use the ROW locking option sparingly.

However, even if you specify DBSPACE locking at ROW level, you should be aware that SQL/DS may automatically promote the locking level to DBSPACE locking (depending on the number of actual locks). To control lock escalation from ROW or PAGE locking to DBSPACE locking, SQL/DS employs the following two parameters:

- **NLRBU** -- number of lock requests allowed for a single user (default value is 1000);
- **NLRBS** -- number of lock requests allowed for the system.

If the number of actual locks is greater than one of these values, SQL/DS automatically locks the whole DBSPACE.

To determine the approximate number of locks acquired during the execution of a data retrieval or manipulation command, estimate the number of rows accessed by SQL/DS (not only those returned) to produce the requested result. When no index is used, SQL/DS has to access every row in the DBSPACE. If an index is used, SQL/DS accesses both the index keys and the data rows to which those index keys point.

Private DBSPACES

If the data stored in a DBSPACE is accessed and updated by only one user, define the DBSPACE as private. Each user may own one or more private DBSPACES. SQL/DS locks PRIVATE DBSPACES at the DBSPACE level. Concurrent access to data contained in a PRIVATE DBSPACE is only possible for READ operations.

Space Requirements for Indexes

As previously mentioned, indexes are stored together with the corresponding tables in the same DBSPACE. Index data is contained in index pages. When you acquire a DBSPACE, define the number of pages to reserve for the insertion of index information. Once the DBSPACE is acquired, this value cannot be changed. To increase or decrease the number of reserved index pages, you must define a new DBSPACE and reload the data from the old DBSPACE.

The default value for index allocation is 33% of the entire DBSPACE. If you do not change the default value, SQL/DS reserves twice as many pages for table data as for index pages.

To determine the space requirements for index data, consider the following:

- For each table you can create one or more indexes. The index can be based on the values contained in one column or it can be created using multiple columns. The primary reasons for creating an index are to ensure uniqueness of the rows in a table and to improve performance. On the other hand, an index causes overhead for its maintenance. Each time the column values on which the index is based are updated, SQL/DS must also update the corresponding key values in the index. You should limit the amount of indexing for those tables that are frequently changed. However, if the data contained in a DBSPACE is generally accessed as read-only, you may increase the percentage of index pages for this DBSPACE to allow the definition of many indexes to improve performance.

- Index entries based on columns defined as VARCHAR or VARGRAPHIC are always expanded by 25% when stored as part of a key in a cluster. Furthermore, SQL/DS adds one byte to the key field to store its actual length.

- If the index is defined as unique, there are as many index entries in the corresponding index as there are rows in the table. For nonunique indexes with multiple occurrences of the index value, SQL/DS stores each distinct key value only once in the index along with all the row pointers for the rows that contain this specific value.

Storage Pool Assignment

When you acquire DBSPACES, they are assigned to a physical allocation of storage called a *storage pool*. When determining the storage pool to which you want to assign a DBSPACE, you should consider the following:

- If the DBSPACE contains read-only data -- typically tables with historic information -- assign them to a nonrecoverable storage pool.

- To avoid potential device contention, place large and frequently accessed tables in different DBSPACES and assign these DBSPACES to different storage pools.
- Assign DBSPACES in relation to their actual and potential size to different storage pools to balance device utilization.

Adding a DBSPACE to a Database

To add a new DBSPACE to a database, you must invoke the SQLADBSP EXEC. During its execution SQLADBSP requests information about the DBSPACES to be added to the database. This information is created either on a CMS file prior to executing the EXEC or dynamically created during runtime. In any case, you must specify the number of PUBLIC, PRIVATE and INTERNAL DBSPACES must be added as well as the number of pages and the storage pool assignment for each.

Once the required information is created, SQLADBSP invokes SQL/DS with the ADD DBSPACE option. This facility allocates page tables in the database directory for the new DBSPACES and updates the SYSTEM.SYSDBSPACES catalog table.

Note: Adding DBSPACE is typically performed by the DBA or a system programmer with the necessary authorization. We have only provided a brief description of the related activities.

Acquiring a DBSPACE

After adding a DBSPACE to the database directory, you may acquire it for use via the ACQUIRE DBSPACE statement. To acquire a PRIVATE DBSPACE you need DBA or, at least, RESOURCE authority. A PUBLIC DBSPACE can only be acquired by the DBA.

The general format of the ACQUIRE DBSPACE statement is as follows:

```
ACQUIRE   PUBLIC    DBSPACE
          PRIVATE
   NAMED  [owner.] dbspace-name
          [(options)]
```

where;

owner   The userid of the user that is the owner of the
                              DBSPACE. If you acquire the DBSPACE for yourself
                              the ownerid may be omitted.

dbspace_name   Do not use 'SYS' in the first three characters of
                the DBSPACE name because 'SYS' identifies
                DBSPACES for system use.

Additionally, you may specify the following options:

NHEADER   *Number of header pages.*
           The default is 8 header pages. You can specify any
           integer number of pages within a range of 1 to 8.

PAGES   *Maximum number of pages in the DBSPACE.*
           The default is 128 pages. You can specify any integer
           number of pages as a multiple of 128 within a range of
           128 to a maximum of approximately 8,000,000.

PCTINDEX   *Percentage of index pages in the DBSPACE.*
           The default is 33. You can specify any number of pages
           within a range of 1 to 100.

PCTFREE   *Percentage of free space for each page in the DBSPACE.*
           The default is 15%. This free space is necessary to allow
           variations in length of updated rows. Free space reserved
           via the PCTFREE option is utilized only during update
           operations. Insert operations are carried out by SQL/DS
           if it is possible to store the row within the page without
           reducing the available free space below the PCTFREE
           percentage. Variations during updates may be caused by
           insertion of real values into columns with NULL values
           or updates of variable length columns. If a row is in-
           creased in length during update and SQL/DS cannot find
           space for the updated row on the same page, the updated
           row is stored in another page and a pointer is placed in
           the original page. Subsequent retrieval of the updated
           row requires at least two I/O operations. **SQL/DS does
           not use this free space for insertion until you change the
           PCTFREE value to a lower value via the ALTER DBSPACE
           statement.** You should therefore reduce the PCTFREE
           value immediately after table data loading. However,
           SQL/DS typically reserves more free space than what you
           specify.

LOCK   *ROW/PAGE/DBSPACE*
           For a PUBLIC DBSPACE you may choose the locking level.
           The default is PAGE level locking. A PRIVATE DBSPACE is
           always locked at DBSPACE level.

STORPOOL   *Identifier of the storage pool.*
Identifies the storage pool to which the DBSPACE has been assigned. If you omit the STORPOOL parameter the DBSPACE is assigned to storage pool 1.

Reorganizing a DBSPACE

Once a DBSPACE has been acquired, SQL/DS does not allow you to allocate additional storage for it or to change the distribution of pages on index and data pages. There are several reasons for reorganizing a DBSPACE including:

- the need to move table data into a larger DBSPACE;
- insufficient space for the creation of new indexes;
- the need to transfer tables from a PRIVATE DBSPACE to a PUBLIC DBSPACE or from a PUBLIC DBSPACE to a PRIVATE DBSPACE -- for example, for test purposes.

Copying one table

If you have to copy only one table from one DBSPACE to another, use the following procedure:

- Use the INSERT statement to copy only non-clustered tables.

  ```
  INSERT INTO .....
  ```

- To copy a large table or a table in clustering sequence, use the DBS facility for unloading and reloading tables:

  ```
  UNLOAD TABLE (table_name)  OUTFILE(filename)

  RELOAD TABLE (table_name) NEW INFILE (filename)
  ```

Note: The filename identifies a dataset defined with a variable blocked spanned (VBS) record format.

Copying multiple tables

To transfer all tables from one DBSPACE to another -- for example, to increase the size -- use the DBS utility but keep in mind the following when a DBSPACE is deleted:

- all indexes created for the tables in the DBSPACE are dropped;
- all synonyms based on the tables in the DBSPACE are dropped;
- all authorizations to access the tables are dropped;

- all applications using the tables are invalidated.
- all referential constraints involving the tables in the DBSPACE are also dropped;

Before dropping a DBSPACE, query the catalog tables to verify if there are applications or views based on the tables or any users with authority to access the tables. The following catalog tables should be queried:

- SYSTEM.SYSCATALOG   Retrieve all tables which match on the DBSPACE name.

- SYSTEM.SYSINDEXES   Retrieve the index name, column-names, index type and clustering information for all indexes in the DBSPACE.

- SYSTEM.SYSSYNONYMS   Query synonym names and the userids of the users who defined them.

- SYSTEM.SYSTABAUTH   Retrieve authorizations on tables and views for users and programs.

- SYSTEM.SYSVIEWS   List defined views.

Reorganization activities

To reorganize a DBSPACE, you should perform the following tasks:

- Unload the old DBSPACE with the following statements:

```
UNLOAD DBSPACE (dbspace_name) OUTFILE (filename)
```

where;

filename   identifies a dataset defined with a variable blocked spanned (VBS) record format .

- Drop the old DBSPACE.
- Define and acquire a new DBSPACE with additional pages by using the ACQUIRE DBSPACE statement.
- Recreate all tables with the CREATE TABLE command;
- Recreate all foreign and primary key definitions via the CREATE TABLE or ALTER TABLE commands;
- Reload the table data from the previously created file with following statement:

```
RELOAD DBSPACE (dbspace_name) NEW INFILE (filename)
```

- Recreate all indexes with the CREATE INDEX statement.
- Recreate all views with the CREATE VIEW statement.

- Authorize the corresponding users for the tables and views with the GRANT statement.
- Inform the users to recreate their synonyms.

Storage Pools

A storage pool is a set of DBEXTENTS. Each DBEXTENT is a CMS *minidisk*. A minidisk is a portion of a DASD volume that is defined under VM/SP by adding a MDISK control statement to the VM/SP directory of the SQL/DS database machine.

An active storage pool owns at least one DBEXTENT. Storage pools are called active when a DBSPACE has been assigned to it.

Storage pools are the link between table data contained in a DBSPACE and the storage devices used to physically store that table data. As we previously discussed, DBSPACES are subdivided into pages of 4K bytes. A storage pool consists of 4K blocks, called SLOTS, to hold used DBSPACE pages. The actual assignment of a used DBSPACE page to a specific slot is managed by SQL/DS and cannot be controlled by the user. By assigning a DBSPACE to a storage pool, you can decide what kind of storage device to use, avoid potential device contention for frequently used data and balance device utilization.

Physical storage allocation for storage pools may be increased by adding another DBEXTENT. New DBEXTENTs, must be defined to the directory of the SQL/DS database and assigned to the storage pool by using the SQLADBEX EXEC statement.

Storage pools are units of physical storage as well as objects for logging and recovery. SQL/DS distinguishes two types of storage pools:

- recoverable storage pools
- nonrecoverable storage pools

For recoverable storage pools, SQL/DS provides complete logging of data manipulation activities on the data stored in the corresponding storage pool and assures full recovery in case of system failures or errors. For those DBSPACES assigned to a non-recoverable storage pool, however, SQL/DS only provides reduced recovery functions. It is left to the user to create backup copies of the data to restore a consistent situation in case of system failure or abend.

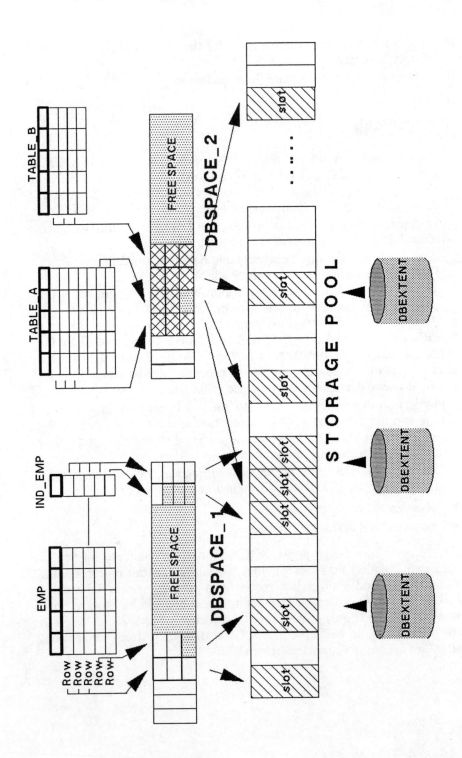

Index

Indexes in SQL/DS reorder the data logically so that it can be accessed without a lengthy sequential search thus improving performance. Additionally, indexes may ensure uniqueness of rows in the table. Only for a clustering index does SQL/DS try to keep the data in logical as well as physical order. For each table you can create one or more indexes. The index can be for one column or it can be created using multiple columns. Even though you may have many indexes defined for one table, you cannot assume that good performance is dependent on the number of indexes. This is especially true if a rows are constantly inserted, deleted or updated. Since any index causes overhead for its maintenance, too many indexes may degrade performance.

Indexes are only used internally by SQL/DS. Even though an index exists for a given table, you cannot be sure that SQL/DS uses the index to access the rows of the table.

Selecting Columns for an Index

When selecting columns for indexing, you should consider the following rules:

- Create an index for columns that are used in WHERE clauses in the most frequently used queries and transactions.
- If a column is used in a JOIN, creating an index for that column can avoid a complete table scan or sort.
- If you frequently check for the existence of a value in a column, you should create an index for that column.
- Avoid creating indexes on long columns (more than 40 bytes) or variable length columns. The result may be more levels in the index page hierarchy, which results in additional I/O.
- Create a unique index on those columns that ensure uniqueness of rows.

Clustering Index

SQL/DS automatically recognizes an index as clustered if the rows in the table are physically stored in logical key sequence. This is accomplished by sorting the input file by the index columns before the DATALOAD operation is performed. In previous releases, SQL/DS grouped all indexes in two categories: clustered and unclustered. For a clustered index, SQL/DS keeps track of the number of rows that are not in clustering sequence. If that number exceeds a certain maximum value, SQL/DS no longer considers the index as clustered. The fact that an index becomes unclustered impacts the following decisions within earlier releases of SQL/DS:

■ *Optimal page selection for INSERT operations.* When a table has a clustering index, SQL/DS attempts to place rows in the DBSPACE pages so that their physical ordering is the same as the corresponding index entries. Even though a table can have several clustering indexes, only the first is used by SQL/DS for inserting new rows. If the first index becomes non-clustered -- e.g., caused by mass inserts of rows -- SQL/DS Version 2 Release 1 and earlier do not use other indexes for selecting free DBSPACES for inserts.

■ *Optimal access path selection.* If a previously clustered index becomes unclustered, the optimizer may no longer consider the index to access data even if the number of rows not in clustering sequence slightly exceeds the allowed maximum. The index in this case still provides better access performance then any other non-clustered index.

SQL/DS Version 2 Release 2 uses a relative clustering measure in percentages between 0% and 100% instead of the binary indicator; clustered and non clustered. This new indicator allows the optimizer to better determine the optimum access strategy if less than 100% of the rows are in clustering sequence. The optimizer also benefits from another improvement in the available statistics on indexed columns, i.e., information on key distribution within a table. In releases prior to SQL/DS Version 2 Release 2, the decisions of the optimizer are based on the assumption of a uniform key distribution for non-unique indexes.

To create a clustering index, execute the following tasks:

■ Order the data on the input data set in clustering sequence.

■ Before executing the data load procedure set the PCTFREE parameter for the DBSPACE to a level high enough to reserve sufficient space to allow future insertion of rows in clustering sequence. Use the ALTER DBSPACE command to change the PCTFREE parameter.

■ Load the data into the table by using the DBS load utility.

■ Create the index by using the CREATE INDEX statement. SQL/DS automatically recognizes the degree of clustering. In previous releases, SQL/DS stored the value 'F' in the CLUSTER column in the SYSTEM.SYSINDEXES catalog table for the first clustering index on the table. For all other clustering indexes the value in the CLUSTER column is changed to 'C'.

■ Reduce the PCTFREE parameter for the DBSPACE by using the ALTER DBSPACE statement to free the reserved space for future insertion of table rows in clustering sequence.

Monitoring indexes

Controlling clustering sequence

If a table with a clustering index is often updated, the clustering level gradually decreases. During the execution of the UPDATE STATISTICS statement, SQL/DS determines the degree of clustering and updates the corresponding catalog tables. You should consider reorganizing the table when the clustering level is lower than 90%. In previous releases, when the clustering level decreased, SQL/DS may decide that the index is no longer clustered and change the value in the CLUSTER column from 'F' to 'W' for the first clustering index (from 'C' to 'N' for other clustering indexes). In this case, you should consider immediately reorganizing the table to reestablish the clustering sequence.

Controlling the number of index levels

After the execution of the UPDATE STATISTICS statement, you should control the number of levels in the index tree. The following query gives you the required value for all indexes on a specific table:

```
SELECT   INAME,   NLEVELS
  FROM   SYSTEM.SYSINDEXES
 WHERE   TNAME = 'table name';
```

If this number exceeds a value of 3, it could have a negative impact on performance (additional I/O operations on the index), and you should consider splitting your table into several tables to reduce the size of the indexes.

Index Options

An index is created using the following statement:

```
CREATE [UNIQUE] INDEX   index name
       ON [creator_prefix.]tablename
          (column_name_1 ASC [,column_name_2 ASC...])
                         DESC                  DESC
       [PCTFREE = integer]
```

where;

UNIQUE   indicates that the index must ensure uniqueness of table rows.

ASC/DESC   orders index entries based on column values in ascending or descending order.

PCTFREE   determines amount of space to be left free on each index page during index creation.

The creation of an index affects the SYSTEM.SYSINDEXES catalog table.

Utilities

Table Loading

SQL provides three different methods to load a table:

■ Using the SQL INSERT statement in an application program, under ISQL or under QMF.

To copy all rows from one table to another, use the following statement:

```
INSERT INTO    [creator_id.] old_table_name
               SELECT *
               FROM    [creator_id.] new_table_name;
```

The table C_EMP for example is created as a reduced copy of the original table EMP:

```
INSERT INTO C_EMP
            SELECT *
            FROM EMP
            WHERE DEPT_NO = 20
               AND SALARY BETWEEN 25000 and 50000;
```

■ Using the ISQL INPUT procedure. This procedure allows you to insert multiple rows (one at a time), entering the table name only once. For a selected column insert, required columns must be named at the beginning. The INSERT statement is re-displayed each time, so that you may type over the fields in the values clause that are different.

The inserted rows are not immediately placed into the tables. In order to physically store the inserted rows, you must quit the ISQL INPUT procedure by typing END or by entering the SAVE command. ISQL offers the possibility of removing all inserts made since the beginning of the INPUT session or since the last SAVE command by entering the BACKOUT statement. The same effect can be obtained by entering CANCEL. The CANCEL command performs a BACKOUT and ends the INPUT session.

- Using the SQL/DS DATALOAD or RELOAD facility to load from sequential datasets or by providing the input via DXT.

The general format for the corresponding commands is as follows:

```
DATALOAD TABLE ([creator_prefix.] table_name)
data-item-1      start_position - end_position
........          .......          .......
........          .......          .......
........          .......          .......
INFILE   (filename)
```

Update Statistics

The information stored in the catalog tables is used by SQL/DS to locate certain objects in the database and to determine the optimum access path to the data to be retrieved to produce a required result.

To retrieve certain rows or certain column values from a table by using the SELECT statement, SQL/DS accesses the corresponding catalog tables to extract all the available information on the corresponding objects. Based on this information, SQL/DS determines the best strategy for data access. For example, when executing a specific query, even if there is an index defined for a table, SQL/DS may decide not to use the index and to perform a sequential read of table rows. Possible reasons for a sequential scan of table rows include the number of rows to be retrieved is too large or the index may have become useless because the tables rows are no longer in index sequence.

It would add too much overhead to SQL/DS operations to update the information about certain objects -- tables, indexes or DBSPACES -- each time a DELETE, UPDATE or INSERT statement are executed. For this reason, you must execute the UPDATE STATISTICS utility on a periodic basis, to update the information stored in the catalog tables.

As a general rule you should execute UPDATE STATISTICS in the following situations:

- When a table has been loaded and the appropriate indexes have been created.
- When a table has been reorganized.
- After excessive data manipulation activities (end of year processing.)
- Before binding new applications and rebinding existing applications that are performance critical.
- On a periodic basis to discover changes in table performance.

The general format of the UPDATE STATISTICS statement is as follows:

```
UPDATE   [ALL] STATISTICS FOR
         TABLE     [creator_id.] table_name
         DBSPACE   [owner.] dbspace_name
```

The output from the UPDATE STATISTICS statement is stored in the following catalog tables:

- SYSTEM.SYSCATALOG
- SYSTEM.SYSDBSPACES

If you specify the keyword ALL, the UPDATE STATISTICS statement produces new information on all columns in the table or DBSPACE. By omitting the ALL keyword, statistics are only refreshed for columns on which indexes have been created.

Querying the Catalog Tables

The CREATE TABLE statement causes SQL/DS to insert rows into the corresponding catalog tables to store information about the new objects. These catalog tables may be queried by the user to verify the table definition or to monitor table growth, overflow of rows and other table characteristics that can influence performance. The following examples illustrate the use of the catalog tables:

- The SYSTEM.SYSCOLUMNS catalog table contains one row for each column in a table. To ascertain the column names, column order, data types and length of all columns in a specific table, enter the following query:

```
SELECT      CNAME, COLNO, COLTYPE, LENGTH
  FROM      SYSTEM.SYSCOLUMNS
 WHERE      TNAME = 'table_name'
   AND      CREATOR = USER
ORDER BY    COLNO;
```

- To list table definitions of your tables use the following query:

```
SELECT      TNAME, NCOLS, REMARKS
  FROM      SYSTEM.SYSCATALOG
 WHERE      TABLETYPE = 'R'
   AND      CREATOR = USER
ORDER BY    TNAME;
```

- When rows are updated they may be written to a page that is different from the original -- for example, update of a variable length column or insert of real values into columns with NULL values. SQL/DS places a pointer in the original row to point to its new location. Retrieval of this row requires at least two I/O operations. For all non-empty tables of a DBSPACE, the following query returns the percentage of rows that overflowed from their original location. When this percentage is higher than 10%, you should consider reorganizing the tables by unloading and reloading them.

```
SELECT      TNAME, ROWCOUNT, NOVERFLOW,
                (NOVERFLOW * 100)/ROWCOUNT
  FROM      SYSTEM.SYSCATALOG
 WHERE      DBSPACENAME = 'dbspace_name'
   AND      ROWCOUNT > 0
ORDER BY    TNAME;
```

DB2 Data Definition Language

Introduction

In this chapter we will discuss the Data Definition Language as well the as logical and physical data structure of DB2. In particular, we will examine the following objects:

- Storage Groups
- Buffer pools
- Table Spaces
- Index Spaces
- Indexes

We will also introduce additional options of the CREATE TABLE statement under DB2 and the utilities required for loading tables and the maintenance of the catalog tables.

Table

Creating Tables

Tables are created using the following CREATE TABLE statement:

```
CREATE TABLE   [creator-prefix.] tablename

(column-name   data-type    ⌈NOT NULL
                             ⌊NOT NULL WITH DEFAULT⌋,

...........    ......    .....................,
...........    ......    .....................,
[PRIMARY KEY (column-name1[,column-name2,...]),]

⌈FOREIGN KEY (column-name3[,column-name4,...])
⌊          REFERENCES tablename-2

            ON DELETE  ⌈RESTRICT
                       ⌊CASCADE
                        SET NULL⌋
                                              ⌋)
[IN database-name.tablespace-name]
[IN DATABASE database-name]
[EDITPROC    program-name]
[VALIDPROC   program-name]
```

Note: For a detailed discussion of the PRIMARY KEY and FOREIGN KEY option see Chapter 5.)

where;

creator_prefix
: The creator_prefix defaults to the userid of the user that is actually executing the CREATE TABLE statement.

tablename
: The tablename may be up to 18 characters long. The first character must be alphabetic (A-z, @, #, $) and the rest either alphabetic, '_', or numeric. The fully qualified name for tables, however, is formed by qualification with the creator_prefix:

: (creator_prefix.tablename).

Column-name
: The column-name may be up to 18 characters long. The first character must be alphabetic (A-z, @, #, $) and the rest either alphabetic, '_', or numeric. The column-name must be unique within a table.

data-type   *See Data Types, pp. 67 ff.*

NOT NULL WITH DEFAULT assigns a default value to those columns for which the user did not supply a value. These defaults are dependent upon the data type:

0	numeric columns
blank	fixed length character columns
empty string	variable length character columns
CURRENT	date/time data type (*DB2 Release 3 and later*)

It is recommended that you provide the database-name and the table-space name in the CREATE TABLE statement. If the database name is omitted, DB2 assumes the default database. If you omit the table space name, DB2 may read every page of the table-space catalog table to check if you are creating a table in a non-existent table space. Then, DB2 automatically creates a table space with the same name as the table itself (*implicitly created table space*).

Edit Routines

An edit routine is declared for a table using the EDITPROC clause of the CREATE TABLE command. Its purpose is to encrypt and/or compress data. DB2 calls this routine every time a row is retrieved from the table and every time a new row is inserted or an existing row is updated. This causes a increase in CPU usage. Other characteristics of the edit routine include the following:

- it must always be written in ASSEMBLER;
- it must be part of the DSN.SSPGM or a concatenated dataset;
- its name may not start with DSN...;
- no SQL statements are allowed in the routine;
- an existing routine cannot be dropped nor can a new one be added after the table has been created;
- no new column may be added to a table that already has an edit routine.

Validation Routines

A validation routine is declared for a table using the VALIDPROC clause of the CREATE TABLE command. Its purpose is to validate data (ranges, etc.) to reduce the amount of application program code. The routine receives control every time a new row is inserted or an existing row is

updated.   Other characteristics of validation routines include the
following:

- it must always written in ASSEMBLER;
- it must be part of the DSN.SSPGM or a concatenated dataset;
- its name may not start with DSN...;
- it may not include SQL statements;
- it may be dropped or added using the ALTER TABLE command.

Altering the Validation Routine

In our discussion of the ALTER TABLE statement we have seen already
that DB2 allows you to add a new column or to add and delete
referential constraints. In this section, we will discuss the use of the
ALTER TABLE command to change the validation routine specified in the
VALIDPROC clause of the CREATE TABLE statement.

The following example shows the structure of the corresponding
ALTER TABLE statement:

```
ALTER TABLE   tablename
         ADD   validation-routine-name
               NULL
```

where;

validation-routine-name - Assigns a new validation routine to the
                table. If you previously defined a routine for the table,
                DB2 disconnects the old one and connect the new one.
                Existing rows are not automatically validated by the new
                validation routine. To make sure that the existing rows
                conform to the new routine, you must run the routine
                against the rows; unload the table with the REORG facility
                (specify UNLOAD ONLY) and reload it with the LOAD
                utility.

NULL   By specifying NULL you can disconnect an existing
                validation routine from the table.

Storage Group

A *Storage Group* is a set of DASD volumes to which you assign a name.
When a storage group is created, you specify the volume serial numbers
of the DASD volumes to be used for your data. By selecting the
appropriate storage group you can enhance performance by placing

frequently used tables on fast DASD devices and more infrequently used tables on slower devices.

The options of the CREATE STOGROUP command are the follow-ing:

```
CREATE   STOGROUP storage group name
         VOLUMES (vol ser numbers)
         VCAT VSAM catalog name
```

Each storage group has a row in the SYSIBM.SYSSTOGROUP and each volume specified has a row in the SYSIBM.SYSVOLUMES.

In designing your storage group, you should be aware of the following:

- All volumes in a storage group must be of the same device type.
- The same volume can be used in more than one storage group.
- At installation time, DB2 provides a default storage group named SYSDEFLT.

Instead of using storage groups you can choose to define your own VSAM ESDS (*see Allocating User Defined Clusters for Table Spaces, pp. 119ff.*). You should always make use of storage groups when defining external storage and let DB2 manage your data sets.

Database

A *Database* is a collection of Table Spaces and Index Spaces. The database serves as an operational unit that can be used for starting and stopping access to tables and indexes. A database is also a unit of authorization. From an application point of view, it is recommended that only related tables are grouped together in a database.

DB2 only allows definitional activity in a database concurrent with prebound application access and update of data not involved in the definition. Concurrent definitional activity is not allowed with activities like BIND, DB2 utilities and dynamic SQL calls. Consideration should be given to creating separate databases for users involved in creating objects within a database.

When you create a database, the only two options you may specify are storage group and buffer pool defaults for subsequent table space and index definitions.

```
CREATE DATABASE   database name
         STOGROUP   storage group name
       BUFFERPOOL   (BP0/ BP1/ BP2 or BP32K)
```

For performance reasons -- e.g., using different buffer pools for tables located in the same database -- these defaults may be overridden with the CREATE TABLESPACE command. Each database has a row in the SYSIBM.SYSDATABASE table.

Buffer Pool

Buffer Pools are areas of virtual storage which DB2 uses to temporarily store pages of table spaces needed for data retrieval or update. When a user wants to access a row of a table, the page containing that row is brought into a buffer. If data is changed, that buffer must be written back to the disk to make the change effective.

During installation, DB2 allows the definition of a maximum of three pools of 4k buffer size (BP0, BP1 and BP2) and only one buffer pool of 32k bytes (BP32K). Your choice of the buffer pool when defining a table space implicitly determines the page size of the table space. The actual number of buffers in a buffer pool is dynamically assigned by DB2, but the number is between a minimum and a maximum defined during installation in the DB2 installation module DSNZPARM. DB2 internally uses BP0 when accessing the catalog tables, DB2 directory databases, and temporary workfiles. For performance critical applications, BP1 or BP2 should be used so as not to interfere with DB2's own use of BP0.

Note: It is recommended that the use of the 32K bytes buffer pool (BP32K) be avoided.

If several different table spaces and indexes are using the same buffer pool, you may expect longer response times depending on the overall size of the buffer pool and the resulting buffer contention.

Table Space

A *Table Space* is a storage unit used to logically allocate one or more tables. Table spaces are physically divided into pages. Each page holds one or more rows of a table. Two page sizes (4K and 32K) are available. The page size is selected through the assignment of the table space to a buffer pool during table space creation. Each table space consists of one entry-sequential dataset (*VSAM/ESDS*) or for partitioned table spaces of 1 to 64 VSAM/ESDS datasets.

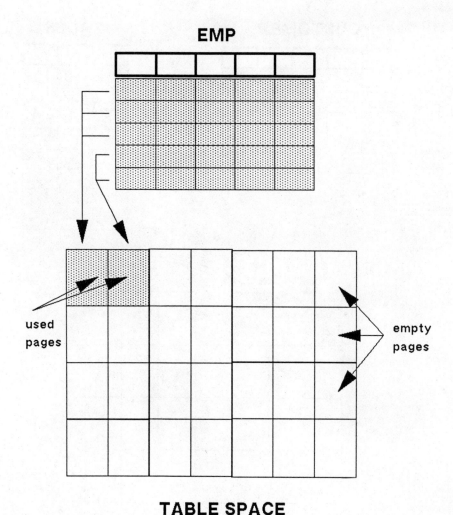

Figure 7.1   Table space

Simple Table Space

A simple table space can hold one or more tables, as illustrated **Figure 7.2**. If there is more than one table in the table space, each page may contain rows from different tables.

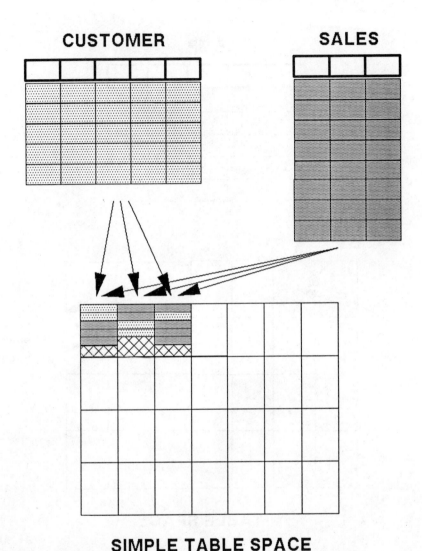

Figure 7.2   Simple table space

For the following reasons, it is advantageous to have only one table per each simple table space:

- If an application uses the LOCK TABLE option to gain exclusive use of a table or if DB2 locks the whole table because of large update activities, other applications or users are prevented from accessing the locked table as well as the entire table space.

- When executing the recovery or reorganization utility program, the complete table space is unavailable for access.
- When an index is not used, the entire table space is scanned. As pages containing data from different tables are all mixed up in the table space, an increased number of I/O operations result from a scan of a table space with more than one table present.
- If a table is dropped, space in the table space is not reclaimed until reorganization is performed. If table creation and deletion are frequent, limit a table space to one table and drop the table space when the table is no longer required.

There are equally good reasons to have more than one table in a given table space:

- Since each table space requires a VSAM/ESDS dataset, fewer table spaces reduce allocation/deallocation cost.
- During execution of the OPEN statement to access a table space, approximately 4K Bytes of virtual storage are allocated by the operating system and only released when the corresponding VSAM dataset is closed.
- If you have numerous small tables, you might gain a performance advantage and save storage space.

Segmented Table Spaces

DB2 Version 2 introduces segmented table spaces to more efficiently store multiple tables and to address the problems created by the use of simple table spaces. Problems encountered in previous releases of DB2 included limited update concurrence because of table space locking, additional I/O activities during table space scan and no reclamation of space allocated to dropped tables without reorganization of the complete table space.

A segmented table space is subdivided into sets of equal size, on contiguously stored pages called segments. The segment size -- i.e., the actual number of pages in each segment -- must be a multiple of 4 and may vary between 4 to 64 pages (page size either 4K or 32K). It is defined via the SEGSIZE option of the CREATE TABLESPACE command. DB2 maintains the information concerning which segments are assigned to single tables in Segment Control Blocks within Space Map Pages. Each segment control block contains the name of the table to which the segment is assigned. The number of physical pages that can be controlled through a space map page depends both on the page (4K or 32k) and segment size.

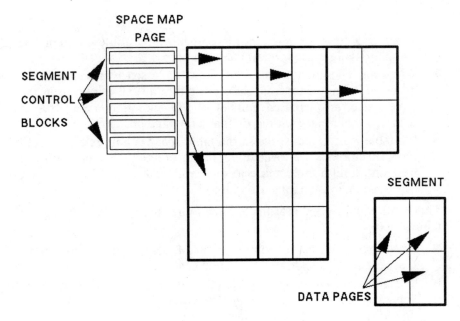

SEGMENTED TABLE SPACE

Figure 7.3   Segmented Table Space - elements

The primary difference between segmented and simple table spaces consists in the allocation of table rows within the table space. Each segment and every page within that segment contains only rows of the table to which the segment is assigned (*see* **Figure 7.3**). New segments are automatically assigned by DB2 to a table when additional storage space is needed -- for example, during insert operations or table load. For an insert of a new row into a table, DB2 selects the optimal segment to store the row based on the following considerations:

- For a table without a clustering index DB2 stores the new row in the first segment with sufficient free space that is already assigned to the table. If no space is available in any of the existing segments, DB2 assigns a new segment to the table and stores the row in it.

- For tables with a clustering index DB2 attempts to maintain the clustering sequence during insert -- i.e., DB2 stores the row in the page containing the closest higher key. If there is no space available in that page, DB2 tries to insert the row into any available page within the same segment. If this fails, the row is stored in the segment that had been assigned last to the table.

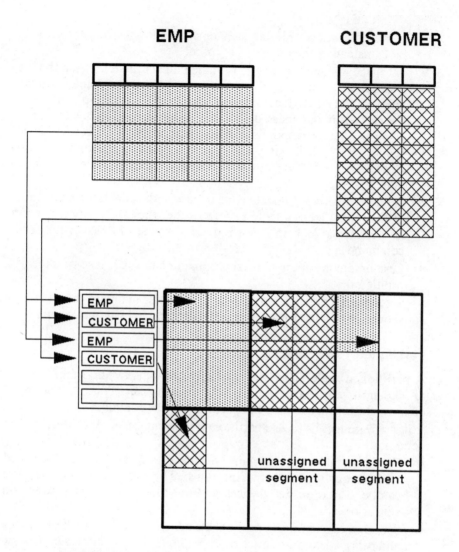

SEGMENTED TABLESPACE : EXAMPLE

Figure 7.4   Segmented Table Space - example

Since the distribution of table data within a segmented table space is known to DB2 through the space map pages, segmented table spaces present the following advantages over the use of simple table space for multiple table storage:

■ Reduced I/O overhead when indexes are not used for table data access. DB2 scans only the segments assigned to the corresponding table instead of the entire table space;

- All space assigned to a table is immediately available when the table is dropped. The same is true when all rows are deleted within a table via the DELETE command without explicitly dropping the table. To carry out the mass deletion of table rows, DB2 accesses and changes the corresponding space map pages. This significantly reduces the I/O, locking, and logging overhead otherwise required to access and delete individual data and index pages within simple table spaces.
- A higher degree of update concurrency within the table space, since DB2 at most locks a table instead of the whole table space (as long as table space locking is not requested in the CREATE TABLESPACE command).
- Less time consuming table space maintenance because of improved utilities.
- Segmented table spaces allow DB2 to better maintain the clustering sequence of table rows during insert and table load operations.

Partitioned Table Spaces

A partitioned table space holds exactly one table. The table space is divided into partitions, based on partitioning key values. You must create a clustering index on the partitioning key column.

It is advantageous to use partitioned table spaces under the following conditions:

- For large tables or if certain portions of a given table are accessed more frequently than other portions. The frequently accessed parts can be stored on fast devices and the other parts or partitions on slower ones.
- An advantage of using partitioned table spaces is that the recovery and reorganization utilities can operate on a partition level. During the reload phase of the Reorganization utility and execution of COPY, RECOVER and LOAD utilities, the locks apply to the entire table space. *(The use of partitioned table space is faster since the reorganization considers only the partition or partitions that have to be organized.)*

EMP

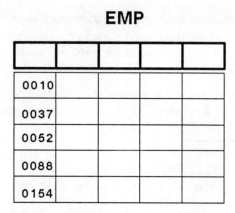

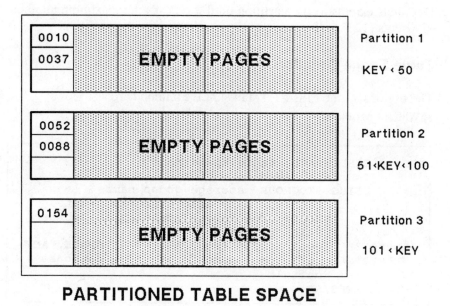

PARTITIONED TABLE SPACE

Figure 7.5 Partitioned table space

The following rules apply to partitioned table spaces:

- The table space can only contain one table.
- The partitioning key column in a table, located in a partitioned table space, cannot be updated. You must delete the row and re-insert it with the updated key column value.

- You must create a clustering index on the partitioning key column.
- You may define up to a maximum of 64 partitions. Each partition is a single ESDS dataset. The maximum size of each partition depends on the number of partitions:

Number of partitions	Maximum space for each partition	Maximum space for tablespace
1 - 16	4 GB	4 - 64 GB
17 - 32	2 GB	34 - 64 GB
33 - 64	1 GB	33 - 64 GB

DB2 adds extents to the partition until it reaches the maximum number of extents (123) or the maximum space allowed for the partition.

Table Space Creation

The options on the CREATE TABLESPACE command are as follows:

a) Without partitions

```
CREATE TABLESPACE   table space name
        IN   database name
        USING STOGROUP   storage group name
            PRIQTY primary allocation in K-bytes
            SECQTY secondary allocation in K-bytes
            ERASE  NO/YES
    LOCKSIZE   level of locking (PAGE, TABLESPACE, ANY)
    BUFFERPOOL bufferpool name to override database
                default
    CLOSE  YES/NO
```

b) Segmented table space

```
CREATE TABLESPACE  table space name
       IN  database name
       USING STOGROUP  storage group name
             PRIQTY  primary allocation in K-bytes
             SECQTY  secondary allocation in K-bytes
             ERASE    NO/YES
       SEGSIZE    integer
LOCKSIZE  level of locking (PAGE, TABLE,
                                   TABLESPACE, ANY)
  BUFFERPOOL  bufferpool name to override database
                                     default
        CLOSE   YES/NO
```

c) Partitioned table space

```
CREATE TABLESPACE   table space name
IN   database name
NUMPARTS integer (PART integer USING STOGROUP
                                    storage group name
              PRIQTY prim. allocation in K-bytes
              SECQTY  sec. allocation in K-bytes
              ERASE    NO/YES ,
              PART integer USING STOGROUP
                                    storage group name..)
   LOCKSIZE  level of locking (PAGE, TABLESPACE, ANY)
   BUFFERPOOL bufferpool name to override database
              default
CLOSE   YES/NO
```

LOCKSIZE Option

TABLESPACE The entire table space is locked in exclusive or share mode. The result is that updating applications utilize less CPU time because the overhead caused by the locking and unlocking of individual pages is avoided, but no other application can access the tablespace. This option is recommended for read only tables and tables that require a low level of concurrency. **You should not use TABLESPACE locking for segmented table spaces.**

TABLE   This new option of the LOCKSIZE keyword was introduced with DB2 Version 2 for segmented table spaces. Only the segments assigned to a table are locked in exclusive or share mode when the table is accessed. This option allows a much higher level of update concurrency within the same table space than the TABLESPACE option.

PAGE   Pages are locked individually. This allows more concurrent usage of the table space. Update applications should issue frequent commits to free resources. Even with this option, if a lock for the entire tablespace or table is needed, the application program may use the LOCK TABLE SQL-statement:

```
LOCK TABLE table-name IN SHARE      MODE
                                 EXCLUSIVE
```

Use the SHARE option, if you are reading a significant number of rows and concurrency is not required with update applications against the same table space. Use EXCLUSIVE if you are updating data to such an extent that it makes the table data meaningless for other applications.

For prebound applications the user is informed by a warning message at BIND time if DB2 selects table space or table locking instead of page-locking.

ANY   It is not recommended to use the ANY clause, because in an interactive environment you are not aware which strategy DB2 has chosen. DB2 chooses the locking level at application plan BIND time. If only one page is affected, DB2 selects page-locking; otherwise, table space or, in case of segmented table spaces, table locking is used.

CLOSE

If the table space is used relatively frequently, you should use the CLOSE NO option to avoid reopening and closing of the dataset. In general, CLOSE YES is recommended for private tables and table spaces accessed only by batch programs.

Table Space Size

In calculating the size of the table space, you should try to keep your table space within the primary allocation. If the secondary allocation has to be used, it is probably not located physically adjacent to the primary allocation.

A method of calculating the disk space required for the allocation of a table space can roughly be accomplished with the following steps:

- For each table, multiply the row length by the number of rows.
- Add this value together for each table in the table space.
- Multiply the total by 2 to include free space, row and page overhead and unused disk-space (e.g., only 4 pages fit on a 19K track of 3350, 10 pages on a 3380).

Allocating User Defined Clusters for Table Spaces

Instead of using storage groups for the allocation of table spaces you can choose to define your own VSAM/ESDS. Consider the following rules:

- The datasets have to be defined before executing the CREATE TABLESPACE statement.
- The clusters have to be defined with the following VSAM options:
  ```
  NIXD RECSZ(4089) CISZ(4096) SHR(3,3)
  ```
- The ALIAS of the VSAM catalog must be specified in the USING VCAT option of the CREATE TABLESPACE statement.
- Secondary volumes for extension of the datasets have to be allocated by the user.
- The DB2 naming conventions for dataset names have to be observed.

The names for table spaces and index spaces are composed as follows: c.so.d.p.i.tnnn

where;

c -	VSAM catalog name or ALIAS
s -	fixed string DSNDB
o -	C if cluster, D if data object
d -	database name
p -	table space name
i -	fixed string I0001
t -	fixed constant A
nnn-	sequence number of dataset

Example:

Under IDCAMS

```
DEFINE CLUSTER NAME (U1.DSNDBC.DB1.TS1.I0001.A001)..
CATALOG(U1).....
```

Under DB2

```
CREATE TABLESPACE TS1
USING VCAT U1
```

You always make use of storage groups when defining external storage and let DB2 manage your data sets.

Table space set

Referential integrity under DB2 Version 2 not only impacts dependent and independent tables, but also the physical objects they are stored in, i.e. the table spaces. A table space set is a group of table spaces that are associated to each other by referential constraints. Let's assume the DEPARTMENT table in our previous example is stored in table space T1, while T2 holds the EMPLOYEE and RELATIONS tables. Since the DEPARTMENT and EMPLOYEE tables are related to each other via the department number (DEPT_NO), T1 and T2 form a table space set.

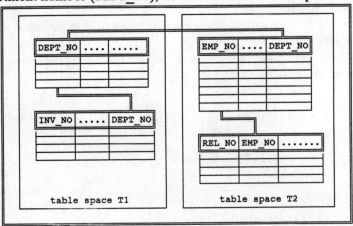

Figure 7.6 Table Space Set

All table spaces that belong to a table space set must be recovered when all of their data is consistent -- i.e. no referential constraints are violated. This point in time is called a 'QUIESCE' point. If the table space set is recovered to a point that does not correspond to a QUIESCE point, or if not all members of the set are recovered, DB2 automatically sets the CHECK PENDING condition for all table spaces within the set that have not been included in the recovery and that contain dependent tables.

Index Space

For each index, DB2 automatically allocates an *index space* when the corresponding index is created. The index space is deleted when the index is dropped. Unlike table spaces, there is no command to create or delete an index space.

Index spaces are physically divided into pages. Each page holds several index entries consisting of a row pointer and the corresponding key value or values for a non-unique index. Only one page size of 4K is available. Each index page is subdivided into subpages. You can specify from 1 to 16 subpages. A subpage is the unit for index locking.

Index

Indexes in DB2 reorder the data logically so that it can be accessed without a lengthy sequential search. Only when there is a clustering index does DB2 try to keep the data in logical and physical order. For each table, you can create one or more indexes. The index can be for one column or it can be created using multiple columns. The primary reason for creating an index is to improve performance. Even though you may define many indexes for a table, you cannot assume that good performance is only dependent on the number of indexes. This is especially true if a table is constantly having rows inserted, deleted or updated. Since any index causes overhead for its maintenance, too many indexes may degrade performance. Another reason for creating an index is to ensure uniqueness of rows in the table -- i.e, for a primary key.

Indexes should always be created before the LOAD operation. The LOAD utility builds them in a more efficient way than the one used if the index is created after the table has been loaded. It may be interesting to generate a temporary index for an existing table -- e.g., year-end reporting, which requires access to a table in a number of different orders -- and delete the index when it is no longer needed. During index creation the table is locked and no concurrent access to that table is permitted until the index generation is complete.

When DB2 creates an index, it uses a structure called a *B-Tree*. A B-Tree structure is a multilevel hierarchical structure characterized by the fact that all paths from the top to the bottom level are exactly of the same length. This means that an index organized as a B-Tree guarantees the same predictable access time and performance for all parts of the index.

As illustrated in **Figure 7.5**, an index is composed of one root, zero or more intermediate pages and a number of leaf pages. The leaf pages contain the real index entries consisting of an indexed column value and a pointer, or for a non-unique index, as many pointers as there are duplicates of this specific column value throughout the table. These pointers are used to physically access the corresponding table data.

Since index entries within the leaf pages are ordered in logical key sequence, DB2 uses this index level if a sequential access to the stored data is required.

Each level above the leaf pages contains one entry for each index page at a lower level consisting of the highest column value in the index page and a pointer to access the page. The root page and the intermediate pages from the index set are used to randomly access the stored table data.

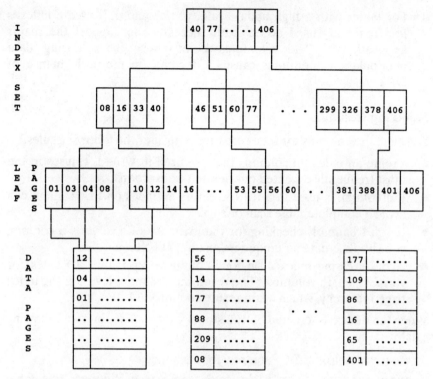

Figure 7.7   B-tree structure for index organization

Indexes are only used internally by DB2.   Even though an index exists for a given table, you cannot be sure that DB2 uses the index to access the rows of the table. However, you can design your program or query so that at least you are not preventing DB2 from using the index.

In designing indexes for tables you should consider the following rules:

- Every table, independent of its size, should have a clustering index defined if the table is often accessed in a specific sequence. For a clustering index, DB2 tries to physically store table rows in the logical key sequence of the index.

- For a simple table space containing two or more tables, you should create an index for each table for the columns that are most frequently used in search conditions.

- In order to limit the number of physical I/O operations, every table space, independent of the number of tables it contains, should have an index defined for each table if the table space occupies more than one cylinder of disk storage.

- For tables with a high update rate, you should only create indexes for frequently used access paths necessary to support the major applications. The maintenance of every index during data manipulation operations causes a decrease in the performance of DB2.

Selecting Columns

To select the columns for index creation, consider the following rules:

- Create an index on columns that are used in WHERE clauses in the most frequently executed queries and transactions.
- If a column is used in a JOIN, creating an index on that column can avoid a complete table scan or sort.
- If you frequently checking for the existence of a value in a column, you should create an unique index on that column.
- Avoid creating indexes on long columns (more than 40 bytes) or variable length columns. The result may be more levels in the index page hierarchy, which again results in more I/O.

When an index is created, DB2 stores information in the following catalog tables:

SYSIBM.SYSINDEXES	one row for each index;
SYSIBM.SYSINDEXPART	if the table space is partitioned, this table contains one row for each partition;
SYSIBM.SYSKEYS	additional information about the columns that comprise an index.

Multiple Column Index

An index can be defined on one or more columns. If you created an index for more than one column, DB2 considers an index for those columns that are not preceded in the WHERE clause by conditions involving higher order columns using a comparison operator other than ' = '.

For example, if an index is defined for three columns (C1, C2 and C3), DB2 uses the index in the following manner:

C1='ABC' and C2=123 and C3>456
Use of index for all three columns

C1='ABC' and C2>123 and C3=456
Use of index only for C1 and C2, since C3 is preceded by the higher ·
order column C2 with a comparison operator other than ' = '

```
C1>'ABC' and C2=123 and C3=456
```
Use of index only for `C1` as `C2` and `C3` are preceded by the higher order column `C1` with a comparison operator other than ' = '

Clustering Index

As previously discussed, if a table is often required in a specific sequence -- e.g., ORDER BY -- or if the rows in a table are often retrieved in logical key sequence, you should consider creating a clustering index. The index should be created on the column(s) that are most frequently used in the WHERE and ORDER BY clauses.

With a clustering index, DB2 tries to store the table rows so that their physical sequence is the same as the logical order of the corresponding index entries. You may define only one clustering index for a table even though a table can have several indexes and some might also fulfill the requirement of a clustering sequence. The clustering index should always be the first one created for a table. If you define a clustering index after you have loaded the table, DB2 does not rearrange the rows until the table space is reorganized.

A clustering index only improves performance if multiple rows are retrieved sequentially in logical key sequence. If only a single row is retrieved, then clustering has no advantage over the use of a normal index.

Options of the CREATE INDEX Statement

An index is created using the following statement:

```
CREATE [UNIQUE] INDEX   index name
       ON tablename (column_name_1 ASC
                                   DESC
                     [,column_name_2 ASC ...])
                                   DESC
       USING STOGROUP storage group name
             PRIQTY primary allocation in K-bytes
             SECQTY secondary allocation in K-bytes
             ERASE    NO
                      YES
       CLUSTER                 (instructs DB2 to build a
                                 clustering index)
       BUFFERPOOL    bufferpool name
       SUBPAGES      number of subpages 1/2/4/8/16
       CLOSE         YES
                     NO
```

The SUBPAGES option is used to specify the size of the subpage for index leaf pages. When an index is updated, a lock is held on the subpage. The default value is 4 subpages in one index page (always 4k pages). You should specify a smaller subpage size (8 or 16) if a high degree of sharing and update concurrency is required for the index. The smaller the subpage size, the lower the lock contention (more than one user wants to lock the same subpages at the same time) but the higher the CPU time requirements. If the index is seldom updated or the level of sharing is very low, you should use a larger subpage size (1 or 2).

Disk Space Requirements for Indexes

To make a rough calculation of the size of an index, you should keep in mind the following:

- The size of an index page is always 4K bytes.
- Each entry in the index leaf pages consists of the key or keys and the row-id where the row-id is 4 bytes. Less space is required if the index entries are non-unique, since the index 'key' value is not repeated.
- DB2 creates enough levels of intermediate index pages until there is a single root page.
- DB2 reserves 10% free space included in each index page during index creation for later insertion of new index entries.
- An index built on a variable length column is expanded to the maximum column length.
- If the indexed column definition does not exclude NULLS, null values are treated as normal index entries.

Monitoring Indexes

Controlling clustering sequence

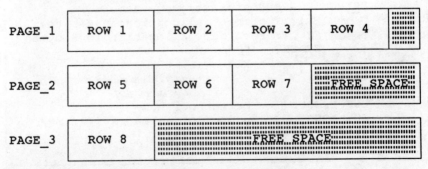

Figure 7.8a   Row insertion in clustering sequence - part 1

If you insert a new row (5.5) into the table, DB2 attempts to maintain the clustering sequence and store the new row between row 5 and 6. Since there is free space available in the corresponding data page, rows 6 and 7 are shifted to the right and the new row is inserted correctly.

| PAGE_1 | ROW 1 | ROW 2 | ROW 3 | ROW 4 | (free space) |

| PAGE_2 | ROW 5 | NEW ROW 5.5 | ROW 6 | ROW 7 | (free space) |

| PAGE_3 | ROW 8 | FREE SPACE |

Figure 7.8b   Row insertion in clustering sequence - part 2

If you want to insert another row -- for example new row 5.75 -- you see that there is not enough space left on the correct data page. DB2 would insert the new row in the nearest data pages with sufficient space -- in our example PAGE_3 -- without maintaining the clustering sequence.

| PAGE_1 | ROW 1 | ROW 2 | ROW 3 | ROW 4 | |

| PAGE_2 | ROW 5 | NEW ROW 5.5 | ROW 6 | ROW 7 | (free space) |

| PAGE_3 | ROW 8 | NEW ROW 5.75 | FREE SPACE |

Figure 7.8c   Row insertion in clustering sequence - part 3

RUNSTATS calculates the decrease and updates the columns NEAROFFPOS and FAROFFPOS of the SYSIBM. SYSINDEXPART catalog table for the index, where:

NEAROFFPOS   indicates the number of times the next row was fetched from a faraway page

FAROFFPOS   indicates the number of times the next row was fetched from a nearby page

After the execution of the RUNSTATS utility, you should use the following query which provides you with the percentage of rows fetched from another page and the total number of rows referenced by the index.

```
SELECT   IXNAME, NEAROFFPOS, FAROFFPOS, CARD,
         (NEAROFFPOS + FAROFFPOS)*100/CARD
  FROM   SYSIBM.SYSINDEXPART
 WHERE   STORNAME = 'storage group name'
   AND   CARD > 0
```

If you don't want DB2 to ignore the index during data retrieval and manipulation operations, you should reorganize the table space if the percentage of rows fetched from another page is greater than 10%. A reorganization of the table space relocates the rows in the correct clustering sequence.

Controlling the number of index levels

As previously discussed, an index under DB2 is created with a multilevel hierarchical sequence. Since the number of index levels has a negative impact on performance (more I/O operations on the index) you should control the dimension of the index tree after each RUNSTATS execution. The following query gives you the required value for all indexes on a specific table:

```
SELECT   NAME, INDEXSPACE, NLEVELS
  FROM   SYSIBM.SYSINDEXES
 WHERE   TBNAME = 'table name'
```

If this number exceeds a value of 3 you might consider splitting your table into several tables to reduce the sizes of the indexes.

Utilities

Table LOAD

DB2 provides you with the following three different methods to load your table:

- Using SQL INSERT in your application program;
- Using SQL INSERT under SPUFI;
- Using the DB2 LOAD facility (the table space is locked) to load from sequential datasets, from SQL/DS unloaded datasets or by providing the input via DXT. If you load data into your table, instruct the LOAD facility to log its activities (LOG YES). This option allows you to restart the facility from the last commit point using the RESTART option. If you specify LOG NO and the LOAD facility fails, you must delete all loaded rows from the table and begin the utility from the beginning.

If you are creating a unique index, it is recommended to sort your input and to eliminate duplicates.

Under DB2 Version 2 the LOAD utility performs various types of data consistency checks:

- *Uniqueness of index* - If you define a unique index on a table the LOAD utility checks the input records for duplicate keys before loading the data. All duplicates, including the first occurrence, are discarded. However, if any of the new records is a duplicate of a key that existed prior to the load, only the new record is eliminated. DB2 does not delete any existing rows. You may instruct DB2 via the DISCARDDN ddname option to copy all duplicate input records to the dataset specified under that ddname. It is also possible using the DISCARDS parameter to define the maximum number of errors that you tolerate during the load process. If this maximum is exceeded, DB2 automatically abends the load.

- *Referential integrity* - In order to assure that the input data does not violate any referential constraint, you may specify ENFORCE YES. With this option the LOAD utility validates the input data against all referential constraints involving the table to be loaded. In case of an error in the input records, for example a foreign key without the corresponding primary key, DB2 eliminates the input data. As we have seen above, you may request DB2 to copy the invalid record to a data set and/or to abend the load process after a certain number of errors. In case you specify ENFORCE NO, DB2 does not check the input data for violations of referential integrity, but marks the table space as 'CHECK PENDING' in the STATUS column of the SYSIBM.SYSTABLESPACE catalog table. The CHECK PENDING condition only applies to table spaces containing dependent tables. The condition indicates that the tables within the table spaces may contain rows that violate referential integrity. CHECK PENDING may be set not only during data load operations, but also by adding a referential constraint on a populated via the ALTER TABLE, or by the CHECK utility. DB2 does not allow data manipulation operations in that table space until the CHECK PENDING condition is removed by the CHECK DATA utility. The CHECK DATA utility discovers violations of referential constraints and optionally deletes invalid rows and their descendents (DELETE YES/NO). You may also require that invalid rows are copied into exception tables (COPY YES/NO). The exception tables must have in addition to the same column definitions as the model tables a four character column to store the row identifier (RID) of the row that violates the referential constraint. The user is requested to previously create these tables via the CREATE TABLE command.

Note: The CHECK PENDING condition may also be turned off by the REPAIR utility. However, REPAIR does not correct invalid rows and it should therefore only be used in extreme cases.

Table UNLOAD

- A table space containing only one table with a clustering index is unloaded using the clustering index.
- A simple table space containing more than one table is always unloaded in physical sequence -- i.e. rows belonging to different tables may be mixed.
- A segmented table space is always unloaded table by table. Tables with a clustering index are unloaded using the clustering index. Without a clustering index tables are unloaded in physical sequence.

RUNSTATS Utility

DB2 uses catalog tables to store all necessary information on physical and logical objects -- e.g., tables, table spaces, indexes, etc. Catalog tables are for data retrieval and to determine the optimum access path.

For example, each time you request the retrieval of certain rows or certain column values from a table by using the SELECT statement, DB2 accesses the corresponding catalog tables to extract all the available information on those objects. Based on this information DB2 determines the best strategy for data access.

Since it would add too much overhead to DB2 operations to update the information about certain objects each time a DELETE, UPDATE and INSERT statement is executed, you should periodically execute the RUNSTATS utility to update the information stored in the catalog tables.

DB2 allows you to use either of the following formats for the RUNSTATS utility:

```
RUNSTATS TABLESPACE tsname

 INDEX (index1,.)    SHRLEVEL  REFERENCE
 ALL                           CHANGE
```

```
RUNSTATS INDEX   indexname1,...[SHRLEVEL REFERENCE]
                                          CHANGE
```

The output from RUNSTATS is stored in the following DB2 catalog tables:

- SYSIBM.SYSTABLEPART
- SYSIBM.SYSTABLESPACE
- SYSIBM.SYSTABLES
- SYSIBM.SYSCOLUMNS
- SYSIBM.SYSINDEXPART
- SYSIBM.SYSINDEXES

RUNSTATS should be executed under the following conditions:

- When a table has been loaded and the appropriate indexes have been created.
- When a table space or index has been reorganized.
- On a periodic basis to discover changes in the table performance.

After the execution of the RUNSTATS utility, you should verify that the database is still efficiently organized. One of the values that should be controlled is the number of relocated rows within a table space. Relocation of rows might occur when a row is increased in length by updating variable length columns and DB2 cannot find space for the updated row on the same page. In such cases, DB2 stores the row in another page and places a pointer on the original page to indicate the new location. To retrieve that row, DB2 needs at least two I/O operations.

Besides the number of relocated pages within a table space, you should also control the amount of unrecovered space caused by dropping tables within table spaces containing more than one table.   The following query provides you with the percentage of dropped space for all the table spaces in a given storage group:

```
SELECT  TSNAME, DBNAME, PERCDROP
  FROM  SYSIBM.SYSTABLEPART
 WHERE  STORNAME = 'storage group name'
   AND  PERCDROP > 0
```

A value of -1 in the PERCDROP column indicates that RUNSTATS has not yet been executed against a given table space.

STOSPACE Utility

The STOSPACE utility program is an online program that records the **actual space allocated** for storage groups, table spaces, and indexes, whereas the RUNSTATS program records the **space actually used** by the same objects.

The format of the STOSPACE command is described as follows:

```
STOSPACE STOGROUP   storage group name
```

The output from STOSPACE is stored in the following catalog tables:

- SYSIBM.SYSSTOGROUP
- SYSIBM.SYSTABLESPACE
- SYSIBM.SYSINDEXES

In each of these tables STOSPACE updates the actual allocated DASD space for the storage group and its related table spaces and indexes. The updated value is stored in the column SPACE in each of these catalog tables.

The following query helps you monitor space utilization:

```
SELECT TSNAME, PQTY, SQTY, SPACE, SPACE*100/(PQTY*4)
  FROM SYSIBM.SYSTABLEPART, SYSIBM.SYSTABLESPACE
 WHERE TSNAME = NAME
   AND PARTITIONS = 0
   AND STORNAME = storage group name
```

This query returns the amount of space used by primary (PQTY) and secondary (SQTY) allocations as well as the relation between total allocated space and primary allocation for table spaces in a given storage group.

The following query provides you with the utilized space as a percentage of the space allocated:

```
SELECT NAME, SPACE,NACTIVE,NACTIVE*PGSIZE *100/SPACE
  FROM SYSIBM.SYSTABLESPACE
  WHERE SPACE > 0
```

The column PGSIZE contains the size of the page in K-Bytes.

Data Retrieval-Simple Query Structures

Introduction

To access data stored in DB2 or SQL/DS tables, you utilize the *Structured Query Language* (SQL). SQL provides you with four statements for data manipulation and retrieval. The type or operation you want to perform is identified by the first clause of each statement: SELECT, INSERT, UPDATE or DELETE. We begin with a comprehensive description of the SELECT statement in this and the following chapter and continue in Chapter 10 with a discussion of additional data manipulation statements: INSERT, UPDATE and DELETE.

At the end of each section, the new SQL language elements will be summarized in a syntax diagram providing a quick overview and to serve as a reference for your own work with DB2 and SQL/DS.

SELECT Statement

The SELECT statement is used to retrieve data from one or more tables and to perform basic operations on the retrieved data.

The SELECT statement contains several clauses:

SELECT   lists the columns you want to retrieve;

FROM   names the table(s) that contain the selected columns;

WHERE   describes condition(s) for selecting rows to satisfy the request;

GROUP BY   indicates the column(s) to be used to group the retrieved data;

HAVING   describes the condition each group must satisfy. It functions in the same manner as a WHERE clause for groups;

ORDER BY   specifies the order in which the selected columns should appear on the output.

The first two clauses of the SELECT statement -- the SELECT and FROM clauses -- are mandatory. You must enter the SELECT clause first and follow it immediately with the FROM clause. **If you use additional clauses for retrieving data, they must be specified in the exact order indicated above.** For example, the ORDER BY clause must always appear as the last clause of a SELECT statement.

SELECT Clause

Selecting all columns - SELECT *

If you do not remember the column names of the columns you want to select from a table or a view or if you want to select all of the existing columns, use the '*' (asterisk) character in the SELECT clause. The asterisk tells DB2 or SQL/DS that you want all columns for all the selected rows.

```
SELECT  *
   FROM  table-name;
```

In the following example, since there is no WHERE clause, DB2 or SQL/DS retrieve all rows and all columns from the indicated table. The result of the query is therefore an exact copy of the base table, as illustrated below.

```
SELECT   *
   FROM   EMP;
```

EMP

EMP_NO	CONTT_SCR	APPT_SCE	SRC_RCP_CDE	LOA
612666	89	5	A	54
866520	166	1	B	51
1474050	145	1	C	50
1621720	135	1	B	48
4174690	161	4	C	45

The above query returns the following result:

RESULT TABLE

EMP_NO	CONTT_SCR	APPT_SCE	SRC_RCP_CDE	LOA
612666	89	5	A	54
866520	166	1	B	51
1474050	145	1	C	50
1621720	135	1	B	48
4174690	161	4	C	45

Figure 8.1   Selecting all columns -- example

By looking at the selected information, you will notice that the result is a table itself. When the data for your query is retrieved from the specified table or tables, DB2 and SQL/DS physically store it in a temporary table called a *result table*. The result table is used to display the selected information on your terminal and is maintained until the end of the session or until you execute another query. The size of the result table depends on the number of rows and columns returned from the query. The larger the result table, the more I/O operations are required to physically store the table and to read its rows for display purposes. Because a greater number of I/O operations has a negative impact on performance, it should be clear to you how important it is to let DB2 and SQL/DS retrieve only the data you really need. Therefore, you should always use the column list, described on the following page, in the SELECT clause to specify only the columns you are interested in. Later on in this chapter, we will discuss the WHERE clause which can be used to limit the information that you want to retrieve.

Selecting Specific Columns (Column List)

If you know the column name of the columns you want to select, specify them in the SELECT clause.

```
SELECT  column-name-1,column-name-2,....
  FROM  table-name;
```

As a result, DB2 and SQL/DS displays only the data from the retrieved rows for the specified columns.

Example: Select all salespersons with the corresponding reference and length of service information from the EMP table.

```
SELECT  EMP_NO, APPT_SCE, LOA
  FROM  EMP;
```

EMP

EMP_NO	CONTT_SCR	APPT_SCE	SRC_RCP_CDE	LOA
612666	89	5	A	54
866520	166	1	B	51
1474050	145	1	C	50
1621720	135	1	B	48
3118370	198	1	C	38
3728880	214	1	D	45
4174690	161	4	C	44
4174690	161	4	C	45

RESULT TABLE

EMP_NO	APPT_SCE	LOA
612666	5	54
866520	1	51
1474050	1	50
1621720	1	48
3118370	1	38
3728880	1	45
4174690	4	44
4174690	4	45

Figure 8.2 Column list -- example

Elimination of Duplicate Rows - DISTINCT

If you select all columns from a table that may contain duplicate rows or
specific columns from a table with unique rows, but omit the key
column(s), the result table returned by DB2 or SQL/DS may contain
duplicate rows. In certain situations this duplication of information may
be desired by the user -- for example, when creating statistics -- and
therefore justified. But if you want to eliminate these duplicate rows
and make sure that each row contains unique data, you have to specify
the DISTINCT keyword on your SELECT statement.

```
SELECT   DISTINCT *
  FROM   table-name;
```

or

```
SELECT   DISTINCT column-name-1,column-name-2,....
  FROM   table-name;
```

Example: Select all salespersons from the EMP table and eliminate
duplicates:

```
SELECT   DISTINCT EMP_NO
  FROM   EMP;
```

EMP

EMP_NO	CONTT_SCR	APPT_SCE	SRC_RCP_	LOA
612666	89	5	A	54
866520	166	1	B	51
1474050	145	1	C	50
1621720	135	1	B	48
3118370	198	1	C	38
3728880	214	1	D	45
4174690	161	4	C	44
4174690	161	4	C	45

```
                RESULT  TABLE

              ┌─────────────────┐
              │   EMP_NO        │
              ├─────────────────┤
              │    612666       │
              │    866520       │
              │   1474050       │
              │   1621720       │
              │   3118370       │
              │   3728880       │
              │   4174690       │
              └─────────────────┘
```

Figure 8.3   DISTINCT keyword -- example

The result table displays all unique salesperson numbers from the EMP table. The number '4174690' which is contained twice in the base table, has been included only once.

FROM Clause

Table Names

With the FROM clause you specify the name(s) of the table(s) from which you want DB2 or SQL/DS to retrieve data. A formal table name consists of two parts:

- The authorization ID (Creator_Prefix) of the person who created the table. This person is also the owner of the table (except for the DBA under SQL/DS, who may create tables and objects for other users).
- The second part of a table name is a name given to the table when it is created. This table name must be unique within one Creator_prefix.

If you have to use tables created and owned by other IDs, you must specify the fully qualified tablename: Creator_prefix.table-name

You may omit the Creator_prefix when using your own tables and select the desired tables by specifying only the table name and allow DB2 and SQL/DS to qualify the table automatically with your own ID. This identification depends on the environment in which you are operating.

System	Environment	User Identification
Only DB2	TSO	Logon ID
	Batch	User parameter in JCL
	IMS MPP BMP	SIGNON ID LTERM PSBNAME
SQL/DS- DB2	CICS	SIGNON ID TERMINAL ID CICS ID TRANSACTION ID User supplied string
Only SQL/DS	explicit CONNECT	USER ID
	implicit CONNECT	LOGON ID

Figure 8.4 SQL/DS and DB2 user identification

If you often select data from fully qualified tables, you may want to establish new, easier names for them. To do this you may use the CREATE VIEW or the CREATE SYNONYM commands described previously. With the CREATE VIEW statement you can assign new name to tables as well as new names to columns that you want to select.

Note: A synonym is only effective for the user who creates it. If many users want to use the same synonyms, they must each define them separately.

A VIEW that assigns a simpler name, both to columns and table, can be created using the following statement:

```
                new table name        new column names

CREATE  VIEW   TABEASY  (COLEASY1,COLEASY2,COLEASY3)
          AS
               SELECT   COL_COMPLEX_1,COL_COMPLEX_2,
                        COL_COMPLEX_3
                FROM    CREATOR.TAB_NAME_COMPLEX
```

If you want to define only an alternate table name you can use the CREATE SYNONYM command:

```
                    new table name          old table name

CREATE  SYNONYM  TABEASY  FOR    CREATOR.TAB_NAME_COMPLEX
```

Selecting Data from More Than One Table

In the examples we have examined so far, the data was selected from only one table. Often, the information you want is contained in more than one table. In that case, you have to use a SELECT statement to retrieve and combine column values from several tables to form a unique row of the *result table*. Operations that select data from two or more tables are called JOIN operations.

To join two tables and select data from both, you must do the following:

- Specify the table names in the FROM clause.
- If the tables have any column names in common, qualify those column names by prefixing them with the name of the table. Column names that are unique don't need a prefix.
- Specify the relationship between the two tables; that is, the JOIN condition in the WHERE clause. **If you omit the WHERE clause, each row of the first table is concatenated to every row in the second table** (the result is a Cartesian Product which you may not want).

The following example shows a JOIN operation between two tables without a JOIN condition (producing a Cartesian Product of table rows).

A company produces three different types of furniture: tables, chairs, and wardrobes. The information about this furniture is stored in the FURNITURE table. Each piece of furniture is available in three different colors. The amount of color needed to paint a piece depends on its surface and the density of the color. The FURNITURE table contains the amount of color, in pounds, needed to paint a single piece while the COLOR table contains the yielding factor and the cost per pound for each color.

To produce a list of the available combinations the following query must be executed:

```
SELECT  *
FROM    FURNITURE, COLOR
```

FURNITURE   COLOR

DESC	PROD COST	COLOR WEIGHT
TABLE	75	1.2
CHAIR	35	0.5
WARDROBE	95	1.8

COLOR	YIELDING	COST_LB
GREEN	1	3.5
RED	1.2	4.2
BLUE	0.8	3.3

RESULT TABLE

DESC	PROD COST	COLOR WEIGHT	COLOR	YIELDING	COST_LB
TABLE	75	1.2	GREEN	1	3.5
TABLE	75	1.2	RED	1.2	4.2
TABLE	75	1.2	BLUE	0.8	3.3
CHAIR	35	0.5	GREEN	1	3.5
CHAIR	35	0.5	RED	1.2	4.2
CHAIR	35	0.5	BLUE	0.8	3.3
WARDROBE	95	1.8	GREEN	1	3.5
WARDROBE	95	1.8	RED	1.2	4.2
WARDROBE	95	1.8	BLUE	0.8	3.3

Figure 8.5   JOIN operation -- example 1

As you can see, each row from the FURNITURE table has been combined with each row from the COLOR table.

To select all columns from one table without explicitly listing them and only specific columns from another second table, you must qualify the ' * ' (to indicate all columns from a table) with the corresponding table name.

Example: To display all rows from the SALES table including the length of service (LOA) information from the EMP table, specify the following query:

```
SELECT  SALES.*, LOA
  FROM  SALES, EMP
 WHERE  SALES.EMP_NO = EMP.EMP_NO
   AND  WEEK  = 8708;
```

SALES   EMP

WEEK	STORE	EMP_NO	MKT_CDE	NET_SALE
8708	75	61266	U	110.22
8708	80	147405	I	45.29
8708	84	417469	G	1147.47
8709	75	86652	R	144.89
8709	77	162172	R	55.83
8709	80	147405	I	32.17
8709	84	417469	G	264.35
8710	933	480186	U	95.04

EMP_NO	LOA
612666	54
866520	51
147405	50
162172	48
311837	38
372888	45
417469	44
417469	45

RESULT TABLE

WEEK	STORE	EMP_NO	MKT_CDE	NET_SALE	LOA
8708	75	61266	U	110.22	54
8708	80	147405	I	45.29	50
8708	84	417469	G	1147.47	45
8708	84	417469	G	1147.47	44

Figure 8.6   JOIN operation -- example 2

JOIN queries can become tedious to type when column names have to be prefixed with table names. SQL allows you to define a temporary label or shortname in the FROM clause by placing the shortname after the table name, separated by a *space*. You can then use these labels in place of the full table names within the query. The above SELECT statement might therefore be written in the following manner:

```
SELECT  P.*, S.LOA
  FROM  SALES P, EMP S
 WHERE  P.EMP_NO = S.EMP_NO
   AND  WEEK  = 8708;
```

This technique is useful to abbreviate the table name in the SELECT clause it also allows you to join the table to itself as though it were two separate tables. *(See Chapter 9, Advanced Query Structures.)*

WHERE Clause

In most of the preceding examples, all the rows of a table were selected. Normally, you want to retrieve only those rows that correspond to certain selection criteria. To do this, use a WHERE clause in your SELECT command. **A WHERE clause always follows the FROM clause.**

```
       SELECT   ......
         FROM   ......
        WHERE   ......
```

With the WHERE clause you can define a search condition that instructs DB2 or SQL/DS to look in the specified column for the desired value. Only those rows are selected for which the column value satisfies the condition.

The following statement illustrates the format of the WHERE clause when you look for a specific value in a column:

```
WHERE column-name comparison-operator constant-value
```

The comparison rules of DB2 and SQL/DS usually require compatible data types: only number to number and character string to character string can be compared. Data types of INTEGER, SMALLINT, DECIMAL and FLOAT are compatible. Also, CHAR, VARCHAR and LONG VARCHAR are compatible.

The required data type of the constant depends upon the data type of the column it is to be compared to. If the column is numeric the literal must contain only numeric data (0-9, ., -, +). SQL/DS allows a numeric column to be compared to an incompatible data type. For example, the string '123' can be compared to a column defined as INTEGER. DB2, however, requires compatible data types. In SQL/DS leading and trailing zeros are ignored for determining the precision and scale, while DB2 uses any leading and trailing zeros of decimal constants in determining the precision and scale of the number.

If the column data type is alphanumeric (CHAR, VARCHAR, or LONG VARCHAR) the constant value has to be enclosed in apostrophes. You don't have to worry about the length of the literal that you compare to a column. SQL/DS and DB2 always perform the comparison of two strings of unequal length using a copy of the shorter string, padded on the right with blanks, to the length of the other string.

For example, if the column NAME of a table is defined as CHAR(20) and you want to search for all individuals with the name SMITH you can write the following:

```
SELECT   NAME,......
   FROM   ......
  WHERE   NAME = 'SMITH';
```

or

```
  WHERE   NAME = 'SMITH          ';
```

The results are the identical. If you compare a character type column (defined as CHAR, VARCHAR or LONG VARCHAR) to a literal longer than the column length, DB2 and SQL/DS do not use any index defined for that column.

Example: Select all rows for week 8708 from the SALES table:

```
SELECT   *
   FROM   SALES
  WHERE   WEEK   = 8708;
```

SALES

WEEK	STORE	EMP_NO	MKT_CDE	NET_SALE
8708	75	612666	U	110.22
8708	80	1474050	I	45.29
8708	84	4174690	G	1147.47
8709	75	866520	R	144.89
8709	77	1621720	R	55.83
8709	80	1474050	I	32.17
8710	933	4801860	U	95.04

RESULT TABLE

WEEK	STORE	EMP_NO	MKT_CDE	NET_SALE
8708	75	612666	U	110.22
8708	80	1474050	I	45.29
8708	84	4174690	G	1147.47

Figure 8.7   WHERE clause comparison with a constant value

In addition to a comparison with a constant value, a WHERE clause can compare a value stored in one column with a value stored in another column. We have already seen this type of comparison in the previous examples for JOIN operations.

```
WHERE column-name1 comparison-operator column-name2
```

When comparing two columns, the general rule described above concerning data type compatibility still remains valid. There is an exception to the padding and comparison rules for character data.

If two columns both defined as variable in length have to be compared, SQL/DS does not pad the shorter column or column value with blanks. Only the first *n* pairs of characters are compared, where *n* is the length of the shorter string. Even if the first *n* pairs of characters are equal and the rest of the longer string is blank, the two strings are not recognized as equal. **Thus, two variable length strings of different length cannot be equal in SQL/DS.** This is not true in DB2; DB2 always applies the extension rule described above, so that the shorter string would be padded with blanks to the length of the longer one. DB2 then compares the two strings, correctly recognizing whether the two are equal or not.

A search condition can use any of the following comparison operators:

Environment	User Identification
Equal to	=
Not equal to	= or <>
Less than	<
Less than or equal to	<=
Not less than	<
Greater than	>
Greater than or equal to	>=
Not greater than	>

Figure 8.8 Comparison operators

All comparison operators can be used to compare both alphanumeric and numeric data. In case of alphanumeric data the following collating sequence is used: {blank}, A-Z, 0-9 (*e.g., {blank} is lower than any character or number and any character is lower than any number*).

If you are joining two tables, try to provide SQL/DS and DB2 with redundant search information to let them choose the best way to do the JOIN. If you cannot do this, at least put the search condition on the table for which the access time can be reduced (the larger table). If the two tables have a one-to-many relationship, put the search condition on the table with unique rows.

Note: If you JOIN *a table to itself, SQL/DS and DB2 do not use the index.*

Ordering Rows of a Result Table - ORDER BY

Normally selected rows are displayed by DB2 and SQL/DS in the order in which they were retrieved from the base table(s). You can control the display order of selected rows by adding an ORDER BY clause to the SELECT statement.

Note: If you use the ORDER BY *clause, it must be the last clause of the* SELECT *command.*

To change the sequence of the rows to the desired order, DB2 and SQL/DS invoke an internal SORT program. As the internal SORT is relatively slow you should be very careful in using the ORDER BY clause especially when you expect the result table to be very large.

When you use the ORDER BY clause without specifying the or-dering sequence, the retrieved rows are ordered in **ascending** order.

You can also organize rows in **descending** order by using the DESC keyword after the column name that you are ordering by.

```
SELECT    .....
  FROM    .....
 WHERE    .....
ORDER BY  column-name DESC;
```

Example: Select all rows from the EMP table and order them by length of service in descending sequence.

```
SELECT    *
  FROM    EMP
ORDER BY  LOA DESC;
```

EMP

EMP_NO	CONTT_SCR	APPT_SCE	SRC_RCP CDE	LOA
612666	89	5	A	54
866520	166	1	B	51
1474050	145	1	C	50
1621720	135	1	B	48
3118370	198	1	C	38
3728880	214	1	D	45
4174690	161	4	C	44
4174690	161	4	C	45

RESULT TABLE

EMP_NO	CONTT_SCR	APPT_SCE	SRC_RCP CDE	LOA
612666	89	5	A	54
866520	166	1	B	51
1474050	145	1	C	50
1621720	135	1	B	48
3728880	214	1	D	45
4174690	161	4	C	45
4174690	161	4	C	44
3118370	198	1	C	38

Figure 8.9 ORDER BY clause -- example 1

If you want to put the selected rows in a sequence based on the values of more than one column, you can specify additional column names in the ORDER BY clause. In this case, you may specify a different ordering sequence (ascending or descending) for each sequencing level.

```
    SELECT   .....
      FROM   .....
     WHERE   .....
  ORDER BY   column-name-1 DESC,column-name-2,column-
             name3 DESC;
```

Example: Select all rows from the EMP table and order them by contract score in descending sequence. Within the same contract score values order by SRC_RCP_CDE in ascending order.

```
SELECT *
   FROM   EMP
ORDER BY   CONTT_SCR DESC, SRC_RCP_CDE;
```

EMP

EMP_NO	CONTT_SCR	APPT_SCE	SRC_RCP_CDE	LOA
612666	89	5	A	54
866520	166	1	B	51
1474050	145	1	C	50
1621720	135	1	B	48
3118370	198	1	C	38
3728880	214	1	D	45
4174690	161	4	C	44
4174690	161	4	C	45

RESULT TABLE

EMP_NO	CONTT_SCR	APPT_SCE	SRC_RCP_CDE	LOA
3728880	214	1	D	45
3118370	198	1	C	38
866520	166	1	B	51
4174690	161	4	A	44
4174690	161	4	C	45
1474050	145	1	C	50
1621720	135	1	B	48
612666	89	5	A	54

Figure 8.10   ORDER BY clause -- example 2

When you order the result table by columns containing NULL values, the NULL entries are always at the top of the result table regardless of whether it is in ascending or descending order.

Instead of using the column name in the ORDER BY clause, you may also specify its sequence number on the SELECT clause:

```
  SELECT   COL1, COL3, COL5
    FROM   .....
   WHERE   .....
ORDER BY   COL5;
```

Since COL5 is the third column named in the SELECT clause, you may also specify the following:

```
  SELECT   COL1, COL3, COL5
    FROM   .....
   WHERE   .....
ORDER BY   3;
```

You may also use column sequence numbers instead of column names if you want to order the displayed rows based on the result of an expression. *(Expressions and calculated values are discussed in Chapter 9 -- Advanced Query Structures.)*

Summary - SELECT Statement - General Format

```
SELECT   [DISTINCT] *
                    column-name1, column-name2,...
                    [tablename1.]*, [tablename2.]column-name-1,
                              [tablename-2.]column name-2,.....
                    [shortname-1.]column-name-1,
                              [shortname-2.]column name-2,.....
   FROM   tablename-1 [shortname-1[, tablename-2 [shortname-2...]]]



                                =
                                >
   WHERE   [NOT] column-name    <            column name
                                >=           constant value
                                <=
                               ¬>
                               ¬<
                           ¬= or <>


   GROUP BY .....
   HAVING   .....
   ORDER BY column-name1 [DESC][,column-name2[DESC]..]
            seq-number1   [DESC][,seq-number2[DESC]....]
```

Data Retrieval - Advanced Query Structures

Introduction

In the previous chapter, we discussed basic elements of the SELECT statement. In this chapter, we will introduce advanced query structures. The examples used to illustrate the purpose of single features and structures are deliberately kept as simple as possible. The major objective of this book is to provide you with the necessary knowledge to operate in a relational environment without the burden of theoretical explanations and descriptions of specific problems used to demonstrate the limitations of SQL language rather than its power.

This chapter is structured as follows:

- Special comparison operators, such as IN, LIKE, BETWEEN;
- JOIN operations;
- UNION operator;
- subqueries as nested queries;
- expressions;
- built in column and scalar functions;
- GROUP BY and HAVING clauses;
- examples.

Special Comparison Operators

In our preliminary discussion of conditions in the WHERE clause, we described the method used to select required rows from a table by comparing the values contained within a certain column to a constant-value or with a value stored in another column. In this chapter, we will introduce special comparison operators that allow you to compare a column value to a list of values, a range, or to partially match a combination of characters.

Values in a List - IN Keyword

The IN keyword lets you select rows that contain a value matching one from a list of values that you supply.

The following rules apply to a list of values:

- separate items by commas;
- enclose values in single quotation marks (' ') if they represent alphanumeric data;
- enclose the entire list in parentheses.

The order of the values in the list does not have any impact on the execution of the comparison operation or the ordering of the selected rows. If you want the result table to be ordered, you must specify the corresponding criteria in the ORDER BY clause.

The use of the IN operator has the same effect as multiple conditions separated by the OR keyword. The following condition:

```
WHERE   NAME IN ('SMITH','WHITE')
```

selects the same rows for the result table as

```
WHERE   NAME  ='SMITH' OR NAME = 'WHITE'
```

The IN operand saves keying time and is easier to understand than multiple conditions.

Example: Retrieve the contract score and length of service information for salespersons 1474050 and 4174690.

```
SELECT  EMP_NO, CONTT_SCR, LOA
   FROM  EMP
  WHERE  EMP_NO IN (1474050, 4174690);
```

EMP

EMP_NO	CONTT_SCR	APPT_SCE	SRC_RCP_CDE	LOA
612666	89	5	A	54
866520	166	1	B	51
1474050	145	1	C	50
1621720	135	1	B	48
3118370	198	1	C	38
3728880	214	1	D	45
4174690	161	4	C	44
4174690	161	4	C	45

RESULT TABLE

EMP_NO	CONTT_SCR	LOA
1474050	145	50
4174690	161	44
4174690	161	45

Figure 9.1 IN keyword - use in the WHERE clause -- example 1

Example: Retrieve the EMP_NO, NAME, and length of service information for salespersons with the names SMITH and NELSON.

```
SELECT EMP_NO, EMP_NAME, LOA
FROM EMP
WHERE EMP_NAME IN ('SMITH', 'NELSON');
```

EMP

EMP_NO	EMP NAME	CONTT_SCR	SRC_RCP_CDE	LOA
612666	SMITH	89	A	54
866520	MILLER	166	B	51
1474050	BROWN	145	C	50
1621720	O'HARA	135	B	48
3118370	WINTER	198	C	38
3728880	WHITE	214	D	45
4174690	NELSON	161	C	44
4174690	NELSON	161	C	45

RESULT TABLE

EMP_NO	EMP_NAME	LOA
612666	SMITH	54
4174690	NELSON	44
4174690	NELSON	45

Figure 9.2 IN keyword - use in the WHERE clause -- example 2

If you are accessing relatively large tables, you should minimize the use of the IN keyword. If performance is critical, you should check if you cannot obtain the same results by substituting the IN operator with the UNION structure.

```
SELECT   .......
   FROM  .......
  WHERE    WEEK IN (8708,8710);
```

```
SELECT   .......FROM...
  WHERE   WEEK = 8708
  UNION
SELECT   ........  FROM ..
  WHERE   WEEK = 8710;
```

Since UNION invokes the SORT to eliminate duplicate rows, the results obtained from the two queries may be different. Besides, the SORT may have a negative effect on performance if more than 100 rows are returned. In DB2 Release 3 and later as well as in SQL/DS Version 2 Release 2, the UNION keyword has been improved. You may specify the ALL keyword, if you want the result table to contain all rows returned by the base queries. No sorting of the result table and elimination of duplicate rows is performed in this case.

In SQL/DS, the second operand of the IN predicate can only be a list of values, as we've seen already, or a subquery that produces as a result two or more values. In DB2, the second operand can also be an expression, such as a formula.

Matching Character Pattern - LIKE Keyword

In addition to selecting rows that completely match a single value or a value from a list of values, you can also retrieve rows that partially match a combination of supplied characters. The LIKE keyword cannot be used with numeric data. In previous releases of DB2 and SQL/DS the LIKE operator could only be used with character columns with a maximum length of 254 bytes.

You can use the following two special characters with the LIKE keyword:

%   The percent character represents *any string of zero or more characters*. If, for example, you are looking for a name that starts with the letter 'W' and ends with the letter 'E', regardless of how many characters there are between them, you may write:

```
WHERE   NAME   LIKE   'W%E'
```

_   The underscore character represents a *single character position*. If, for example, you are looking for a name that ends with the letter 'E' with exactly four (4) preceding unknown characters, you may write:

```
WHERE   NAME   LIKE   '_ _ _ _E'
```

If you need to match the special characters '%' and '_' in the text, you may use the ESCAPE keyword under SQL/DS Version 2 Release 2.

Example: Select all employees with a 'T' in any position of their name.

```
SELECT   EMP_NO, EMP_NAME
  FROM   EMP
 WHERE   EMP_NAME LIKE '%T%';
```

EMP

EMP_NO	EMP_NAME	CONTT_SCR	SRC_RCP_CDE	LOA
612666	SMITH	89	A	54
866520	MILLER	166	B	51
1474050	BROWN	145	C	50
1621720	O'HARA	135	B	48
3118370	WINTER	198	C	38
3728880	WHITE	214	D	45
4174690	NELSON	161	C	45

RESULT TABLE

EMP_NO	EMP_NAME
612666	SMITH
3118370	WINTER
3728880	WHITE

Figure 9.3 LIKE keyword use in the WHERE clause -- example 1

Example: Select all employees with a six-letter name and an 'I' in the second position.

```
SELECT  EMP_NO, EMP_NAME
  FROM  EMP
 WHERE  EMP_NAME LIKE '_I____';
```

EMP

EMP_NO	EMP_NAME	CONTT_SCR	SRC_RCP_CDE	LOA
612666	SMITH	89	A	54
866520	MILLER	166	B	51
1474050	BROWN	145	C	50
1621720	O'HARA	135	B	48
3118370	WINTER	198	C	38
3728880	WHITE	214	D	45
4174690	NELSON	161	C	45

RESULT TABLE

EMP_NO	EMP_NAME
866520	MILLER
3118370	WINTER

Figure 9.4   LIKE keyword - use in the WHERE clause -- example 2

If you are accessing relatively large tables, you should minimize the use of the LIKE predicate in the WHERE clause because SQL/DS and DB2 may not utilize an index for a column that is used in conjunction with LIKE. If performance is critical, you should try to substitute LIKE with other operators, such as BETWEEN, that takes advantage of an existing index.

```
WHERE   NAME LIKE 'S%'
equals
WHERE   NAME BETWEEN 'SA' AND 'SZ'
```

The alphanumeric literals 'SA' and 'SZ' are padded to the correct length of the column.

Even with BETWEEN, depending on the complexity of the SQL statement, SQL/DS may not use the index. Anyway, your chances are better than with the LIKE operand.

Selecting Values from a Range - BETWEEN...AND Keywords

The BETWEEN .. AND .. keyword sequence allows you to select rows that contain values within a range. Use the BETWEEN operand to specify the lower and upper boundaries. The lower limit must be specified first, then the upper limit. The boundary values are included into the range. For example, if you are looking for names starting with the letters A, B, C, you can specify the following:

```
WHERE   NAME BETWEEN 'A' AND 'C'
```

The BETWEEN operand can be used for both alphanumeric and numeric data.

Example: Select all salespersons with NET_SALES in a range from $50 to $200.

```
SELECT  EMP_NO
FROM    SALES
WHERE   NET_SALE BETWEEN 50 AND 200;
```

SALES

WEEK	STORE	EMP_NO	MKT_CDE	NET_SALE
8708	75	612666	1	110.22
8708	80	1474050	2	45.29
8708	84	4174690	4	1147.47
8709	75	866520	3	144.89
8709	77	1621720	3	55.83
8709	80	1474050	2	32.17
8709	84	4174690	4	264.35
8710	933	4801860	3	95.04

RESULT TABLE

EMP_NO
612666
866520
1621720
4801860

Figure 9.5 BETWEEN ... AND keywords - use in the WHERE clause -- example

Multiple Conditions - The Boolean Operators AND and OR

At times, you may find it necessary to specify more than one search condition in a WHERE clause to retrieve the desired rows from a table.

- The AND keyword connects two conditions that must <u>both</u> be true in order to select the corresponding row.
- The OR keyword connects the conditions. Only <u>one</u> of the search conditions needs to be satisfied to select a row.

You can combine AND and OR in the same query to specify as many search conditions as are necessary to select the desired rows.

Example: Select all rows from the EMP table for employee 3728880 where the contract score is 214.

```
SELECT   *
   FROM   EMP
  WHERE   EMP_NO = 3728880 AND CONT_SCR = 214
```

EMP

EMP_NO	CONTT_SCR	APPT_SCE	SRC_RCP_CDE	LOA
612666	89	5	A	54
866520	214	1	B	51
1474050	145	1	C	50
3728880	135	1	B	48
3118370	198	1	C	38
3728880	214	1	D	45
4174690	161	4	C	44
4174690	161	4	C	45

RESULT TABLE

EMP_NO	CONTT_SCR	APPT_SCE	SRC_RCP_CDE	LOA
3728880	214	1	D	45

Figure 9.6   Boolean operators -- example 1

Example: Select all rows from the EMP table for employee 3728880 or where the contract score is 214.

```
SELECT   *
   FROM   EMP
  WHERE   EMP_NO = 3728880 OR CONT_SCR = 214
```

RESULT TABLE

EMP_NO	CONTT_SCR	APPT_SCE	SRC_RCP_CDE	LOA
866520	214	1	B	51
3728880	135	1	B	48
3728880	214	1	D	45

Figure 9.7   Boolean operators -- example 2

When specifying multiple conditions, you may find it necessary to use parentheses to group them together to control the sequence in which conditions must be applied.   This is called *logical precedence*. Parentheses also allow you to clarify the meaning of the WHERE clause and make complex conditions more readable and understandable.

When parentheses are nested, SQL/DS and DB2 interprets the conditions starting with the innermost level.

Negation of Conditions - NOT Keyword

You can negate any group of search conditions by enclosing the conditions in parentheses and preceding the group with the keyword NOT.

Using the NOT keyword means that you want to select all rows *except* those identified by the condition specified.   **The NOT clause must precede the entire condition and not only the comparison operator.**

```
WRONG------WHERE--NAME--NOT-=-'SMITH'

RIGHT       WHERE   NOT   NAME = 'SMITH'
```

To negate a single comparison operator (= , < , >) you must use the symbol ' '

If you use the other SQL operators -- such as LIKE, IN, BETWEEN -- the NOT keyword may directly precede these operators. The following clauses are accepted by DB2 and SQL/DS as equivalent:

```
WHERE   NAME NOT IN ('SMITH','BROWN')
WHERE   NOT NAME IN ('SMITH','BROWN')
```

or

```
WHERE   NAME NOT LIKE 'SM%'
WHERE   NOT NAME LIKE 'SM%'
```

or

```
WHERE   NAME NOT BETWEEN 'SA' AND 'SZ'
WHERE   NOT NAME BETWEEN 'SA' AND 'SZ'
```

Example: Select all rows from the EMP table except those for salesperson 3728880 or where the contract score is 214.

```
SELECT  *
  FROM  EMP
 WHERE  NOT (EMP_NO = 3728880 OR CONT_SCR = 214)
```

EMP

EMP_NO	CONTT_SCR	APPT_SCE	SRC_RCP_CDE	LOA
612666	89	5	A	54
866520	214	1	B	51
1474050	145	1	C	50
3728880	135	1	B	48
3118370	198	1	C	38
3728880	214	1	D	45
4174690	161	4	C	44
4174690	161	4	C	45

RESULT TABLE

EMP_NO	CONTT_SCR	APPT_SE	SRC_RCP_CDE	LOA
612666	89	5	A	54
1474050	145	1	C	50
3118370	198	1	C	38
4174690	161	4	C	44
4174690	161	4	C	45

Figure 9.8   NOT keyword -- example

NULL Values in Conditions

Any field value in a table, regardless of its data type, may have the special value NULL. A NULL value may be thought of as an unknown value. NULL values can be prohibited by specifying NOT NULL for the desired columns during table creation.

Since a NULL value cannot be greater than, equal to or less than any other value specified in a search condition, a row containing NULL values would never be retrieved. DB2 and SQL/DS provide you with a special comparison operator to use in the search condition of the WHERE clause to explicitly test for NULL values.

To select values from rows that contain NULL values, specify the following:

```
WHERE   column-name IS NULL
```

The following search conditions will not give you the desired result:

```
WHERE column-name = 'NULL'
```

WRONG   **or**

```
WHERE column-name = NULL
```

In the first case both DB2 and SQL/DS would search the specified column for the character string NULL to verify the condition while the second condition is simply invalid.

You may modify the IS NULL comparison operator with the keyword NOT, by specifying the following:

```
WHERE   column-name IS NOT NULL
```

In this case, only the rows containing valid or known values in the specified column are returned.

NULL values contained in a column that is specified in the GROUP BY clause causes some trouble in SQL/DS because **each row of a grouping column containing a NULL value is a separate group.** In DB2, starting with Release 2, NULL values are identical for the purpose of grouping.

JOIN Operations

In a relational database system single tables are related to each other by the values stored in columns that are based on the same kind of data.

For example, the tables SALES and EMP each have a column that contains the account number of the employee. This account number allows you to relate rows from the SALES to rows in the EMP table.

To select rows from one or more tables, as we have already seen in a previous chapter, you name the tables with the FROM clause. You can then use the corresponding column names -- eventually qualified with the table name or an associated short name -- throughout all the other clauses of the SELECT statement.

Assume you want to know the amount of sales of all salespersons with APPT_SCE equal to 5. By looking at the EMP table we find that only the salesperson 612666 has the required value in the APPT_SCE column. By looking at the SALES table, you can see that salesperson 612666 had sold for $110.12 in week 8708.

In this way, we have related one row of the SALES table to another row in the EMP table by searching for matching values in the account number column. In the same way, DB2 and SQL/DS perform a JOIN operation.

Example:

```
SELECT   S.EMP_NO, LOA, WEEK, NET_SALE
  FROM   EMP S, SALES P
 WHERE   S.EMP_NO  =  P.EMP_NO
```

EMP

EMP_NO	CONTT_SCR	APPT_SCE	SRC_RCP_CDE	LOA
612666	89	5	A	54
866520	166	1	B	51
1474050	145	1	C	50
1621720	135	1	B	48
3118370	198	1	C	38
3728880	214	1	D	45
4174690	161	4	C	44
4924690	161	4	C	45

SALES

WEEK	STORE	EMP_NO	MKT_CDE	NET_SALE
8708	75	612666	1	110.22
8708	80	1474050	2	45.29
8708	84	4174690	4	1147.47
8709	75	866520	3	144.89
8709	77	1621720	3	55.83
8709	80	1474050	2	32.17
8709	84	4174690	4	264.35
8710	933	4801860	1	95.04

RESULT TABLE

EMP_NO	LOA	WEEK	NET_SALE
612666	54	8708	110.22
866520	51	8709	144.09
1474050	50	8708	45.29
1474050	50	8709	32.17
1621720	48	8709	55.83
4174690	44	8708	1147.47
4174690	44	8709	264.35

Figure 9.9   JOIN operation - example 1

In the above example, we have used the ' = ' operator in the join condition. This particular kind of join is called an 'EQUI-JOIN'. Although there are several other types of JOIN conditions, the EQUI-JOIN is the most common type.

Sometimes it is necessary to join a table to itself. A classic example is the selection of all employees whose salary exceeds their corresponding manager's salary. Suppose that we have the following employee table:

EMPNO	NAME	JOB	MGRNO	SALARY
10001	SMITH	REPRESENTATIVE	10048	45000
10002	BROWN	SALESPERSON	10048	23000
10003	WHITE	SECRETARY	10048	43000
10004	GREEN	REPRESENTATIVE	10048	32000
10020	BLAKE	SALESPERSON	10048	25000
10021	GARDEN	SALESPERSON	10048	24500
10023	WINTER	MANAGER	10023	88000
10030	HOUSE	JANITOR	10023	18000
10045	JONES	REPRESENTATIVE	10048	37000
10047	FRANKS	SECRETARY	10023	35000
10048	O'HARA	MANAGER	10023	42500
10049	JOHNSON	BOOKKEEPER	10023	32000

To find all the employees whose salary exceeds their corresponding manager's salary, execute the following query:

```
SELECT   W.NAME, W.SAL, M.NAME, M.SAL
  FROM   EMP W, EMP M
 WHERE   W.MGRNO = M.EMPNO
   AND   W.SALARY > M.SALARY
```

This query produces the following result table:

NAME	SALARY	NAME	SALARY
SMITH	45000	O'HARA	42500
WHITE	43000	O'HARA	42500

Figure 9.10   JOIN operation -- example 2

When two tables are joined, DB2 or SQL/DS first concatenates each row from the first table to each row in the second table. Based on the information supplied in the WHERE clause, it decides whether this combination is valid and desired or not. If you omit the WHERE clause, each combination is considered valid and the number of rows in the result table is a product of the number of rows of each joined table. This result is called a Cartesian Product, which is not what you were looking for, so a JOIN condition should be specified.

UNION

In the previous chapter, we described how two or more tables can be joined together in a single SELECT statement so that we obtain one result table. In this section, we will describe how two or more SELECT statements, each producing its own result table, can be combined in a single query by using the UNION keyword.

When you use the UNION clause, DB2 or SQL/DS executes each single SELECT statement producing an *interim result table*. These multiple interim result tables are then combined to the *combined result table*. All duplicate rows are automatically eliminated.

Example: Suppose you have a SALES table for two different geographical regions: PART_NORTH and PART_SOUTH. To select the information about week 8708 from both tables and combine the retrieved rows in a single result table, use the following query:

```
     SELECT    WEEK,    STORE  , EMP_NO, NET_SALE
       FROM    PART_NORTH
      WHERE    WEEK = 8708
UNION
     SELECT    WEEK,    STORE  , EMP_NO, NET_SALE
       FROM    PART_SOUTH
      WHERE    WEEK = 8708;
```

PART_NORTH

WEEK	STORE	EMP_NO	NET SALE
8708	75	612666	110.2
8708	80	1474050	45.2
8708	84	4174690	1147.4
8709	75	866520	144.8
8709	77	1621720	55.8
8709	80	1474050	32.1
8709	84	4174690	264.3
8710	933	4801860	95.0

PART_SOUTH

WEEK	STORE	EMP_NO	NET SALE
8708	92	894353	0.0
8708	947	7020350	614.2
8708	935	7114690	147.4
8708	75	6567520	185.8
8709	84	1560668	25.8
8709	92	894353	15.9
8709	947	7020350	67.3
8710	933	2037927	133.8

RESULT TABLE

WEEK	STORE	EMP NO	NET SALE
8708	75	612666	110.2
8708	80	1474050	45.2
8708	84	4174690	1147.4
8708	92	894353	0.0
8708	947	7020350	614.2
8708	935	7114690	147.4
8708	75	6567520	185.8

Figure 9.11   UNION operation -- example 1

The result table no longer reflects the source of the sales figures (NORTH or SOUTH).

Constants may be used to identify the rows that are provided from the single tables. Constant values that the user wants to be included in the rows of the result table must be enclosed in single quotation marks (' ') and are required to be of the same length.

The above query can be modified as follows:

```
SELECT 'NORTH   ', WEEK, STORE, EMP_NO,NET_SALE
   FROM PART_NORTH
  WHERE  WEEK = 8708
UNION
  SELECT 'SOUTH   ', WEEK, STORE, EMP_NO,NET_SALE
   FROM PART_SOUTH
  WHERE  WEEK = 8708;
```

RESULT TABLE

	WEEK	STORE	EMP_NO	NET_SALE
NORTH	8708	75	612666	110.2
NORTH	8708	80	1474050	45.2
NORTH	8708	84	4174690	1147.4
SOUTH	8708	92	894353	0.0
SOUTH	8708	947	7020350	614.2
SOUTH	8708	935	7114690	147.4
SOUTH	8708	75	6567520	185.8

Figure 9.12   UNION operation -- example 2

The difference between a JOIN operation and the use of the UNION keyword consists in different forms of aggregation. The *JOIN operation* permits you to build a row of the result table by *horizontally* combining single columns from different tables while the UNION keyword produces a *vertical* combination of result tables. With the UNION keyword, a set of rows selected through the execution of one SELECT statement is appended to the set of rows selected through the execution of another SELECT statement. Duplicate rows in the interim result tables are eliminated.

There are several restrictions that apply to the use of the UNION keyword in previous releases of DB2 and SQL/DS:

■ To combine multiple result tables they have to be *identical in column composition*. This means that the following must apply

   ● Each SELECT statement combined by the UNION keyword must retrieve the same number of columns.

   ● Corresponding columns in the single SELECT statement must be identical as far as the data type and length of each column is concerned.

- Corresponding columns must be NULL compatible; both must either accept or not accept NULL values in order to be combined.

■ You may order your rows of the *combined result table*, but not of the single *interim result tables*. If you use the ORDER BY clause, it may appear only once throughout all the SELECT statements that are part of the union. It must be the last clause of the whole group following the last SELECT statement. To specify the columns you want DB2 or SQL/DS to order the result by, you must use the column sequence number. You may not use column names, as they normally vary on each SELECT statement in the union.

■ You can use UNION only on outer-level SELECT statements; the UNION keyword may never appear on a SELECT statement in a subquery.

The limitations described above have been partly removed in the new releases. The following description of the new UNION keyword provides an overview of these improvements:

■ You may specify UNION ALL if you want to display all rows retrieved by the base queries without elimination of duplicates. It is also possible to combine the UNION and UNION ALL keywords in the same statements. The order of execution determines whether the final result table contains duplicates or not. You can change the order of execution by using parentheses.

■ Corresponding columns may be combined whether they allow nulls or not.

■ The new releases provide a number of conversion rules to produce the corresponding columns in the result table in case the length and data type attributes of the base columns are different. Columns may be combined even if they do not have exactly the same data type. It is sufficient that their data types are comparable; all character data types may be mixed and any number can be joined with any other number. The new conversion rules are described below.

Example: Suppose you want to know all stores served by all salespersons during week 8708 and 8709.

```
SELECT    STORE, EMP_NO
  FROM    SALES
 WHERE    WEEK = 8708

 UNION    ALL

SELECT    STORE, EMP_NO
  FROM    SALES
 WHERE    WEEK = 8709;
```

RESULT TABLE
UNION

STORE	EMP_NO
75	612666
80	1474050
84	4174690
75	866520
77	1621720

RESULT TABLE
UNION ALL

STORE	EMP_NO
75	612666
80	1474050
84	4174690
75	866520
77	1621720
80	1474050
84	4174690

Figure 9.13   UNION and UNION ALL -- example

The following is an overview over the conversion rules that apply in the new releases:

Rules for character columns --   If you want to combine two character columns the following rules apply:

- If both columns are of fixed length, the result column will be of the same data type. The length of the result column corresponds to the maximum length of both columns. The values derived from the shorter column are padded on the right with blanks to the length of the longer column.
- If both columns are of variable length, the result column will be of the same data type. The length of the result column corresponds to the maximum length of both columns.
- Only character columns of the same data type can be combined.

Rules for numeric columns. The following table shows the data type of the result column depending on the data type of the base columns:

	SMALLINT	INTEGER	DECIMAL	SPFP *)	DFP *)
SMALLINT	SMALLINT	INTEGER	DECIMAL	DPFP *)	DPFP *)
INTEGER	INTEGER	INTEGER	DECIMAL	DPFP *)	DPFP *)
DECIMAL	DECIMAL	DECIMAL	DECIMAL	DPFP *)	DPFP *)
SPFP *)	DPFP *)	DPFP *)	DPFP *)	SPFP *)	DPFP *)
DPFP *)	DPFP *)	DPFP *)	DPFP *)	DPFP *)	DFP *)

* SPFP - Single Precision Floating Point
* DPFP - Double Precision Floating Point

Rules for date/time columns - To combine Date/Time columns, the data type of all columns must be identical.

The following restrictions still apply to the use of the UNION keyword even in the new releases.

- Each SELECT statement combined by the UNION keyword must retrieve the same number of columns.

- The ORDER BY clause must be the last clause of the whole group following the last SELECT statement.

- You can use UNION only on outer-level SELECT statements; the UNION keyword may never appear on a SELECT statement in a subquery.

- The UNION keyword may not be used to create a view; the SELECT statement, on which the definition of the view is defined, is considered a subquery.

- The UNION keyword may not be used to copy data from one or more input tables using the INSERT statement. The SELECT statement, on which the definition of the view is defined, is considered a subquery.

Subqueries

In the queries we have seen so far, we have used either a constant value or a column name in the WHERE clause because we already knew what value or values to look for. In some cases, we have to consult another table to get the desired values for the search condition. We can execute our first query to return the required values and record them manually.

In a second step, we can build our real query with the now completed search condition and execute it.

But there is an easier way!

One of the reasons why SQL is so powerful is that you can build complex queries out of several simple queries. We have already seen this when we used the UNION keyword to combine the intermediate result tables of several single queries to one combined result table. It is also possible to nest queries in the WHERE clause; the WHERE clause itself can contain another query, called a *subquery*. The first SELECT command, also called *main query or outer-level SELECT*, uses the inner query in the search condition to select the desired rows.

Subqueries must be enclosed in parentheses, but they do not need to be indented. The use of indentation throughout this manual is only introduced to make the queries more readable.

When you use a subquery, DB2 or SQL/DS executes it first and places the value(s) resulting from the subquery directly into the WHERE clause. Subqueries can be nested; each subquery may contain another subquery in the corresponding search condition. In addition, you may specify multiple conditions in the WHERE clause using the AND or OR keywords. Each single condition can include a subquery. Subqueries may also be used in INSERT, UPDATE and DELETE statements

Subqueries Returning Only One Value

If you are sure that the subquery returns only one value -- for example, as a result of a built-in function or an arithmetic expression -- you can use the subquery immediately following any of the comparison operators. DB2 or SQL/DS evaluates the search condition the same way as if you had supplied a constant value.

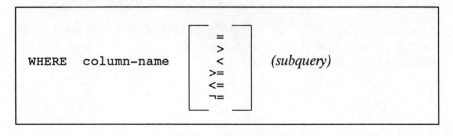

Example: Retrieve all salespersons that have sold more than the average sales.

```
SELECT   *
  FROM   SALES

 WHERE   NET_SALE >
         (SELECT AVG(NET_SALE)
           FROM SALES);
```

SQL executes the inner query first and produces an intermediate result table:

SALES

WEEK	STORE	EMP_NO	MKT_CDE	NET_SALE
8708	75	612666	1	110.22
8708	80	1474050	2	45.29
8708	84	4174690	4	1147.47
8709	75	866520	3	144.89
8709	77	1621720	3	55.83
8709	80	1474050	2	32.17
8709	84	4174690	4	264.35
8710	933	4801860	1	95.04

INTERMEDIATE RESULT TABLE

AVG(NET SALE)
236.91

Figure 9.14   Subqueries returning only one value -- example - part 1

In a second step, SQL substitutes the intermediate result table in the WHERE condition of the outer query and executes the outer SELECT producing the final result table:

```
SELECT   *
  FROM   SALES

 WHERE   NET_SALE  >   236.91
```

FINAL RESULT TABLE

WEEK	STORE	EMP_NO	MKT_CDE	NET_SALE
8708	84	4174690	4	1147.47
8709	84	4174690	4	264.35

Subqueries Returning a Set of Values

If a subquery returns a set of values (that is zero, one or many values) you must use the ANY or ALL keywords in combination with the comparison operator that precedes the subquery (You may also use the IN keyword discussed previously).

The ALL clause indicates that the value contained in the indicated column must be compared to all the values returned by the subquery.

```
                        ┌        ┐
                        │   =    │
                        │   >    │
WHERE   column-name     │   <    │   ALL (subquery)
                        │  >=    │
                        │  <=    │
                        │  ¬=    │
                        └        ┘
```

If, for example, you choose the greater than ' > ' operator, the value contained in the specified column must be greater than all the values returned by the subquery -- i.e., it must be greater than the highest value returned by the subquery. If the subquery returns an *empty set* of values (no values), the condition is also true.

Correspondingly, the ANY keyword is used to say that the value in the named column must compare (depending on the comparison operator chosen) to any of the values returned from the subquery. In DB2 Release 3 and SQL/DS Version 2 Release 2 you may also use according to the ANSI/SQL standard the SOME keyword instead of ANY.

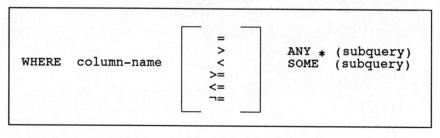

```
                        ┌        ┐
                        │   =    │
                        │   >    │   ANY * (subquery)
WHERE   column-name     │   <    │   SOME   (subquery)
                        │  >=    │
                        │  <=    │
                        │  ¬=    │
                        └        ┘
```

(*) Introduced in DB2 Release 3 and SQL/DS Version 2 Release 2.

If, for example, you again choose the greater than ' > ' operator, the value contained in the specified column must be greater than at least one of the values selected by the subquery -- i.e., it must be greater than the lowest value returned by the subquery. If the subquery returns an empty set of values (no values) then the condition has not been satisfied.

Example: Retrieve all salespersons that have sold more than the average sales of at least one week

```
SELECT   *
  FROM   SALES
 WHERE   NET_SALE  > ANY
         (SELECT AVG(NET_SALE)
            FROM SALES
          GROUP BY  WEEK);
```

SQL/DS executes the inner query first and produces an intermediate result table:

SALES

	WEEK	STORE	EMP_NO	MKT_CDE	NET_SALE
I	8708	75	612666	1	110.22
	8708	80	1474050	2	45.29
	8708	84	4174690	4	1147.47
II	8709	75	866520	3	144.89
	8709	77	1621720	3	55.83
	8709	80	1474050	2	32.17
	8709	84	4174690	4	264.35
III	8710	933	4801860	1	95.04

INTERMEDIATE RESULT TABLE

AVG(NET_SALE)
434.33
124.31
95.04

Figure 9.15 Subqueries returning a set of values -- example - part 1

In the second step of the process, SQL substitutes the intermediate result table in the WHERE condition of the outer query and executes the outer SELECT producing the final result table:

```
SELECT   *
FROM     SALES

WHERE    NET_SALE   > ANY (    434.33
                               124.31
                                95.04    )
```

FINAL RESULT TABLE

WEEK	STORE	EMP_NO	MKT_CDE	NET_SALE
8708	75	612666	1	110.22
8708	84	4174690	4	1147.47
8709	75	866520	3	144.89
8709	84	4174690	4	264.35
8710	933	4801860	1	95.04

Figure 9.16   Subqueries returning a set of values -- example - part 2

The IN keyword has the same meaning and can be substituted for the '= ANY' combination, and NOT IN means the same as '¬ = ALL'. DB2 and SQL/DS allow the use of the IN keyword because it is designed to treat a list of values.

```
SELECT   *
FROM     EMP
WHERE    EMP_NO   IN
         (SELECT EMP_NO
               FROM SALES
               WHERE NET_SALE BETWEEN 50 AND 200);
```

SALES

WEEK	STORE	EMP_NO	MKT_CDE	NET_SALE
8708	75	612666	1	110.22
8708	80	1474050	2	45.29
8708	84	4174690	4	1147.47
8709	75	866520	3	144.89
8709	77	1621720	3	55.83
8709	80	1474050	2	32.17
8709	84	4174690	4	264.35
8710	933	4801860	1	95.04

INTERMEDIATE RESULT TABLE

EMP_NO
612666
866520
1621720
4801860

Figure 9.17   Use of the IN keyword in subqueries - part 1

SQL replaces the intermediate result table in the WHERE condition of
the outer query, executes the outer SELECT and produces the following
final result table:

```
SELECT   *
   FROM   EMP

   WHERE   EMP_NO   IN (    612666
                           866520
                          1621720
                          4801860
                                      )
```

FINAL RESULT TABLE

EMP_NO	CONTT_SCR	APPT_SCE	SRC_RCP_CDE	LOA
612666	89	5	A	54
866520	166	1	B	51
1621720	135	1	B	48

Figure 9.18   Use of the IN keyword in subqueries - part 2

Considerations in the Use of Subqueries

Although the subqueries represent a powerful element of the SQL language, you should consider the following when using them:

- If you are using a subquery in a SELECT statement, DB2 or SQL/DS may not use an available index. Whenever possible, you should consider using JOIN operations instead of subqueries.

```
SELECT   NAME,PHONE
    FROM   TEMPL                          subselect
   WHERE   EMPNO IN
           (SELECT MGRNO FROM TDEPT)


SELECT   NAME, PHONE
    FROM   TEMPL, TDEPT                    join
   WHERE   EMPNO = MGRNO
```

- Since performance degrades when using subqueries, you should not use more than three (3) levels of nested subqueries.
- Although a subquery can return a set of rows, it can only select values from one column. This means that the SELECT statement in the subquery can specify only one column, one of the built-in functions or an arithmetic expression.
- A subquery cannot include an ORDER BY clause.
- A subquery can include the GROUP BY and HAVING clauses. This extension is introduced with DB2 Release 3.
- If you use a subquery in a SELECT statement, the subquery can be based on the same table or view as the outer-level SELECT statement. This is not true when using a subquery with an UPDATE, INSERT or DELETE statement.

EXISTS Keyword

The EXISTS keyword verifies that at least one row can be found that satisfies the search condition in the subquery. Since the subquery in this case does not return any values, you do not have to specify column names in the SELECT clause of the subquery (simply specify SELECT *).

```
WHERE  EXISTS  subquery
```

If the condition is satisfied, DB2 or SQL/DS retrieves the rows indicated by the outer-level SELECT statement.

You can also negate the EXISTS condition by using the NOT keyword.

The following example illustrates the use of the EXISTS keyword. If, for example, you want all the accounting numbers of employees who had actually served customers during the last week but are missing in the EMP table, you may use the following SELECT statement:

```
SELECT   P.EMP_NO
  FROM   SALES P
 WHERE   NOT EXISTS
         (SELECT  *
            FROM  EMP S
           WHERE  S.EMP_NO = P.EMP_NO);
```

Beginning with SQL/DS Version 2 Release 1, the search for the inner SELECT terminates when at least one row satisfying the search condition of the inner SELECT is found. In the previous releases it does not terminate processing until all rows satisfying the inner SELECT are found.

Correlated Subqueries

The subqueries that we have so far examined are executed only once by DB2 or SQL/DS. The returned value or values are substituted in the right side of the search condition in the WHERE clause of the outer-level SELECT statement. The outer-level SELECT statement is then executed normally.

When you use a correlated subquery, it is evaluated for each row of the table or view specified in the outer-level SELECT. In this case, the WHERE clause of the subquery contains a column value from a column in the table or view used in the outer-level SELECT. As this value changes, DB2 or SQL/DS has to re-execute the subquery for each row of the table/view in the outer-level SELECT.

A correlation subquery differs from a normal subquery in that you specify a correlation name after the table name in the FROM clause of the outer SELECT. The correlation name is a variable that identifies the current row of the correlated table. To specify the correlation, you must prefix the column name in the WHERE clause of the subquery with the correlation name.

Suppose you want to retrieve the EMP_NO of all the salespersons that sold more products than the average of their store during the last week. Your SELECT statement would be as follows:

```
SELECT   EMP_NO
  FROM   SALES PAR
 WHERE   SALES >
           (SELECT   AVG(SALES)
              FROM   SALES
             WHERE   STORE = PAR.STORE);
```

Although the above query looks simple, it takes DB2 or SQL/DS numerous I/O operations to execute it correctly and to produce the desired result table.

Make certain that there is no other way to obtain the needed information before using a correlated subquery.   In the previous example you could choose the following alternative solution:

1. Create a temporary table to store the results from the inner query:

```
CREATE   TABLE TEMP
         (STORE      CHAR(5)
          AVGSALES   DECIMAL(10,2));
```

2. Store the result of the above subquery in the temporary table using the INSERT statement:

```
INSERT   INTO      TEMP
         SELECT   STORE, AVG(SALES)
           FROM   SALES
          GROUP   BY STORE;
```

3. Join the SALES table with the TEMP table obtaining the same result you would obtain from the use of correlated query:

```
SELECT   ACCTNO
  FROM   SALES P, TEMP T
 WHERE   P.STORE = T.STORE
         AND
         SALES > AVGSALES;
```

SQL Expressions

An SQL statement can contain arithmetic expressions. An arithmetic expression consists of column names and/or constant numeric values connected by arithmetic operators. You can use any of the following operators:

ARITHMETIC OPERATOR	DESCRIPTION
+	Addition
−	Subtraction
*	Multiplication
/	Division

DB2 and SQL/DS executes your expressions according to the rule that multiplication '* ' and division '/' have precedence over addition '+' and subtraction ' − ' unless parentheses are used. .Using parentheses allows you to better clarify the meaning of your expression.

Arithmetic calculations can be done on any kind of numeric data, but you cannot use alphanumeric data in these expressions. DB2 and SQL/DS considers each and every column defined with CHAR, VARCHAR, LONG VARCHAR, or graphic as alphanumeric data, even if these columns contain numeric values -- e.g., phone numbers.

Using Expressions in the WHERE Clause

You can use an arithmetic expression as part of the condition in the
WHERE clause.

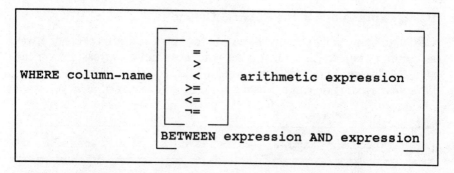

Example: Select furniture/color combinations from the COMBINATIONS
table with production costs less than $80:

```
SELECT   DESC, COLOR
  FROM   COMBINATIONS
 WHERE   (((COLOR_WEIGHT * YIELDING) * COST_LB) +
         PROD_COST) < 80;
```

COMBINATIONS

DESC	PROD COST	COLOR WEIGHT	COLOR	YIELDING	COST_LB
TABLE	75	1.2	GREEN	1	3.5
TABLE	75	1.2	RED	1.2	4.2
TABLE	75	1.2	BLUE	0.8	3.3
CHAIR	35	0.5	GREEN	1	3.5
CHAIR	35	0.5	RED	1.2	4.2
CHAIR	35	0.5	BLUE	0.8	3.3
WARDROBE	95	1.8	GREEN	1	3.5
WARDROBE	95	1.8	RED	1.2	4.2
WARDROBE	95	1.8	BLUE	0.8	3.3

RESULT TABLE

DESC	COLOR
TABLE	GREEN
TABLE	BLUE
CHAIR	GREEN
CHAIR	RED
CHAIR	BLUE

Figure 9.19   Use of expressions in the WHERE clause

Keep in mind that when you use an expression in a condition of the WHERE clause that DB2 or SQL/DS does not use an index on a column that is compared to an arithmetic expression.

Using Expressions in the SELECT Clause

Calculated values can be displayed for the retrieved rows the same way as column values. You must code your arithmetic expressions on the SELECT clause along with the names of the columns that you want to have displayed. You can use as many arithmetic expressions as you want in a query.

```
SELECT column-name-1, expression-1, column-name2,...
```

Example: Based on the COMBINATIONS table, calculate the corresponding costs for color and the total production cost for tables:

```
SELECT  DESC, COLOR, (COLOR_WEIGHT * YIELDING) *
        COST_LB,  ((COLOR_WEIGHT * YIELDING) *
        COST_LB) + PROD_COST
  FROM  COMBINATIONS
 WHERE  DESC = 'TABLE';
```

COMBINATIONS

DESC	PROD COST	COLOR WEIGHT	COLOR	YIELDING	COST_LB
TABLE	75	1.2	GREEN	1	3.5
TABLE	75	1.2	RED	1.2	4.2
TABLE	75	1.2	BLUE	0.8	3.3
CHAIR	35	0.5	GREEN	1	3.5
CHAIR	35	0.5	RED	1.2	4.2
CHAIR	35	0.5	BLUE	0.8	3.3
WARDROBE	95	1.8	GREEN	1	3.5
WARDROBE	95	1.8	RED	1.2	4.2
WARDROBE	95	1.8	BLUE	0.8	3.3

RESULT TABLE

DESC	COLOR		
TABLE	GREEN	4.2	79.2
TABLE	RED	6.05	81.05
TABLE	BLUE	3.17	78.17

Figure 9.20   Using expressions in the SELECT clause -- example

Column names are used as display headings for query results. If the SELECT clause contains an arithmetic expression, it depends on the ONLINE query tool that you are using as to whether or not there is a column header automatically generated for columns containing results from expressions.

SPUFI No heading for expressions

QMF under VM The column header is 'EXPRESSION n' where n is the sequence number of the expression. This means that the first column containing calculated values are 'EXPRESSION 1', the second 'EXPRESSION 2', etc.

QMF under MVS The column header is 'COLn' where n is the sequence number of the expression. This means that the first column containing calculated values are 'COL1', the second 'COL2', etc.

Using Expressions in the ORDER BY Clause

If you want to order the result table based on values calculated with an arithmetic expression, use the column number of the result column instead of the column name.

```
SELECT column-name-1, expression-1, column-name-2
   FROM    .....
   WHERE   .....
   ORDER BY 2;
```

Built-in Column Functions

The argument of a built-in column function is a list containing all values of a specific column for a table or subset of a table (if the GROUP BY clause is specified). The result is a single value representing the sum, average, minimum, or maximum of these values.

In the arithmetic expressions that we have seen so far, we have calculated certain values for *individual rows* of the result table. You can also select summary information about *groups of rows*.

The following statements are five SQL built-in column functions available in DB2 and SQL/DS that you can use with a SELECT statement:

SUM([DISTINCT] column name)
> Returns the total value for the specified column within the set of selected rows.

MIN([DISTINCT] column name)
> Returns the lowest value for the specified column within the set of selected rows.

MAX([DISTINCT] column name)
> Returns the highest value for the specified column within the set of selected rows.

AVG([DISTINCT] column name)
> Returns the average value for the specified column within the set of selected rows.

COUNT(*)
> Returns the number of selected rows for the specified column.

COUNT(DISTINCT column name)
> Returns the number of distinct values for the specified column within the set of selected rows. If you use DISTINCT with multiple columns, each unique combination of column values is considered.

A built-in column function only applies to the rows that satisfy the search condition in the WHERE clause. If the column on which the function is based contains NULL values, DB2 and SQL/DS ignore them for calculating or determining the corresponding value except for the function COUNT(*). The COUNT(*) function finds the number of rows that satisfy the search condition, whether or not they contain NULL values. It is important to remember when you use, for example, the COUNT(*), AVG and SUM functions together. If the column contains NULL values, the value returned by COUNT(*) multiplied by the calculated average, may not give the value returned by the SUM function. The COUNT DISTINCT function, instead, counts NULL values only once.

Another difference between COUNT(*) and the other functions is that when no rows are selected (empty set), COUNT(*) returns 0, while the other functions returns a NULL value.

The result of processing a built-in column function is always one value for each group of rows. This means that if you do not use the GROUP BY clause in the SELECT statement, each specified function returns only one value for the whole result table. In other words, when you are not using the GROUP BY clause you cannot combine built-in column functions and single column values. The use of a built-in column function in conjunction with the display of single rows causes an error.

```
Wrong        SELECT   EMPNO, NAME, AVG(SALARY)
             FROM   EMPLOYEE;
```

In the above example, both DB2 and SQL/DS would return an error message, because the content of the desired result table is not clear. While the first two columns specify a listing of all selected rows of the result table, the use of the AVG function returns only a single value.

With the use of the GROUP BY clause, each built-in function returns one value for each group of rows. You also have to make sure that all the other columns specified in the SELECT statement produce one value for each group. To ensure this, include in the SELECT clause only those columns that are also specified in the GROUP BY clause.

The SUM and AVG functions can only be applied to numeric columns. A column is considered numeric if it is defined INTEGER, SMALLINT, DECIMAL or FLOAT. Columns that contain alphanumeric data can only be used with the MIN, MAX and COUNT functions, as can numeric columns. Remember, when you use the MIN and MAX functions with character data, DB2 or SQL/DS use the EBCDIC collating sequence: {blank}, A-Z, 0-9.

You can specify the DISTINCT keyword with any built-in function - except for COUNT(*) - if you don't want duplicate rows to be considered for the calculation.

Examples of Built-in Column Functions:

EMP

EMP_NO	CONTT_SCR	APPT_SCE	SRC_RCP_CDE	LOA
612666	89	5	A	54
866520	214	1	B	51
1474050	145	1	C	50
3728880	135	1	B	48
3118370	198	1	C	38
3728880	214	1	D	45
4174690	161	4	C	44
4174690	161	4	C	45

■ Count the number of rows in the EMP table:

```
SELECT   COUNT(*)   FROM   EMP;
```

8

■ Count the number of distinct values in the SRC_RCP_CDE column:

```
SELECT   COUNT(DISTINCT SRC_RCP_CDE)
   FROM   EMP;
```

(Distinct values are 'A', 'B', 'C', 'D')

4

Figure 9.21   Built-in column functions - COUNT DISTINCT

■ Sum the length of service information for different values in SRC_RCP_CDE:

```
SELECT   SRC_RCP_CDE, SUM(LOA)
   FROM   EMP
GROUPBY   SRC_RCP_CDE;
```

SRC_RCP_CDE	
A	54
B	99
C	177
D	45

Figure 9.22   Built-in column functions - SUM

- Calculate the average length of service for salespersons with a SRC_RCP_CDE equal to 'C'.

```
SELECT    AVG(LOA)
  FROM    EMP
 WHERE    SRC_RCP_CDE = 'C';
```

```
44.25
```

Figure 9.23   Built-in column functions - AVG

- Select all salespersons that are working for the company for a period longer than the minimum length of service:

```
SELECT    EMP_NO
  FROM    EMP
 WHERE    LOA >
            (SELECT    MIN(LOA)
               FROM    EMP);
```

EMP_NO
612666
866520
1474050
3728880
4174690
4174690

Figure 9.24   Built-in column functions - MIN

Built-in Scalar Functions for Data Manipulation

While a built-in column function has as its argument a list containing all values of a specific column for a table or subset of a table, the argument of a scalar function consists of a single value representing either a column value or a constant.

There are several built-in scalar functions for data handling and manipulation available in DB2 Release 3 and later as well as in SQL/DS Version 2 Release 2.

We will discuss these functions using the following modified SALES table:

SALES

WEEK	STORE	EMP_NO	FIRST NAME	LAST NAME	MKT CDE	NET SALE
8708	75	612666	JOHN	SMITH	1	110.22
8708	80	1474050	WALTER	BROWN	2	45.29
8708	84	4174690	BILL	WHITE	4	1147.47
8709	75	866520	HENRY	MORRISON	3	144.89
8709	77	1621720	ROBERT	LEMON	3	55.83
8709	80	1474050	WALTER	BROWN	2	32.17
8709	84	4174690	BILL	WHITE		264.35
8710	933	4801860	DAVID	BLUE	1	95.04

DECIMAL (V1, V2, V3) The DECIMAL function transforms the number represented by V1 into a decimal number of V2 digits with a scale of V3. The function can be used for example to reduce the number of unwanted decimals generated by a built-in column function or to change the representation of a floating point number in the result table.

INTEGER (V1) The INTEGER function selects only the integer portion of V1 disregarding any decimals. No rounding is performed. For example INTEGER (123.9) and INTEGER(123.1) both result in 123.

DIGITS (V1) The DIGITS function selects only the decimal portion of V1. DIGITS is the complementary function to the INTEGER function.

HEX (V1) The HEX function displays the content of V1 in hexadecimal format. The value V1 can be of any type with a maximum length of 254 bytes. This function may be used by a programmer to analyze the hexadecimal content of a field in case of data error.

FLOAT (V1) The FLOAT function transforms the number V1 into a double precision floating-point representation to increase the precision during calculations.

LENGTH (V1) The LENGTH function calculates the actual length of its argument including blanks and leading zeros.

SUBSTR (V1,V2 [,V3]) With the SUBSTR function it is possible to select a portion of the string V1 beginning in position V2. The value V3 indicates the length of the desired string in characters. If V3 is omitted the result includes all characters of V1 to the right of V2. For example:

```
SUBSTR('1987/09/21',1,4) results in 1987
SUBSTR('1987/09/21',9) results in 21
```

V1 || V2 The || operator concatenates two character or graphic strings. The strings may be two column values or a column value and a constant.

VALUE (V1,V2) The VALUE function allows substitution of NULL values that occur in V1 by the character string supplied in V2. For example:

```
SELECT EMP_NO, VALUE (MKT_CODE,'NA')
```

Inserts the string NA (not assigned) into the corresponding column value if there no is Market Code associated with a representative.

STRIP (V1[[,V2][,V3]]) The STRIP function is available only under SQL/DS Version 2 Release 2. It eliminates leading (V2 = L) or trailing (V2 = T) or trailing and leading (V2 = B, also default) characters from a string V1. The third argument V3 identifies the character to be removed. The default is blank.

TRANSLATE (V1[[,V2][,V3][,V4]]) The TRANSLATE function is available only under SQL/DS Version 2 Release 2. TRANSLATE alters characters in the string V1 according to the input (V2) and output (V3) translate tables. If V2 and V3 are both missing the string V1 is translated to uppercase. If the tables V2 and V3 are not of equal length, the shorter table is padded with blanks or the optional character V4 to the size of the larger table.

The scalar functions described above can be used either separately or combined with built-in column functions.

Examples of Built-in Scalar Functions:

■ Display the average net sales per week with one decimal digit:

```
SELECT    WEEK, DECIMAL(AVG(NET_SALES),7,1)
  FROM    SALES
GROUP BY  WEEK;
```

RESULT TABLE

WEEK	
8708	434.3
8709	124.3
8710	95.0

Figure 9.25   Scalar function: DECIMAL

■ Retrieve the sum and average net sales per week. Display only the integer portion.

```
SELECT    WEEK, INTEGER (AVG(NET_SALES)),
          INTEGER (SUM(NET_SALES))
  FROM    SALES
GROUP BY  WEEK;
```

RESULT TABLE

WEEK		
8708	1302	434
8709	497	124
8710	95	95

Figure 9.26   Scalar function: INTEGER

■ Retrieve the first initial of the first name and the last name for all representatives in week 8709.

```
SELECT  EMP_NO, SUBSTR(FIRST_NAME,1,1), NAME
  FROM  SALES
 WHERE  WEEK = 8709;
```

RESULT TABLE

EMP_NO		LAST NAME
866520	H	MORRISON
1621720	R	LEMON
1474050	W	BROWN
4174690	B	WHITE

Figure 9.27   Scalar functions - SUBSTR

■ Retrieve the first initial of the first name and concatenate it to the
last name for all representatives in week 8709.

```
SELECT EMP_NO, SUBSTR(FIRST_NAME,1,1) |'. '| NAME
  FROM SALES
WHERE  WEEK = 8709;
```

RESULT TABLE

EMP_NO	
866520	H. MORRISON
1621720	R. LEMON
1474050	W. BROWN
4174690	B. WHITE

Figure 9.28   Scalar function - CONCATENATION

■ Retrieve the Market Code assigned to all salespeople during week
8709. If the market code is unknown, display 'X'.

```
SELECT EMP_NO, VALUE (MKT_CDE,'X')
FROM SALES
WHERE  WEEK = 8709;
```

RESULT TABLE

EMP_NO	MKT_CDE
866520	3
1621720	3
1474050	2
4174690	X

Figure 9.29   Scalar function - VALUE

■ Retrieve all distinct representatives and their corresponding market
code. Translate the market code according to the following scheme:

MKT_CDE (INPUT)	OUTPUT	DESCRIPTION
1	M	Metropolitan
2	U	Urban
3	S	Suburban
4	R	Rural

```
SELECT DISTINCT EMP_NO,
       TRANSLATE (MKT_CDE,'1234','MUSR')
FROM SALES;
```

RESULT TABLE

EMP_NO	
612666	M
1474050	U
4174690	R
866520	S
1621720	S
4801860	M

Figure 9.30   Scalar function - TRANSLATE

Built-in Scalar Functions for Date/Time Operations

Concepts

With the releases of DB2 Release 3 and SQL/DS Version 2 Release 1 the supported data types have been extended to include the date and time formats. The following new data types have been added:

DATE   The DATE consists of three parts: year, month, and day. The external representation in a report varies depending on the specified format:

```
ISO  -  (YYYY-MM-DD)
USA  -  (MM/DD/YYYY)
EUR  -  (DD.MM.YYYY)
JIS  -  (YYYY-MM-DD)
LOCAL
```

TIME   The TIME may be displayed in the following formats:

```
ISO  -  (HH.MM.SS)
USA  -  (HH:MM  AM or PM)
EUR  -  (HH.MM.SS)
JIS  -  (HH:MM:SS)
LOCAL
```

TIMESTAMP   TIMESTAMP is a single seven-part value, which represents date and time by year, month, day, hour, minute, second, and microsecond. The timestamp is provided in the following format:

```
YYYY-MM-DD-HH-MM-SS-NNNNNN
```

The correct display and validation of date and time values have always presented a problem in previous releases. Depending on the requirements of the user or application program, partial solutions of the problem had to be achieved by storing these values with a user defined format as numeric or character strings, either in single or multiple columns. The new data types discussed above, allow you to efficiently store date and time values completely independent of the desired external representation.

Besides the new datatypes, DB2 and SQL/DS recognize the following values as valid date or time representations:

- Column values from columns defined as DATE, TIME, or TIMESTAMP;
- Values returned by the DATE, TIME or TIMESTAMP scalar functions discussed below;

■ Values contained in the new special registers CURRENT TIME, CURRENT DATE, CURRENT TIMESTAMP. These special registers return a value based on a CPU clock reading.

■ An expression returning a date or time value.

■ String representations of date and time values in any of the following formats:

TYPE	FORMAT NAME	FORMAT
Date *(at least 8 characters)*	ISO or JIS USA EUR LOCAL	YYYY-MM-DD MM/DD/YYYY DD.MM.YYYY *User format defined at installation*
Time *(at least 4 characters)*	ISO or EUR JIS USA LOCAL	HH.MM[.SS] [1] HH:MM[:SS] [1] HH[:MM] AM or PM [2] *User format defined at installation*
Time-stamp *(at least 16 characters)*		YYYY-MM-DD- HH.MM.SS[.NNNNNN] [3]

(1) If the user does not specify seconds, SQL/DS and DB2 assume zero seconds.

(2) If the user does not specify minutes, SQL/DS and DB2 assume zero minutes.

(3) Microseconds NNNNNN may be omitted.

Figure 9.31 String representations of date and time values

The following rules apply to all of the formats on the previous page:

■ The first digit of a character string representing a date, time or timestamp may not be blank.

■ The character string may contain any number of trailing blanks.

■ Leading zeros for month, day, and hour may be omitted.

The following comparison rules apply to the use of date/time values in the WHERE clause:

- A date may only be compared to another date or a character string representing a date in one of the allowed formats. Since DB2 and SQL/DS do not provide automatic conversion among different date/time data types the DATE scalar function must be used to convert a timestamp or a character representation of a timestamp into a valid date.

- A time may only be compared to another time or a character string representing a time in one of the allowed formats. Analogously to what we already said for date comparisons the TIME scalar function must be used to convert a timestamp or a character representation of a timestamp into a valid time.

- A timestamp may only be compared to another timestamp or a character string representing a timestamp in one of the allowed formats.

- All date or time comparisons are chronological.

Before we discuss the available date/time scalar functions and the related arithmetic expressions we have to introduce the concept of *durations*. A duration is an interval of time expressed in years, months, days, etc. DB2 and SQL/DS distinguish between three different types of durations:

1. *Labeled or simple duration*

   A labeled duration represents a number of years, months, days, hours, etc. It consists of a value followed by the unit identification. The following keywords are recognized as unit type identifiers (Labels):

   - YEAR(S)
   - MONTH(S)
   - DAY(S)
   - HOUR(S)
   - MINUTE(S)
   - SECOND(S)
   - MICROSECOND(S)

   The value preceding the unit type identifier may be a numeric constant, an expression or a column value. **Labeled durations may only be used within date/time expressions that involve at least one date or time value.**

The following are examples of valid date/time expressions including labeled durations:

```
SELECT   *  FROM  ORDER
   WHERE  DATE_ORD + 5 DAYS > DATE_DELIVERY
```

```
SELECT  ORDER_NO, (DATE_ORD + 1 MONTH + 1 DAY),
        DATE_DELIVERY
   FROM  ORDER
```

2. *Date duration*

A date duration is the result of the subtraction of one date from another. This result is expressed as an 8 digit decimal number with scale 0 (DECIMAL (8,0)) that has to be read as YYYYMMDD. For example the value 00010515 represents a duration of 1 year, 5 months, and 15 days.

3. *Time duration*

A time duration is a 6 digit decimal number with scale 0 representing a number of hours, minutes, and seconds as the result of the subtraction of two time values.

Scalar Functions

In this section, we will provide a detailed description of the date/time scalar functions and their meanings.

CHAR (V1 [,V2])   The CHAR function produces a character representation -- i.e., for display purposes -- of a date/time value contained in V1 according to the format specified by the user in V2. V1 may be any of the following:

- a date,
- a time,
- a timestamp,
- a character string representing a date, a time, or a timestamp in any of the allowed formats.

V2, if used, must be ISO, USA, EUR, JIS, or LOCAL. If V2 is omitted the default format is used.

DATE (V1)

The DATE function converts the value V1 to a valid date. V1 may be any of the following:

- a date;
- a timestamp;
- a character string representing a date entered according to the allowed formats (e.g., ISO format YYYY-MM-DD);
- a character string of length 7 representing a date in the form YYYYDDD;
- a positive number containing the number of days passed from the base date December 31, 0000;
- an expression returning a date.

DAY (V1)

The DAY function returns the day portion of V1 as a binary integer. V1 must be a date, timestamp, or a date duration -- Number defined as DECIMAL (8,0).

DAYS (V1)

The DAYS function returns the number of days passed between the base date December 31, 0000 and the date represented by V1. V1 must be one of the following:

- a date,
- a timestamp, or
- a character string representing a date entered according to the allowed formats (e.g., ISO format YYYY-MM-DD).

HOUR (V1)

The HOUR function returns the hour portion of V1 as a binary integer. V1 must be a time, timestamp, or a time duration (Number defined as DECIMAL (6,0)).

MINUTE (V1)

The MINUTE function returns the minute portion of V1 as a binary integer. V1 must be a time, timestamp, or a time duration (Number defined as DECIMAL (6,0)).

MICROSECOND (V1)

The MICROSECOND function extracts the microsecond portion of a timestamp V1.

MONTH (V1)

The MONTH function returns the month portion of V1 as a binary integer. V1 must be a date, timestamp, or a date duration (Number defined as DECIMAL (8,0)).

SECOND (V1)   The SECOND function returns the second portion of V1 as a binary integer. V1 must be a time, timestamp, or a time duration (Number defined as DECIMAL (6,0)).

TIME (V1)   The TIME function converts the value in V1 to a valid time. V1 may be any of the following:

- time;
- timestamp;
- character string representing a time entered according to the allowed formats (e.g., ISO format HH.MM.SS);
- an expression returning a time.

TIMESTAMP (V1, [V2]) The TIMESTAMP function converts the value in V1 to a valid timestamp. V1 may be any of the following:

- a timestamp;
- a character string representing a timestamp (e.g., ISO format YYYY-MM-DD-HH.MM.SS),
- a character string of 8 characters representing a 'store clock' value for a timestamp,
- a character string of 14 characters representing a timestamp in the format YYYYMMDDHHMMSS).

If you specify both V1 and V2, V1 must contain a date or a character representation of a date (e.g., YYYY-MM-DD) while V2 must be a time or a character equivalent of a time value (e.g., HH.MM.SS).

YEAR (V1)   The YEAR function returns the year portion of V1 as a binary integer. V1 must be a date, timestamp or a date duration (Number defined as DECIMAL (8,0)).

Date Arithmetics

SQL/DS and DB2 allow date/time values to be used within arithmetic expressions based on the addition and subtraction operators. The following rules apply to arithmetic expressions involving date values:

- If any operand of an expression, using the addition operator, is a date, the other operands may only be a date duration or a labeled duration of years, months or days. The result of the expression is always a date:

Date + date duration   → date
Date + labeled duration   → date
Date duration + date   → date
Labeled duration + date   → date

You should always keep in mind that labeled durations may only be used within date/time expressions that involve one date or time value.

WRONG   DATE_ORD + (3 MONTH + 1 DAY)

The above statement is not valid since the expression in parenthesis does not include a date value. The correct syntax for the same statement is:

```
DATE_ORD   +   3 MONTH   +   1 DAY
                   or
(DATE_ORD + 3 MONTH)   +   1 DAY
```

- You may not subtract a date from a duration.

```
        ┌─ Labeled duration - date
WRONG   │      or
        └─ date duration      - date
```

- If you subtract one date from another the result of the expression is always a date duration.

                 date - date → date duration

At least one of the operands must be a date value (date column value or a date value obtained from the DATE scalar function). The other operand may also be a character string representation of a date. The following are examples of valid expressions:

```
DATE_DELIVERY          - DATE_ORD
DATE_DELIVERY          - '3/01/1988'
DATE ('03/01/1988') - '2/15/1988'
```

If the first operand of an expression using the subtraction operator is a date and the second operand is a duration, the result of the expression is always a date:

                date - date duration   → date
                date - labeled duration   → date

All discussed date operations are performed according to the calendar --
i.e., only valid dates are allowed. In certain situations, this may lead to
unexpected results for the user. For example, if a month is added to a
date with the following statement:

DATE_ORD + 1 MONTH

SQL/DS and DB2 calculate the new date based on the assumption that
the result should be the same day of the next month. If this leads to a
bad date the day portion of the result is automatically corrected to
represent the last day of that month:

DATE ('08-31-88') + 1 MONTH → 09-30-88

This does not mean that adding one month to the last day of a month
always returns the last day of the next month:

DATE ('09-30-88') + 1 MONTH → 10-30-88

Since subtraction rules are defined analogously we may find that the
following expression does not return the original date:

```
DATE + n MONTH - n MONTH

DATE ('08-31-88') + 1 MONTH - 1 MONTH → 08-30-88
```

The same situation results when adding a duration of years to a date
representing February 29th of a leap year.

```
DATE ('02-29-88')  + 1 YEAR  → 02-28-89
```
and
```
DATE ('02-29-88') + 1 YEAR - 1 YEAR → 02-28-88
```

Time Arithmetics

Arithmetic expressions involving time values follow a set of rules similar
to those already discussed for date arithmetics.

- If any operand of an expression using the addition operator is a time
  the other operands may only be a time duration or a labeled
  duration of hours, minutes, or seconds. The result of the expression
  is always a time.

Time + Time duration	→ Time
Time + labeled duration	→ Time
Time duration + Time	→ Time
Labeled duration + Time	→ Time

  In all cases any overflow of hours is discarded.

  ```
  TIME ('23:10:00') + 4 HOURS  → 03:10:00
  ```

- You may not subtract a time from a duration

WRONG ⎡── Labeled duration - Time
⎢   or
⎣── Time duration   - Time

- If you subtract one time value from another the result of the expression is always a time duration.

Time - Time → Time duration

At least one of the operands must be a time value (Time column value or a time value obtained from the TIME scalar function). The other operand may also be a character string representation of a time. The following are examples for valid expressions:

```
TIME_START         -   TIME_END

TIME_START         -   '02:30:00'

TIME ('12:00:00')  -   '08:00:00'
```

- If the first operand of an expression using the subtraction operator is a time and the second operand is a time duration, the result of the expression is always a time:

Time - Time duration   → Time

Time - labeled duration → Time

In all cases any underflow of hours is discarded:

```
TIME ('09:15:30')   -   10 HOURS   →   23:15:30
TIME ('15:20:30')   -   200000     →   19:20:30
```

Arithmetics Involving TIMESTAMPS

Timestamps can be incremented or decremented by any type of duration (labeled durations, date, or time durations). You may not add or subtract one timestamp from another since SQL/DS and DB2 do not define an object like a *timestamp duration*.

The following is a list of valid expressions using timestamps:

Timestamp	+	Date duration	→	Timestamp
Timestamp	+	Time duration	→	Timestamp
Timestamp	+	Labeled duration	→	Timestamp
Date duration	+	Timestamp	→	Timestamp
Time duration	+	Timestamp	→	Timestamp
Labeled duration	+	Timestamp	→	Timestamp

The result of all expressions shown above is always a timestamp. In all cases date and time arithmetics are performed as described above the only difference being that a possible overflow or underflow in the hour portion is not ignored but reflected in the date part of the result.

```
TIMESTAMP ('1988-02-29-23.10.00.000000') + 4 HOURS

        →   1988-03-01-03.10.00.000000
```

The GROUP BY Clause

Example: Compute the average and sum of sales during campaign 8708 and 8709 from the SALES table.

SALES

WEEK	STORE	EMP_NO	MKT_CDE	NET_SALE
8708	75	612666	1	110.22
8708	80	1474050	2	45.29
8708	84	4174690	4	1147.47
8709	75	866520	3	144.89
8709	77	1621720	3	55.83
8709	80	1474050	2	32.17
8709	84	4174690	4	264.35
8710	933	4801860	1	95.04

You may obtain the desired information by executing the following queries:

```
SELECT    WEEK, AVG(NET_SALE), SUM(NET_SALE)
  FROM    SALES
 WHERE    WEEK = 8708
```

WEEK		
8708	434.33	1302.98

```
SELECT    WEEK, AVG(NET_SALE), SUM(NET_SALE)
  FROM    SALES    WHERE    WEEK = 8709
```

WEEK		
8709	124.31	497.24

The same information can be obtained with a single query using the GROUP BY clause. The GROUP BY clause divides the result table into groups of rows with matching values in the grouping column(s). DB2 or SQL/DS then applies the specified built-in column functions to each group of values.

```
SELECT    WEEK, AVG(NET_SALE), SUM(NET_SALE)
FROM      SALES
WHERE     WEEK IN (8708, 8709)
GROUP     BY WEEK;
```

WEEK		
8708	434.33	1302.98
8709	124.31	497.24

Figure 9.32   GROUP BY clause -- example 1

When using a GROUP BY clause, you may specify the grouping column on the SELECT clause in addition to the built-in column functions. This is because the value contained in the grouping column is an attribute of the group as well as the results returned from the functions.

NULL values contained in a column specified in the GROUP BY clause causes some trouble in SQL/DS because in SQL/DS, **each row of a grouping column containing a NULL value is a separate group.** In DB2, starting with Release 2, NULL values are identical for the purpose of grouping.

The application of the GROUP BY clause does not have the same effect as the ORDER BY clause. GROUP BY simply divides single values into groups without changing the sequence of the retrieved rows for the grouping column. For this reason, it may not return the rows in the desired sequence. If you want to be sure that the result table is ordered, you have to specify ORDER BY.

The GROUP BY clause must follow the WHERE clause or the FROM clause, when there is no WHERE clause specified in the SELECT statement.

```
                              ┌─       ─┐
                              │ AVG     │
                              │ SUM     │
   SELECT name1[,name2],  ... │ MIN     │  (name-3)
                              │ MAX     │
                              │ COUNT   │
                              └─       ─┘
   FROM      .....
   WHERE     .....
   GROUP BY name1[,name2...]
```

The HAVING Clause

You can use the HAVING clause to specify a search condition that each selected group must satisfy. It acts like a WHERE clause, the only difference being that the HAVING clause is not applied to single rows but to groups defined in the GROUP BY clause. The search condition specified in the HAVING clause must test properties of the whole group.

The attributes or properties of groups are the values contained in the grouping columns and the values returned from the execution of the built-in column functions. For this reason you may use built-in column functions in addition to the normal search condition that we specified in the WHERE clause.

The HAVING clause can also include the DISTINCT keyword (as long as you have not used it anywhere else in the same SELECT statement), multiple conditions connected with AND or OR and the NOT keyword for negating conditions.

The HAVING clause is evaluated before the built-in functions or expressions in the SELECT clause are executed. This enables you to eliminate groups with values that may otherwise cause arithmetic errors during the evaluation of the SELECT clause.

Summary - SELECT Statement

```
SELECT [DISTINCT] *
                  column-name-1, column-name-2,.....
                  [tablename-1.]*, [tablename-2.]column-name-1,
                          [tablename-2.]column-name-2,.....
                  [shortname-1.]column-name-1,
                          [shortname-2.]column-name-2,.....
                                                           ,T
          column-name-1 ┌ column-name-2            ┐
                        │               [,...]     │ ...
          expression-1  │ expression-2             │
                        └                          ┘
                                        ┌ AVG  ┐
                                        │ SUM  │
          col-name-1[,col-name-2],      │ MIN  │ (col-name-3)...
                                        │ MAX  │
                                        └ COUNT┘

   FROM  tablename-1 [shortname-1[, tablename-2 [shortname-2...]]]

                          ┌ ┌          ┐                            ┐
                          │ │ =        │                            │
                          │ │ >        │   column-name              │
                          │ │ <        │   constant-value           │
                          │ │ >=       │                            │
   WHERE  [NOT] column-name│ │ <=       │   arithmetic expression    │
                          │ │ ¬=       │   [ANY/ALL] (subquery)     │
                          │ │ LIKE     │        [SOME]  (subquery)  │
                          │ └          ┘                            │
                          │ IS [NOT] NULL                           │
                          │ IN  (constant-1,constant-2...)          │
                          │     (subquery)                          │
                          │     (expression-1,expression-2..)       │
                          │ BETWEEN upper-limit AND lower-limit     │
                          │         expression     expression       │
                          └ ────────── condition-1 ──────────────── ┘

   ┌ ┌                  ┐      ┐
   │ │ AND  condition-2 │ .... │
   │ │ OR               │      │
   └ └                  ┘      ┘
```

(continued)

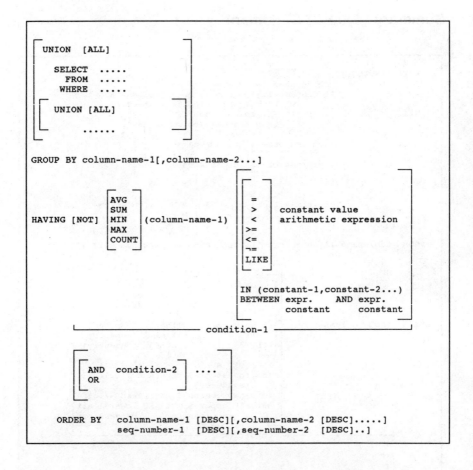

Representation of Manipulation Schemes Using SQL

In the previous examples, we have seen how subsets of data stored in the database can be selected, manipulated and aggregated by using built-in functions or arithmetic expressions,.

For the solution of a certain number of problems this approach is sufficient. But there are many other problems that cannot be solved so easily. Most of these problems are more complex and frequently repeated and usually require at least two steps to reach a solution:

1. Select the data from the data sets where it is physically stored. A relational DBMS -- such as DB2 or SQL/DS, is ideal for performing this task.

2. Perform more or less complex calculations on the retrieved data to produce a final result, such as a report in listed or graphical form.

This step is usually performed by specialized products on the mainframe or PC, such as COBOL, SAS, AS, LOTUS 1-2-3, etc.

In this section, we will show that relational products like DB2 or SQL/DS combined with QMF can also be used, to a certain extent, to perform involved calculations and produce final reports. This does not mean that we are convinced that advanced products -- such as COBOL, SAS, AS, LOTUS, etc. -- can be generally replaced by SQL (in conjunction with QMF). But we do believe that SQL is such a powerful and highly flexible tool that it is always worth considering.

Example 1

Suppose you have the following situation: A company's detail accounting information is stored in a table with the following structure;

- **KEY** column   Identifies the type of detail accounting information;

- **VALUE** column   Contains the value expressed in dollars for each type of detail accounting information.

Your task is to produce a company's balance by aggregating detail values contained in the accounting information table. To do this, you would normally write a program that extracts the needed information from the table and produces the desired aggregated values. The following example shows you a way to obtain the same information using only SQL and relational expressions.

TAB1
Detail Accounting Information

KEY	VALUE
V1	1000.00
V2	543.50
V3	1250.00
V4	770.80
V5	999.90

To produce the balance, you must calculate the totals:

```
T1 = V1 + V2 + V5
T2 = V3 + V4
```

Since we are operating exclusively in a relational environment, there is no immediate way to perform these simple calculations by using only SQL. We have to introduce a new table where we store the relations between detail values and totals. In other words, this table represents the manipulation scheme for the totals we have to produce.

SCHEME1
Manipulation Scheme

KEY	TOTAL
V1	T1
V2	T1
V3	T2
V4	T2
V5	T1

This table says that the keys V1,V2 and V5 relate to the total T1, while keys V3 and V4 relate to the total T2

Our first step is to combine the two tables by using a JOIN operation:

```
SELECT  A.KEY, VALUE, TOTAL
  FROM  TAB1 A, SCHEME1 B
 WHERE  A.KEY = B.KEY;
```

Executing the above query we obtain the following intermediate result table:

INTERMEDIATE RESULT TABLE

KEY	VALUE	TOTAL
V1	1000.00	T1
V2	543.50	T1
V3	1250.00	T2
V4	770.80	T2
V5	999.90	T1

Now, if we use the built-in function SUM on the VALUE column and group by TOTAL, we obtain the desired result table with the sums we had to calculate.

```
SELECT    TOTAL, SUM(VALUE)
  FROM    TAB1 A, SCHEME1 B
 WHERE    A.KEY = B.KEY
GROUP BY  TOTAL;
```

FINAL RESULT TABLE

TOTAL	
T1	2543.40
T2	2020.80

You can also produce a more complex manipulation scheme. Suppose you have to calculate the following formulas for your balance:

$$T1 \ = \ \frac{V1 \ + \ V2}{V5} \ * \ constant \ value$$

$$T2 \ = \ \frac{V3 \ + \ V4}{V5} \ * \ constant \ value$$

The table containing the manipulation scheme now looks like the following:

SCHEME2
Manipulation Scheme

TOTAL	KEY1	KEY2	KEY3	CONST
T1	V1	V2	V5	100
T2	V3	V4	V5	100

```
SELECT TOTAL, ((A.VALUE + B.VALUE / C.VALUE) * CONST
  FROM TAB1 A, TAB1 B, TAB1 C, SCHEME2
 WHERE A.KEY = KEY 1 AND
       B.KEY = KEY 2 AND
       C.KEY = KEY 3
```

We obtain the required result table.

FINAL RESULT TABLE

TOTAL	
T1	154.40
T2	202.10

Example 2

Suppose you have a company's monthly sales stored in a table SALES created with the following statement:

```
CREATE TABLE SALES
  (YY      CHAR(2)   NOT NULL,
   MM      CHAR(2)   NOT NULL,
   AMOUNT  NUMBER(4) NOT NULL);
```

The SALES table contains the following values for the period 1985 -1986:

TABLE SALES
Detail Sales Information

YY	MM	AMOUNT
85	01	1000
85	02	1200
85	03	1300
85	04	1400
85	05	1500
85	06	1600
85	07	1700
85	08	1750
85	09	1800
85	10	1850
85	11	1900
86	01	2000
86	02	2200
86	03	2300
86	04	2400
86	05	2500
86	06	2600
86	07	2700
86	08	2750
86	09	2800
86	10	2850
86	11	2900
86	12	2950

Your task is to produce a quarterly report with the following structure for each row:

column 1:   literal 'n QUARTER' where n varies from 1 to 4

column 2:   Year

column 3-5: Sales for 1st, 2nd and 3rd month within the quarter

column 6:   average sales for the quarter

column 7:   increase or decrease of sales during the quarter

To generate the above report you may write a procedure with the listed tasks:

1) Read three records and store the sales information internally;
2) Perform the requested calculations (average and difference);
3) Print one row for the corresponding quarter;
4) Go to 1 until all records are read;
5) End.

If we want to solve our problem by only using SQL, we encounter the following problems:

- SQL does not allow the use of column values from different rows in an expression. For example, it is not possible to calculate the average by writing the following:

    `(AMOUNT-1 + AMOUNT-2 + AMOUNT-3) / 3`

    where `AMOUNT-1`, `AMOUNT-2`, and `AMOUNT-3` are contained in different rows of the source table.

- SQL does not support values returned from BUILT-IN functions (such as AVG) to be mixed up with single column values (unless these columns are specified in the GROUP BY clause).

There is a way to produce the requested report by using a JOIN operation and the UNION keyword as shown in the query below. Executing this query we obtain the required result table:

	YY	AMOUNT	AMOUNT	AMOUNT		
1 Quarter	85	1000	1200	1300	1167	300
2 Quarter	85	1400	1500	1600	1500	200
3 Quarter	85	1700	1750	1800	1750	100
4 Quarter	85	1850	1900	1950	1900	100
1 Quarter	86	2000	2200	2300	2167	300
2 Quarter	86	2400	2500	2600	2500	200
3 Quarter	86	2700	2750	2800	2750	100
4 Quarter	86	2850	2900	2950	2900	100

```
    SELECT   '1 QUARTER ', A.YY, A.AMOUNT, B.AMOUNT,
             C.AMOUNT, (A.AMOUNT+B.AMOUNT+C.AMOUNT)/3,
             A.AMOUNT - C.AMOUNT
    FROM     SALES A, SALES B, SALES C
    WHERE    A.YY = B.YY
    AND      A.YY = C.YY
    AND      A.MM = '01'
    AND      B.MM = '02'
    AND      C.MM = '03'
    UNION
    SELECT   '2 QUARTER ', A.YY, A.AMOUNT, B.AMOUNT,
             C.AMOUNT, (A.AMOUNT+B.AMOUNT+C.AMOUNT)/3,
             A.AMOUNT -C.AMOUNT
    FROM     SALES A, SALES B, SALES C
    WHERE    A.YY = B.YY
    AND      A.YY = C.YY
    AND      A.MM = '04'
    AND      B.MM = '05'
    AND      C.MM = '06'
UNION
    SELECT   '3 QUARTER ', A.YY, A.AMOUNT, B.AMOUNT,
             C.AMOUNT, (A.AMOUNT+B.AMOUNT+C.AMOUNT)/3,
             A.AMOUNT - C.AMOUNT
    FROM     SALES A, SALES B, SALES C
    WHERE    A.YY = B.YY
    AND      A.YY = C.YY
    AND      A.MM = '07'
    AND      B.MM = '08'
    AND      C.MM = '09'
UNION
    SELECT   '4 QUARTER ', A.YY, A.AMOUNT, B.AMOUNT,
             C.AMOUNT,(A.AMOUNT+B.AMOUNT+C.AMOUNT)/3,
             A.AMOUNT -C.AMOUNT
    FROM     SALES A, SALES B, SALES C
    WHERE    A.YY = B.YY
    AND      A.YY = C.YY
    AND      A.MM = '10'
    AND      B.MM = '11'
    AND      C.MM = '12'

ORDER BY 2, 1;
```

10

SQL Data Manipulation Language

Introduction

In the previous chapters we have seen how to create new tables and query existing ones. In this chapter, we will introduce the commands for data manipulation. SQL/DS and DB2 provide you with the following data manipulation statements:

INSERT   -   allows you to add one or more rows to a table.

UPDATE   -   allows you to change column values in one or more rows of a table.

DELETE   -   allows you to remove one or more rows from a table.

INSERT Statement

Inserting a Single Row into a Table

The simplest form of the INSERT statement consists of an INSERT INTO clause and a VALUES clause:

```
INSERT INTO   table-name
              view-name
     VALUES   (list of values for all columns of
               the table or view)
```

Using this INSERT statement you have to provide column values for all the columns of the table or view. The values have to be in the same order in which the columns were defined when the table was created (The same order in which columns are displayed when you use the SELECT * to select all columns from a table or view). The single column values in the VALUES clause have to be separated by a comma and the whole list has to be enclosed in parentheses.

If a column is defined as alphanumeric (CHAR, VARCHAR, LONG VARCHAR) the supplied value has to be enclosed in apostrophes. If the supplied value for a column defined CHAR is shorter than the column length, DB2 or SQL/DS extends it to the right with blanks. If you supply a value longer than the maximum column length, DB2 and SQL/DS return an error message and does not insert the row.

If a column is defined as numeric (INTEGER, DECIMAL, FLOAT) DB2 requires a compatible data type for the constant. SQL/DS, however, allows the insert of a numeric column value with a constant of an incompatible data type. For example, the string '123' can be used to insert a value into a column defined as INTEGER.

If a table contains columns defined as NULL or NOT NULL WITH DEFAULT you must provide a NULL value for those columns. Specify the NULL keyword for each column you want to be null. NULL values must be coded in the corresponding column position.

```
INSERT INTO .....                               •
      VALUES  ('ABC',NULL,123,'DEF')
                      |
              ┌───────┘
              NULL value
              inserted into
              second column
```

Inserting values can become rather tedious because you have to supply values, explicit or NULL, for all columns in the correct sequence. DB2 and SQL/DS allow you to list the names of the columns you want to supply values for. You must enclose both the list of column names and the list of values in parentheses.

```
INSERT INTO   table-name
              view-name
              [(column-name-1[, column-name-2]...)
      VALUES  (value-1 [, value-2 .....])
```

When you supply the column names, you need not list them based on their position in the table; you may choose any order you want. The corresponding values in the VALUES clause have to be coded in the same order as the listed column names.

There are several reasons for specifying a 'column name list' when inserting rows into a table including the following:

- The INSERT statement becomes more readable and is self-descriptive.
- You can immediately verify that the supplied values are in the correct column order.
- When the INSERT statement is part of a program, it is more independent from physical changes of the table that has to be updated.

If a column permits NULL values or you defined the column not nullable with a default value, you may omit the column from the 'column name list' and you do not have to specify a value for it. When inserting a new row DB2 or SQL/DS automatically assign a NULL value or the corresponding default value for those columns. Even if you insert a row into a view that doesn't contain all the columns of the underlying tables, DB2 and SQL/DS insert NULL values into the missing columns of the base table. (This is not true if your view definition contains the 'WITH CHECK OPTION' clause under DB2.) In any case, you have to list all the columns defined NOT NULL in the 'column name list' or on the view definition and you must supply values for them.

Insert Into a Table Without Clustering Index

Example: Insert the following row into the SALES table:

new row	8708	82	866520	4	167.87

```
INSERT   INTO SALES
         (WEEK, STORE, EMP_NO, MKT_CDE,
         NET_SALE)

         VALUES
         (8708, 82, 866520, '4', 167.87)
```

SALES

	WEEK	STORE	EMP_NO	MKT_CDE	NET_SALE
row 1	8708	75	612666	1	110.22
row 2	8708	80	1474050	2	45.29
row 3	8708	84	4174690	4	1147.47
row 4	8709	75	866520	3	144.89
row 5	8709	77	1621720	3	55.83
row 6	8709	80	1474050	2	32.17
row 7	8709	84	4174690	4	264.35
row 8	8710	933	4801860	1	95.04

Figure 10.1   INSERT into a table without a clustering index - example - part 1

Suppose that the rows from the SALES table are actually stored in three different pages. Only page_2 and page_3 contain enough free space to store an additional row:

PAGE_1	ROW 1	ROW 2	ROW 3	ROW 4	░░░
PAGE_2	ROW 5	ROW 6	ROW 7	░FREE SPACE░	
PAGE_3	ROW 8	░░░░░░FREE SPACE░░░░░░			

Figure 10.2   INSERT into a table without a clustering index - example - part 2

To insert a new row into a table without a clustering index DB2 and SQL/DS use the default insertion rule -- i.e., a new row is placed in the first page with enough free space.

PAGE_1	ROW 1	ROW 2	ROW 3	ROW 4	▓▓▓

PAGE_2	ROW 5	ROW 6	ROW 7	NEW ROW	▓▓▓

PAGE_3	ROW 8	▓▓▓▓▓▓▓▓▓FREE SPACE▓▓▓▓▓▓▓▓▓

Figure 10.3 INSERT into a table without a clustering index - example - part 3

Insert Into a Table with a Clustering Index

Example: Insert the following row into the SALES table:

new row	8709	76	866520	3	230.99

```
INSERT INTO SALES
        (WEEK, STORE, EMP_NO, MKT_CDE,NET_SALE)

VALUES
(8709, 76, 866520, '3', 230.99)
```

Suppose that the rows from the SALES table are actually stored as shown:

PAGE_1	ROW 1	ROW 2	ROW 3	ROW 4	▓▓▓

PAGE_2	ROW 5	ROW 6	ROW 7	▓▓FREE SPACE▓▓

PAGE_3	ROW 8	▓▓▓▓▓▓▓▓▓FREE SPACE▓▓▓▓▓▓▓▓▓

Figure 10.4 INSERT into a table with a clustering index - example - part 1

To insert a new row into a table with a clustering index, DB2 and SQL/DS try to store new rows in logical key sequence. For example, if you defined a clustering index on the columns WEEK, STORE, and

`EMP_NO,` both DB2 and SQL/DS insert the new row as shown below:

PAGE_1	ROW 1	ROW 2	ROW 3	ROW 4	▓

PAGE_2	NEW ROW	ROW 5	ROW 6	ROW 7	▓

PAGE_3	ROW 8	▓▓▓FREE SPACE▓▓▓

Figure 10.5   INSERT into a table with a clustering index - example - part 2

Copying Data from Other Tables

You can use the INSERT command to store the result of a query in a table. One of the uses of this kind of INSERT statement is to temporarily store summary data obtained from a query executed on a large table. To do this, substitute the VALUES clause and the list of data values with a subselect. The SELECT statement is equal to a SELECT statement for normal data retrieval. This means that you can use any keywords, built-in functions and expressions that you like.

If you use a subselect, only the columns and rows retrieved by that SELECT statement are inserted into the new table. Remember that you have to use the CREATE TABLE command to create the new table before rows can be inserted.

```
INSERT INTO  table-name
             view-name
             [(column-name-1[, column-name-2]...)
     subselect
```

When inserting data using a subselect

- The rows you select cannot be from the same table you insert into. DB2 or SQL/DS won't process the INSERT statement if the tables are the same.
- The number of columns named implicitly or explicitly on the INSERT statement must be the same as the number of columns listed in the SELECT statement.
- The selected columns must be compatible in data type with the columns you want to insert.

- You may not use the UNION keyword to combine multiple SELECT statements within the subselect used to insert rows from another table.
- If DB2 or SQL/DS detects an error while executing the INSERT statement, the operation is stopped and no data is inserted into the table.
- You can insert rows obtained by using a JOIN operation to select data from more than one table.
- When inserting new rows you cannot control the sequence of the inserted rows. The ORDER BY keyword is invalid within a subquery used to insert rows from another table.

For example, to produce a reduced copy of the EMP table, use the following statement:

```
INSERT   INTO C_EMP

         SELECT   *
         FROM   EMP
         WHERE   WEEK > 8707
         AND    BRTH_YEAR = 27;
```

INSERT Statement - General Format

```
INSERT INTO     table-name
                view-name
                [(column-name-1[, column-name-2] ...)
    VALUES      (value-1 [, value-2 .....])
    subselect
```

Considerations

There are certain considerations that you should keep in mind when using the INSERT statement:

- If the table has a unique index, DB2 or SQL/DS return an error if you attempt to insert a row that duplicates the key of another row already in the table. If there is no unique index defined for the table the row is inserted without error.

■ Concurrent access to data using SQL data manipulation statements under DB2 is controlled by locking table spaces and index spaces. Locking is required on the table space that contains the table where you want to insert the new rows. In addition, even a lock at index level is necessary, because the new rows generate new index entries for the inserted key fields. The type of table space lock DB2 chooses is mainly dependent on the LOCKSIZE option specified during table space creation (LOCKSIZE options are: TABLESPACE, TABLE, PAGE, ANY) and the number of rows that have to be inserted. Remember that when specifying LOCKSIZE = TABLESPACE all data in all tables of a table space is locked and therefore no concurrent access to the same data is allowed.

The locking level under SQL/DS depends on the type of DBSPACE. A PRIVATE DBSPACE is always locked at DBSPACE level during data manipulation operations. SQL/DS allows locking of PUBLIC DBSPACES at ROW, PAGE, and DBSPACE level. By specifying ROW level locking for table data pages, SQL/DS automatically locks index pages at key level. The default index page locking is at PAGE level. However, even if you specify DBSPACE locking at ROW level, you should be aware that, depending on the number of actual locks, SQL/DS might automatically increase the locking level to DBSPACE locking.

■ The following limitations apply for the use of views in insert operations:

● If you use a JOIN operation to define a view (whether two or more tables/views are joined together or a table/view is joined to itself) the view's data can only be selected. **You cannot insert data into a view that is based on a JOIN operation.**

● You cannot insert data into a view if the view definition includes one of the following:

  ▸ Built-in functions (AVG, MIN, MAX, SUM, COUNT)

  ▸ GROUP BY clause

  ▸ DISTINCT keyword

  ▸ 'WITH CHECK OPTION' clause

● If you use an arithmetic expression in the definition of the view, you cannot update that column or insert rows to the base table but you can select and delete rows or update the other columns.

■ If you insert many rows into a table with a defined clustering index you should control the clustering level frequently. DB2 or SQL/DS may not find enough space for the new rows on the correct pages and store them on other pages. This would cause a decrease in the clustering level.

UPDATE Statement

If you want to modify the contents of one or more columns in one or more rows, you must use the UPDATE statement. This statement acts like a SELECT clause; DB2 or SQL/DS retrieve all the rows that satisfy the condition in the WHERE clause and generate a temporary result table. Then, they execute the desired updates specified in the SET clause and write the updated rows from the result table back to the base table. If DB2 or SQL/DS detects an error while performing these tasks, they stop updating and return an error message. No rows in the table are changed.

The result of an UPDATE statement is one or more modified column values in zero, one, or more rows of the table or view, depending on how many rows satisfy the search condition in the WHERE clause.

The general format of the UPDATE statement is as follows:

UPDATE ....   names the table or view that has to be updated.

SET   ....   names the columns you want updated and assigns a new value to the specified columns.

WHERE ....   specifies a search condition to select the rows that have to be updated.

If you omit the WHERE clause, DB2 or SQL/DS updates each row in the table or view with the supplied column values.

Updating a Single Row

To update a single row you have to specify a search condition that selects one and only one row. That is the case, for example, if you are looking for a specific value in the key column.

Updating Multiple Rows

You can also update multiple rows by specifying a search condition in the WHERE clause that identifies more than one row.

When modifying many rows with a single UPDATE statement you have to be very careful in specifying the correct search condition, because once your statement has been executed by DB2 or SQL/DS it is very hard to undo the changes (unless you saved a copy of the table before the update).

To update multiple ranges of values you have to make sure that your updates are in the right sequence. To illustrate this concept, we use the following simplified employee table:

EMPNO	NAME	JOB	MGRNO	SALARY
10.001	SMITH	REPRESENTATIVE	10048	45000
10002	BROWN	SALESPERSON	10048	23000
10003	WHITE	SECRETARY	10048	43000
10004	GREEN	REPRESENTATIVE	10048	32000
10020	BLAKE	SALESPERSON	10048	25000
10021	GARDEN	SALESPERSON	10048	24500
10023	WINTER	MANAGER	10023	88000
10030	HOUSE	JANITOR	10023	18000
10045	JONES	REPRESENTATIVE	10048	37000
10047	FRANKS	SECRETARY	10023	35000
10048	O'HARA	MANAGER	10023	42500
10049	JOHNSON	BOOKKEEPER	10023	32000

Suppose you want to increase the salaries by the following percentages:

```
        SALARY RANGE
      FROM          TO                    INCREASE
   $      0  - $ 24999      by            10 %
   $ 25000  - $ 44999      by            15 %
   $ 45000  - $   max      by            20 %
```

To modify the corresponding rows in the employee table, you have to execute the following three UPDATE statements, one for each range of values:

```
UPDATE    EMP
    SET   SALARY = SALARY * 1.1
  WHERE   SALARY < 25000;
```

```
UPDATE    EMP
    SET   SALARY = SALARY * 1.15
  WHERE   SALARY BETWEEN  25000 AND 44999;
```

```
UPDATE    EMP
    SET   SALARY = SALARY * 1.2
  WHERE   SALARY > 45000;
```

Figure 10.6   UPDATE statement - example

If you execute the above UPDATE statements in the indicated order, you do not obtain a correct result because BROWN and GARDEN, whose original salaries are lower than $25,000, receive an increase of 10% by executing the first UPDATE statement. This change their salaries to $25,300 and $26,950 respectively. When executing the second UPDATE they again re-enter in the specified range and they are again considered eligible for the increase of 15%. The same thing would happen to WHITE and O'HARA, because they would receive both the 15% and the 20% increases.

Summarizing the above example, we can establish the following rule: If you have to update multiple rows of a table by ranges of values and the search condition and the SET clause specify the same column (in our example the SALARY column) the sequence of the necessary UPDATE statements depends on the following types of variation:

increase   Order the ranges in descending order and start updating the table with the highest range. Then, update the rows selected for the next lower range and so on.

decrease   Order the ranges in ascending order and start updating the table with the lowest range. Then, update the rows selected for the next higher range and so on.

UPDATE Statement - General Format

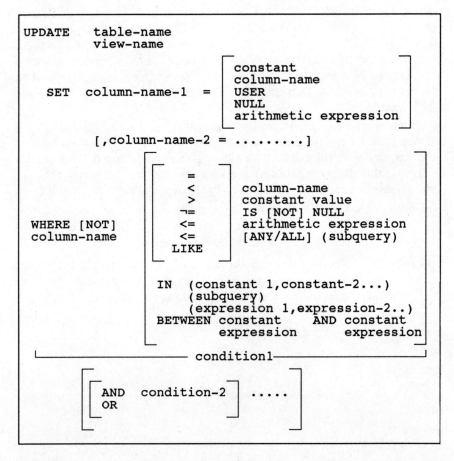

```
UPDATE    table-name
          view-name

                                  ┌─                                ─┐
                                  │ constant                         │
                                  │ column-name                      │
    SET   column-name-1   =       │ USER                             │
                                  │ NULL                             │
                                  │ arithmetic expression            │
                                  └─                                ─┘

          [,column-name-2 = .........]

                      ┌─          ─┐
                      │     =      │
                      │     <      │   column-name
                      │     >      │   constant value
                      │     ¬=     │   IS [NOT] NULL
    WHERE [NOT]       │    <=      │   arithmetic expression
    column-name       │    <=      │   [ANY/ALL] (subquery)
                      │   LIKE     │
                      └─          ─┘

                      IN   (constant 1,constant-2...)
                           (subquery)
                           (expression 1,expression-2..)
                      BETWEEN constant      AND constant
                              expression        expression

      └─────────────────── condition1───────────────────┘

    ┌─                          ─┐
    │ AND   condition-2          │   .....
    │ OR                         │
    └─                          ─┘
```

The values assigned to a column in the SET clause may contain the following:

column-name The value in the column -- column-name-1 -- is replaced with the value of another column of the same row.   The two columns have to be defined with a compatible data type.

constant   The value in the column -- column-name-1 -- is replaced with the supplied constant.   If a column is defined as alphanumeric (CHAR, VARCHAR, LONG VARCHAR) the supplied value has to be enclosed in apostrophes.   If the value in a character column is shorter than the column length, DB2 or SQL/DS extend it on the right with blanks. If you supply a value longer than the maximum column length, DB2 and SQL/DS return an error message and do not update the row.

If a column is defined as numeric (INTEGER, DECIMAL, FLOAT) DB2 requires a compatible data type for the constant. SQL/DS allows the update of a numeric column value with a constant of an incompatible data type. For example, the string '123' can be used to update a column defined as INTEGER.

USER   The value in the column -- column-name-1 -- is replaced with the identification of the current user. This may be used to store the identification of the user who is responsible for the update.

NULL   Deletes the current column value -- column-name-1. Remember that the column has to be defined as nullable in the CREATE TABLE statement. Otherwise if the column is defined as NOT NULL, both DB2 or SQL/DS return an error message.

arithmetic   The value in the column -- column-name-1 -- is
expression   replaced with the result from the arithmetic expression. The expression may contain column names and/or constants.

Considerations

The following considerations should be kept in mind when using the UPDATE statement:

- If a variable length row is increased in length during update and DB2 or SQL/DS cannot find space for the updated row on the same page, the row is stored in another page and a pointer placed in the original page. Subsequent retrieval of the updated row require two I/O operations.

- Concurrent access to data using SQL data manipulation statements under DB2 is controlled by locking table spaces and index spaces. Locking is required on the table space that contains the table where you want to update rows. The type of table space lock DB2 chooses is mainly dependent on the LOCKSIZE option specified during table space creation (LOCKSIZE options are: TABLESPACE, TABLE, PAGE, ANY) and the number of rows that have to be updated. Remember that when specifying LOCKSIZE = TABLESPACE all data in all tables of a table space is locked and therefore no concurrent access to the same data is allowed. Anyway, even if you specify LOCKSIZE = PAGE you cannot be sure that DB2 does not promote the locking level to a table space lock. This occurs if the number of rows to be updated is very high and the number of locked pages thereby increases.

The locking level under SQL/DS depends on the type of DBSPACE. A PRIVATE DBSPACE is always locked at DBSPACE level during data manipulation operations. SQL/DS allows locking of PUBLIC DBSPACES at ROW, PAGE and DBSPACE level. By specifying ROW level locking for table data pages, SQL/DS automatically locks index pages at key level. The default index page locking is at PAGE level. However, even if you specify DBSPACE locking at ROW level, you should be aware that, depending on the number of actual locks, SQL/DS might automatically increase the locking level to DBSPACE locking.

■ The following limitations apply for the use of views in update operations:

● If you use a JOIN operation to define a view (whether two or more tables/views are joined together or a table/view is joined to itself) the view's data can only be selected. **You cannot update data in a view that is based on a JOIN operation.**

● You cannot update data using a view, if the view definition includes one of the following:

▶ Built-in functions   (AVG, MIN, MAX, SUM, COUNT)
▶ GROUP BY clause
▶ DISTINCT keyword
▶ 'WITH CHECK OPTION' clause

In the above cases, you can only select the data by using the view.

● If you use an arithmetic expression for a column in the definition of the view, you cannot update that column, but you can select and delete rows or update the other columns.

DELETE Statement

The DELETE statement is used to delete one or more rows from a table. DELETE only removes entire rows and not single columns. If you want to delete a column from a table you have to use the procedure described in Chapter 5. *(See Performing Other Changes pp. 80 ff.)*

The result of a DELETE statement is the removal of zero, one, or more rows of the table or view, depending on how many rows satisfy the search condition in the WHERE clause. If DB2 or SQL/DS detects an error while executing the DELETE command, they return an error message and do not remove any row.

The DELETE statement consists of a DELETE clause followed by an optional WHERE clause:

DELETE FROM   Names the table or view that you want to delete rows from.

WHERE   Specifies a search condition to select the rows that have to be deleted.

The WHERE clause of the DELETE statement can contain the same search conditions as the WHERE clause of an UPDATE or SELECT statement. You can also use a subquery to select specific rows for removal. **A DELETE command without the WHERE clause causes DB2 or SQL/DS to delete all the rows of the specified table or view.**

Deleting a Single Row

To delete a single row you have to specify a search condition that selects one and only one row. This is the case, for example, if you are looking for a specific value in the key column.

Deleting Multiple Rows

You can also delete multiple rows by specifying a search condition in the WHERE clause that identifies more than one row.

You have to be very careful if you specify a DELETE statement to remove multiple rows. Once your statement has been executed by DB2 or SQL/DS it is very hard to undo the changes (unless you saved a copy of the table before the delete was executed).

DELETE Statement - General Format

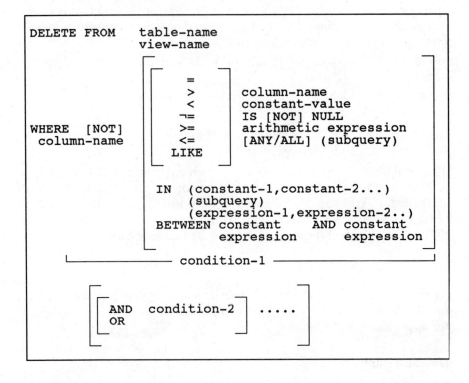

Chapter

11

SQL Language Elements for Security

Introduction

Under SQL/DS and DB2 each user may perform only those activities --
such as creating tables, selecting data, etc. -- for which he has been authorized, either explicitly or implicitly.

SQL/DS and DB2 distinguish between administrative and individual
authorities. Administrative authorities are arranged in a hierarchy. At
the head of this hierarchy is the database administrator (DBA). Under
SQL/DS, this authority is assigned to the userid SQLDBA during database
generation. There is one DBA for each SQL/DS database. All other authorities are derived directly from the DBA or through other previously
authorized users.

Under SQL/DS, all authorizations are only valid within a single
database machine and are stored in SQL/DS catalog tables of that
database. As SQL/DS allows the definition of more than one database
you have as many authorization structures as there are defined databases. The authorization scheme of one database is completely independent from the authorization structures generated in other databases.

In DB2 the security hierarchy is much more sophisticated. At its top
we find the *System Administrator*. This specially privileged user is desig-
nated during the installation process. A System Administrator always
possesses SYSADM authority. A user with SYSADM privilege may perform any valid operation within the installed DB2 system. Although

there may be several users with SYSADM authority, there is only one System Administrator. The difference between the System Administrator and other users with SYSADM privilege is that the SYSADM authority cannot be revoked from the System Administrator without reinstallation of the product.

Under the System Administrator, we find the System Operator (SYSOPR), authorized to perform certain functions from the console, and one or more Data Base Administrators (DBADM). Within a database, a user with DBADM authority may perform any legal command -- such as accessing data, granting or revoking specific authorities, etc. Additionally, two other authorities may be granted for each database: the Data Base Controller (DBCTRL) and Data Base Maintenance (DBMAINT). Users with these privileges are allowed to execute certain database utilities (RECOVER, STOP, START, etc.) but they may not access the data (at least not based on these privileges).

Individual authorities relate to single activities -- such as creating tables or views and selecting or updating data. In the following section, we will discuss only the individual authorities and the corresponding SQL statements to pass these authorities to other users.

Accessing the SQL/DS Databases

Access to the SQL/DS database can be limited in the following ways:

■ Controlling access to the virtual database machine at system level via IUCV control commands in the VM/SP directory.

■ Controlling access to the database machine at virtual machine level performing an authorization check to verify the user authorization to access the database.

In the latter case, a user may connect himself explicitly by issuing the SQL CONNECT command followed by a userid and password. SQL/DS searches the catalog tables for the supplied userid. If the user has CONNECT authority and the password matches the entry in the catalog tables, the user is connected and may perform all the activities for which he is authorized.

If the user does not use the SQL CONNECT statement, SQL/DS searches the catalog tables using the userid specified in the CP LOGON procedure. In this case, no password check is performed. This way of connecting to an SQL/DS database machine is called *implicit connect* and is the most commonly used way to establish a connection.

In either case the DBA has to grant CONNECT authority to the user with the following statement:

```
GRANT CONNECT TO        userid-1  [,userid-2 .....]
                        ALLUSERS

[IDENTIFIED BY          password-1 [,password-2 .....]
```

If the IDENTIFIED BY clause is omitted, the user may only connect himself implicitly. By using the ALLUSERS keyword, you grants implicit connect authority to all users.

To revoke a user's authority to access the SQL/DS database machine, you must issue the following command:

```
REVOKE CONNECT FROM   userid-1 [,userid-2 .....]
```

Each time a GRANT CONNECT statement is executed, SQL/DS updates the information contained in the SYSTEM.SYSUSERAUTH catalog table. This table can only be accessed by users with DBA authority. All other users must query the view SQLDBA.SYSUSERLIST. This view contains all columns from the SYSTEM.SYSUSERAUTH table except for the password.

To ascertain your own authorizations, issue the following query:

```
SELECT  *
  FROM  SQLDBA.SYSUSERLIST
 WHERE  NAME = USER;
```

RESOURCE Authority Under SQL/DS

If a user has been granted RESOURCE authority, he may acquire a PRIVATE DBSPACE and create tables in his own private DBSPACE as well as in PUBLIC DBSPACES. A private DBSPACE has to be defined by the DBA. To grant RESOURCE authority, use the following statement:

```
GRANT RESOURCE TO     userid-1 [,userid-2 .....]
```

By granting RESOURCE authority to a user, the user may define the amount of space for his own private DBSPACES. In this way the DBA would lose control over the use of disk resources. We recommend that PRIVATE DBSPACES be defined and acquired for the user by the DBA without granting RESOURCE authorities. Even if the DBSPACE is acquired for you by the DBA, you may still create tables but only in your own DBSPACES.

Accessing DB2

Within DB2 each user is recognized by his or her authorization-ID (USER-ID). This authorization-ID corresponds to the `creator_prefix` discussed previously that DB2 utilizes to automatically qualify objects created by the user.

Environment		User Identification
TSO		Logon ID
Batch		User parameter in JCL
IMS	MPP	SIGNON ID LTERM
	BMP	PSBNAME
CICS		SIGNON ID TERMINAL ID CICS ID TRANSACTION ID User supplied string

DB2 can only be accessed via one of the following MVS subsystems: TSO, IMS, or CICS. Since DB2 uses the LOGON-ID that you use to sign-on to one of these subsystems, the DB2 user identification depends on the environment in which you are operating.

Note: A detailed description of how the different subsystems establish the connection with DB2 can be found in the appropriate IBM manuals.

Privileges Held by the Creators of Objects

Access to SQL/DS or DB2 entitles the user all privileges that were granted to public use. It does not include the ability to create tables or other objects, unless the DBA or another user with the appropriate authority grants the necessary authority. For example, within SQL/DS this is achieved either by giving you the RESOURCE authority or by acquiring a DBSPACE with your userid.

When a table is created under DB2 or SQL/DS, its creator automatically gains complete control over it (DB2 Version 2 distinguishes between the owner and the creator of an object. In the following discussion we will assume that the creator and the owner are the same userids). For example, if you create a new table you are automatically authorized to INSERT, DELETE, UPDATE, or QUERY its rows, to delete the entire table using the DROP command or to change its structure with the ALTER command. The privilege a user possesses on all objects created by him is called an *implicit privilege*. **Implicit privileges cannot be revoked.**

If you want other users to perform some of these activities, such as selecting or changing data, you have to grant them the corresponding privileges.

You can grant and revoke authorities to and from single authorization IDs or you can specify a group of users on one statement. You may also give certain privileges to all SQL/DS or DB2 users by specifying PUBLIC in the GRANT statement.

The GRANT Statement

You can use the GRANT statement to authorize other users to perform certain activities. Within DB2 there are several sets of GRANT statements to control different privileges (not only for tables and views but also for databases, plans, systems, etc.). In this section, we will discuss only those privileges that can be granted on tables and views. The general format of the GRANT statement is as follows:

GRANT	To specify the type of privilege you want to grant to another user.
ON	To identify the object on which the above privileges are granted.
TO	To specify the user or list of users you want to authorize to perform certain tasks.

Granting Table/View Privileges

You may authorize other users to perform data retrieval and/or modification operations on those tables and views that you own or that you are authorized to operate on. To do this, you must specify in the GRANT statement the type of SQL command you want the other user to be able to execute:

- SELECT
- INSERT
- UPDATE
- DELETE
- ALTER
- INDEX

If you want other users to perform all of the above operations on your own tables, you may specify this by using the ALL keyword. Under DB2 and SQL/DS Version 2 Release 2, ALL indicates that you want to pass all privileges to other users that you yourself own on tables or views. For example, if you have SELECT and UPDATE privileges for the C_SALES table, using the ALL keyword within the GRANT statement allows you to pass on these privileges to other users. This means that you authorize them to retrieve and update data contained in this table. Within the SQL/DS releases prior to Version 2 Release 2, ALL is only a syntactical shorthand for SELECT, INSERT, UPDATE, DELETE, ALTER, and INDEX. For this reason, SQL/DS prior to Version 2 Release 2 in the above example would return an error message, since you only possess the SELECT and UPDATE authority. Furthermore, ALL includes ALTER and INDEX privileges that are not defined for views; using the ALL keyword results in an error message if you try to use this keyword to pass privileges on views.

If you want to allow users to pass the granted privileges on to others, you must specify the WITH GRANT OPTION clause as the last clause of the GRANT statement. The following examples show how the GRANT statement is used to pass certain privileges to other users.

- Authorize all table privileges on table C_SALES to the users CLASS01, CLASS02, CLASS03, CLASS04.

```
GRANT ALL
      ON   C_SALES
      TO   CLASS01, CLASS02, CLASS03, CLASS04;
```

- Allow user CLASS01 to retrieve rows from the C_SALES table and give him the capability to pass the privilege to other users.

```
        GRANT   SELECT
            ON  C_SALES
            TO  CLASS01
        WITH GRANT OPTION;
```

■ Give user CLASS01 UPDATE privilege for the columns MKT_CDE and NET_SALE of the C_SALES table. Note that UPDATE privileges on specific columns cannot be granted with GRANT OPTION and cannot be revoked.

```
GRANT UPDATE (MKT_CDE, NET_SALE)
        ON  C_SALES
        TO  CLASS01;
```

■ To further limit the access capabilities of other users -- for example, to a subset of rows-- you have to use a view. Suppose you want to authorize user CLASS02 to retrieve information on sales weeks only for the region NORTH. Your first step is the creation of the following view:

```
CREATE VIEW V1
        AS
            SELECT  *
            FROM  C_SALES
            WHERE  REGION = 'N';
```

You may then allow user CLASS02 to retrieve rows from the view V1.

```
GRANT SELECT
            ON  V1
            TO  CLASS02;
```

In the same way you may limit data retrieval capabilities to a subset of columns or to a subset of rows and columns.

■   Authorize user to add new columns to your table and to insert rows.

```
GRANT ALTER,  INSERT
      ON   C_SALES
      TO   CLASS03;
```

You may also pass a privilege for other tables if the access authority has been granted to you with the GRANT OPTION. You should be aware that once these privileges are revoked from you, all the other users that you authorized automatically lose their privileges, too.

Let's suppose User-A authorizes you to retrieve data from his own table-A, with the GRANT OPTION.

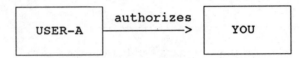

You may then grant the privilege with GRANT OPTION to User-B, who may authorize User-C. The authorization chain would appear as follows:

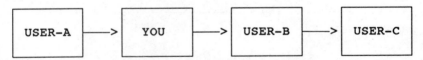

If you revoke the privilege from User-B, C automatically loses his privilege, too. This is because C was authorized by B, who does not possess the authority anymore. If A revokes your authorization, both B and C would immediately lose their privileges.

The GRANT Statement - General Format

```
      ALTER
      DELETE
      INDEX
GRANT INSERT                                    ,.....
      SELECT
      UPDATE
      UPDATE (column-name1 [,column-name2...])
      ALL
   ON [creator-ID.] table-name
      [creator-ID.] view-name
   TO userid-1 [,userid-2 .......]
      PUBLIC
   [WITH GRANT OPTION]
```

In DB2, you may not pass the UPDATE privilege on a column using the GRANT OPTION.

Querying Catalog Tables

All information about user privileges on tables and views are stored in the following catalog tables:

SQL/DS	DB2
SYSTEM.SYSTABAUTH	SYSIBM.SYSTABAUTH
SYSTEM.SYSCOLAUTH	SYSIBM.SYSCOLAUTH
SYSIBM.SYSUSERAUTH	

If you want to know your own privileges, you may issue the following query:

SQL/DS	DB2

```
SELECT *                        SELECT *
   FROM SYSTEM.SYSTABAUTH          FROM SYSIBM.SYSTABAUTH
   WHERE GRANTEE = USER;           WHERE  GRANTEE = USER;
```

If you want to determine what privileges you have granted to other users, issue the query:

SQL/DS	DB2

```
SELECT   *                          SELECT   *
   FROM   SYSTEM.SYSTABAUTH            FROM SYSIBM.SYSTABAUTH
  WHERE   GRANTEE = USER              WHERE GRANTEE =USER
    AND   GRANTEE ¬= USER               AND GRANTEE ¬=USER
    AND   GRANTEETYPE = ' ';            AND GRANTEETYPE=' ';
```

GRANTEETYPE equals blank (' ') means that you a looking for users and not for programs.

DB2-SQL/DS Comparison

FUNCTION	DB2	SQL/DS
Table size	A table is stored in a table space. The maximum amount of storage that can be allocated to a table space is 64 GB.	A table is stored in a DBSPACE. The maximum size of a DBSPACE is 32 GB.
Table row length	As one row must fit within a page, the maximum table row length depends on the page size chosen for data storage: 4K- maximum row size 4056 Bytes 32K- maximum row size 32714 Bytes	Although the maximum record length is approximately 4070 Bytes, a single row with long string columns can involve many records.
Variable length columns	A column defined as VARCHAR may contain a variable length character value of up 32,674 characters and can therefore be a long string column.	A column defined as VARCHAR may contain a variable length character value of up 255 characters and can therefore never be a long string column.

FUNCTION	DB2	SQL/DS
Default values	During table creation a column may be defined as NOT NULL WITH DEFAULT. The used default value depends on the column data type.	SQL/DS does not support default values.
Table routines	DB2 supports two types of table routines: ■ EDITPROC ■ VALIDPROC	
Table locking	DB2 allows three levels of locking: ■ PAGE ■ TABLE ■ TABLESPACE The locking level is defined during table creation.	SQL/DS allows three levels of table locking for PUBLIC DBSPACES: ■ ROW ■ PAGE ■ DBSPACE PRIVATE DBSPACES are always locked at DBSPACE level. The locking level is defined during DBSPACE acquisition.

FUNCTION	DB2	SQL/DS
Index	The index always resides in a separate data set (INDEX SPACE).	The index is always stored logically and physically together with the corresponding table (same DBSPACE).
	The index is identified as clustering by the CLUSTER keyword of the CREATE INDEX statement. A clustered index is required for a partitioned table space.	An index is automatically recognized as being clustered if the logical key sequence corresponds to the physical data sequence. To determine the physical location of new inserted rows SQL/DS distinguishes between the first clustered index and all other clustered index.
	Version 2 introduces a relative clustering indicator in percentages between 0 and 100	SQL/DS V2 R2 introduces a relative clustering measure in percentages between 0 and 100 to improve access path selection.
	(*See also Index Locking and* CREATE *statement.*)	(*See also Index locking and* CREATE *statement*)
Index locking	DB2 locks indexes at SUBPAGE level. The number of subpages for each 4K index page is defined during index creation. The minimum sub-page size is 256 Bytes.	SQL/DS normally locks indexes at PAGE level. For PUBLIC DBSPACES with table locking at row level, indexes are locked at key level.

FUNCTION	DB2	SQL/DS
Index length	The absolute maximum key length is 255 Bytes. This maximum is reduced if index pages are subdivided in more than 8 subpages. The maximum key length for partitioned indexes is 40 Bytes. Key values based on variable length columns are padded to the maximum column length.	The maximum key length is 255 Bytes. Key values based on variable length columns are always extended by 25%.
Synonyms	Synonyms are automatically dropped when the corresponding table or view is dropped.	Synonyms may only be explicitly dropped with the DROP statement.
Comparison operators	The second operand of the IN operator may be a subquery, expression, or a list of constant values.	The second operand of the IN operator may only be a subquery or a list of constant values.

FUNCTION	DB2	SQL/DS
Comparison rules	DB2 requires compatible data types.	SQL/DS requires compatible data types. When comparing two variable length strings, SQL/DS will not pad the shorter string with blanks. Thus, two variable length strings of different length cannot be equal. The data type of an integer constant is considered a character string when compared to a character column; a decimal value when compared to a decimal column.
CREATE statement	If the IN clause of the CREATE TABLE statement is omitted, a tablespace is implicitly created in the default database.	If the IN clause of the CREATE TABLE statement is omitted, SQL/DS attempts to create the table in a PRIVATE DBSPACE owned by the user. If the user does not own any PRIVATE DBSPACE, an error message is returned. The following statements are not supported: ■ CREATE TABLESPACE ■ CREATE DATABASE ■ CREATE STOGROUP

FUNCTION	DB2	SQL/DS
DROP statement	The DROP INDEX statement may not be used to drop a partitioned index. For a partitioned index you must drop the table space. Synonyms are dropped not only explicitly using the DROP SYNONYM statement, but also implicitly when the corresponding table or view is dropped. A view is dropped automatically if the user does not hold anymore the SELECT authority required for the creation of the view. The following statements are not supported: ■ DROP DBSPACE	Synonyms may only be dropped explicitly using the DROP SYNONYM statement. A view is dropped automatically if the user does not hold any privilege on the base tables on which the view is defined. The following statements are not supported: ■ DROP STOGROUP ■ DROP DATABASE ■ DROP TABLESPACE

FUNCTION	DB2	SQL/DS
ALTER statement	The ALTER TABLE statement may be used to add a new column to an existing table, to add or delete a referential constraint, and to delete or change the assigned validation routine. You may not add a new column to a table that has an editing routine assigned to it or a long string column. The ALTER DBSPACE statement is not supported.	The ALTER TABLE statement may only be used to add a new column to an existing table and to add or delete a referential constraint. The following statements are not supported: ■ ALTER INDEX ■ ALTER STOGROUP ■ ALTER TABLESPACE

FUNCTION	DB2	SQL/DS
GRANT Statement	The GRANT statement is used to pass individual authorities on tables or views to other users. The following privileges are supported: SELECT, INSERT, UPDATE, DELETE, ALTER, INDEX, or ALL. Under DB2, the ALL keyword stands for all privileges that you own on tables and views. The ON clause may be followed by a list of objects you want to grant authority on to other users.	The GRANT statement is used to pass individual authorities on tables or views to other users. The following privileges are supported: SELECT, INSERT, UPDATE, DELETE, ALTER, INDEX, or ALL. In SQL/DS prior to V2 R2, the ALL keyword is only a syntactical shorthand for all the above individual privileges. For this reason the ALL keyword causes an error when specified for a view. The ON clause may be followed only by a single table or view name.
Scalar Functions		The following scalar functions are supported only under SQL/DS V2 R2: ■ STRIP ■ TRANSLATE

FUNCTION	DB2	SQL/DS
Catalog Tables	DB2 uses 30 catalog tables. Catalog tables are prefixed with SYSIBM. Catalog tables are incompatible with SQL/DS even when the tables describe similar objects in both systems.	SQL/DS uses 15 catalog tables. Catalog tables are prefixed with SYSTEM. Catalog tables are incompatible with DB2 even when the tables describe similar objects in both systems.
Update of catalog tables	Catalog tables are updated during the execution of the RUNSTATS and STOSPACE utilities. Certain catalog tables may be updated directly by the user to simulate for example a production environment for test purposes. These updates are overwritten during next run of RUNSTATS.	Catalog tables are updated during the execution of the UPDATE STATISTICS command.

Bibliography

Codd, E.F., *Relational Database: a practical foundation for productivity.* Communications for the ACM, Feb. 1982, Vol.25, Number 2

Codd, E.F., *Extending the database relational model to capture more meaning*, ACM TODS, No.4

Codd, E.F., *Further Normalization of the data base relational model*, in *Data Base Systems*, Prentice-Hall, 1972

Date, C.J., *Relational Database: Selected writings*, Addison-Wesley, 1986

Date, C.J., *A Guide to SQL Standard*, Addison-Wesley, 1987

Dictionary of Computing, IBM 1986

Kent, William, *A simple guide to five normal forms in relational database theory*, Communications of the ACM, Feb. 1983, Vol. 26, Number 2

SQL/DS Version 2 Release 1

    General Information for VSE

    Concepts and Facilities for VSE

    System Planning and Administration for VSE

    Data Base Planning and Administration for VSE

    Terminal User's Guide

DB2 Version

    General Information Manual

    SQL Learner's Guide

    System Planning and Administration Guide

    Data Base Planning and Administration Guide

    Command and Utility Reference

Index

special characters
% use with LIKE 167
* multiplication sign 192
+ addition sign 192
- subtraction sign 192
/ division sign 192
_ use with LIKE 167
|| concatenation operator 201
< less than 158
<= less equal 158
= equal 158
> greater than 158
>= greater equal 158
¬ not sign 158
¬< not less 158
¬= not equal 158
¬> not greater 158

A

Access methods
BSAM 7
limitations 7
QSAM 7
ACQUIRE DBSPACE statement
LOCK keyword 100
NHEADER keyword 100
PCTFREE keyword 100
PCTINDEX keyword 100
STORPOOL keyword 101
syntax 100
ALL keyword
see DB2 utility - RUNSTATS
use in the UPDATE STATISTICS
statement
use with subqueries 185
ALLUSER keyword 242
ALTER TABLE statement
adding a new column 77
adding a new foreign key 79
adding a new primary key 79
ALTER TABLE special options
under DB2 116
deleting an existing foreign key 80
deleting an existing primary key 80
AND keyword 170
ANY keyword 185
ANY option
see LOCKSIZE keyword

Apostrophe
comparison of alphanumeric data
155
use with IN keyword 164
Arithmetic expressions
use in update 237
use within views 232, 238
Arithmetic operators
* multiplication sign 192
+ addition sign 192
- subtraction sign 192
/ division sign 192
AS keyword
view creation 87
Attribute 65
Authorization
see special authorities
see GRANT statement
AVG function 196

B

BETWEEN keyword 169
BIND 117
Boolean Operators
AND 170
OR 170
Buffer 55
BUFFERPOOL
description under DB2 118
BUFFERPOOL keyword
index creation under DB2 136
use in database creation under DB2
118
Built-in column functions
AVG 196
COUNT 196
MAX 196
MIN 196
SUM 196
use within views 91, 232, 238
Built-in scalar function
CHAR 208
DATE 209
DAY 209
DAYS 209
DECIMAL 200
DIGITS 200
FLOAT 200
HEX 200
HOUR 209
INTEGER 200

LENGTH 200
MICROSECOND 209
MINUTE 209
MONTH 209
SECOND 210
STRIP 201
SUBSTR 201
TIME 210
TIMESTAMP 210
TRANSLATE 201
VALUE 201
YEAR 210
|| concatenation function 201

C

CASCADE keyword
  see delete rules 75, 79
CHANGE keyword
  see DB2 utility - RUNSTATS
CHAR function 208
CHECK DATA
  see DB2 utilities
CHECK PENDING condition 131,
      139
CLOSE keyword
  in table space creation 128
  index creation under DB2 136
CLUSTER keyword
  index creation under DB2 136
Collating sequence 158, 197
Column
  multiple column index under DB2
  134
  names 75, 77, 88, 114, 152
  new names 151
  prefixing column names 152
  selecting all 146
  selecting columns for index creation
    under DB2 134
    under SQL/DS 105
  selecting specific 148
Column list
  use in the INSERT statement 227
Column value 24, 66
Combined result table 177
Comparison operators
  < 158
  <= 158
  = 158
  > 158

>= 158
BETWEEN keyword 169
description 157
IN keyword 164
LIKE keyword 167
¬< 158
¬= 158
¬> 158
use with multiple column index
under DB2 134
Concurrent data access 232, 237
CONNECT authority 242
Connecting to a data base 242
Connecting to SQL
  explicit 242
  implicit 242
Correlated subquery 190
Correlation name 190
COUNT function 196
CREATE statement
  CREATE DATABASE under DB2
  117
  CREATE INDEX 108, 136
  CREATE STOGROUP 117
  CREATE SYNONYM 83, 90
  CREATE TABLE 114
  CREATE VIEW 87
CREATE statement under SQL/DS
  CREATE TABLE 74
  CREATE VIEW 87
Creator_prefix 75, 83, 90, 114, 150
Current date 69, 205, 206
Current time 70, 205, 206
CURRENT TIMESTAMP 206

D

DASD 52, 54
Data base
  definition 11
Data base machine 50
Data base management system
  benefits 11
  definition 11, 14
Data independence 11
Data model
  definition 14
  Hierarchical 17
  Network 20
  Relational 24
Data reliability 10

Data security 10
Data type
    compatible data types for use with
    the UNION keyword 179
    updating data 237
    see also DB2 or SQL/DS data type
DATABASE concept under DB2
    see DB2 database
DATABASE keyword
    table creation under DB2 114
    use in database creation under DB2
    118
Date 69, 205
Date arithmetics 210
DATE function 209
Date/Time function
    CHAR 208
    DATE 209
    DAY 209
    DAYS 209
    HOUR 209
    MICROSECOND 209
    MINUTE 209
    MONTH 209
    SECOND 210
    TIME 210
    TIMESTAMP 210
    YEAR 210
DAY function 209
DAY(S) duration label 207
DAYS function 209
DB2 catalog tables
    SYSIBM.SYSCOLUMNS 77, 141
    SYSIBM.SYSCOLAUTH 249
    SYSIBM.SYSDATABASE 118
    SYSIBM.SYSINDEXES 134, 141,
    142
    SYSIBM.SYSINDEXPART 134,
    137, 141
    SYSIBM.SYSKEYS 134
    SYSIBM.SYSSTOGROUP 142
    SYSIBM.SYSSTOGROUP table
    117
    SYSIBM.SYSTABAUTH 77, 82,
    249
    SYSIBM.SYSTABLEPART 141
    SYSIBM.SYSTABLES 77, 141
    SYSIBM.SYSTABLESPACE 141,
    142
    SYSIBM.SYSUSAGE 82

SYSIBM.SYSVOLUMES 117
DB2 data type
    CHAR 155
    compatible data types 72
    conversion between data types 71
    DATE 69, 205
    DECIMAL 68
    default values 115
    DOUBLE PRECISION 68
    FLOAT 67
    GRAPHIC 69
    inserting data 226
    INTEGER 67
    LONG VARCHAR 69, 155
    LONG VARGRAPHIC 69
    REAL 68
    SMALLINT 67
    TIME 70, 205
    TIMESTAMP 70, 205
    use in WHERE clause 71, 155
    use of index 156
    VARCHAR 68, 155
        considerations on use 72
        use with index 73
    VARGRAPHIC 69
DB2 database
    creation 117
    overview 117
DB2 utilities
    CHECK DATA
        COPY option 140
        DELETE option 140
        function 139
    LOAD
        Changes under DB2 V2 139
        DISCARDDN option 139
        DISCARDS parameter 139
        ENFORCE parameter 139
        LOG option 139
    REPAIR 140
    RUNSTATS
        overview 140
        use 141
    STOSPACE
        overview 142
        use 142
DBADM authority 242
DBCTRL authority 242

DBEXTENT
  description 103
  general overview 52
DBMAINT authority 242
DBSPACE
  ACQUIRE DBSPACE statement
  99
  adding to a data base 99
  description 93
  determining approximate number of
  locks 97
  determining number of HEADER
  pages 96
  determining size 95, 96
  general overview 54
  locking 54, 97
  names 100
  PRIVATE 54, 97
  PUBLIC 54, 97
  reorganizing 101
  storage pool assignment
    considerations 98
  types 97
  UNLOAD DBSPACE statement
  102
DBSPACE pages
  HEADER 93
  INDEX 93
  TABLE 93
DECIMAL data type
  precision 68
DECIMAL function 200
Delete rules
  CASCADE 62, 74, 75, 79
  RESTRICT 62, 74, 75, 79
  SET NULL 62, 74, 75, 79
DELETE statement
  deleting a single row 239
  deleting multiple rows 239
  FROM clause 239
  General format 240
DESC keyword 158
Dependency
  see Normalization
Difference
  see relational operators
DIGITS function 200
DISTINCT keyword 149
  limitations in views 91

use with built-in column function
197
use within views 232, 238
DROP statement
  DROP SYNONYM 83, 90
  DROP TABLE 83
  DROP TABLESPACE under DB2
  83
  DROP VIEW 90
DSNZPARM
  DB2 installation module 118
Duration
  Date 208
  Labeled 207
    DAY(S) 207
    HOUR(S) 207
    MICROSECOND(S) 207
    MINUTE(S) 207
    MONTH(S) 207
    SECOND(S) 207
    YEAR(S) 207
  Simple 207
  Time 208

E

Edit routines under DB2 115
Editing data under DB2
  see edit routines
EDITPROC keyword 115
  table creation under DB2 114
ERASE keyword
  index creation under DB2 136
ESCAPE keyword under SQL/DS 167
EXEC
  SQLADBEX 103
  SQLADBSP 95
EXISTS keyword 189
Expression
  use with the IN keyword 167
  use within views under SQL/DS 91

F

Field value 24, 66
FLOAT function 200
FOR keyword
  synonym creation 83
Foreign key
  concept 40, 60
  table creation 75

FROM clause
 DELETE statement 239
 SELECT statement 150

G

GRANT statement
 GRANT CONNECT 242
 GRANT RESOURCE 243
 IDENTIFIED BY clause 242
 overview 245
 syntax 249
GROUP BY clause
 description 214
 use within views 91, 232, 238

H

HAVING clause 216
HEX function 200
Hierarchical data model
 characteristics 20
 definition 17
 hierarchic path 18
 hierarchical sequence 18
HOUR function 209
HOUR(S) duration label 207

I

IDENTIFIED BY clause
 GRANT statement 242
IN keyword
 description 164
 table creation 114
 table creation under DB2 75
 table creation under SQL/DS 75
Index
 clustering 56
 clustering index under DB2 122, 124, 135
 creating a unique index under DB2 139
 creation for foreign key 76, 79
 creation for primary key 75
 disk space requirements under DB2 136
 general overview 56
 index generation for primary keys under SQL/DS 60
 index page under DB2 131
 key distribution 106
 monitoring under DB2

clustering sequence 136
 number of index levels 138
 monitoring under SQL/DS
 number of index levels 107
 multiple column index under DB2 134
 rules for index creation under DB2 133
 space allocation under SQL/DS 94
 space requirements under SQL/DS 98
 special names for primary key indexes under SQL/DS 60
 use of under DB2
 matching data types 71
INDEX keyword
 see DB2 utility - RUNSTATS
Index space 55
 description 131
Index under SQL/DS
 monitoring
 clustering sequence 107
INFILE keyword
 of the RELOAD DBSPACE statement 102
 of the RELOAD TABLE statement 101
INSERT statement
 copying data 230
 description 226
 general considerations 231
 inserting multiple rows 230
 inserting single rows 226
 INTO clause 226
 Locking considerations 232
 VALUES clause 226
 use for table load 108, 138
INTEGER function 200
Interim result table 177
Intersection
 see relational operators
INTO keyword
 use in INSERT statement 226
ISQL
 ISQL INPUT command
 BACKOUT 108
 CANCEL 108
 END 108
 SAVE 108

limitations for the use of variable
length columns 69

J

JOIN
see also relational operators
JOIN operations
description 152, 174
difference between JOIN and
UNION 179
use in views 91, 232, 238

K

Key
foreign key 40, 60
primary key 40, 60

L

Labeled duration
see duration
Leaf-page
of an index under DB2 136
LENGTH function 200
LIKE keyword 167
ESCAPE under SQL/DS 167
LOAD utility under DB2
see DB2 utilities
LOCK keyword
acquiring DBSPACE 100
LOCK TABLE option 120, 128
Locking 52
DBSPACE 54
LOCKSIZE keyword
ANY option 128
PAGE option 128
TABLE option 128
TABLESPACE option 127

M

Machine
database 50, 103
user 50
virtual 50
Main query 183
MAX function 196
MDISK control statement 52, 103
MICROSECOND function 209
MICROSECOND(S) duration label
207
MIN function 196

Minidisk
DEBEXTENT 52
directory 52
log 52
MINUTE function 209
MINUTE(S) duration label 207
MONTH function 209
MONTH(S) duration label 207
Multiple column index 134

N

Names
Column 75, 77, 88, 114, 152
DBSPACE 100
table 75, 114, 150
table shortname 152
Network data model
characteristics 22
definition 20
link 20
NHEADER keyword
acquiring DBSPACE 100
Normalization
characteristics 41
definition 41
disadvantages of unnormalized
relations 42, 44
First normalized form
description 43
problems 45
functional dependency 45
Second normalized form
description 45
problems 47
Third normalized form
description 47
NOT keyword 172, 190
NOT NULL WITH DEFAULT
description under DB2 115
limitations for primary key definition
75, 79
NULL
disk storage requirements 73
grouping NULL values in SQL/DS
174, 215
NOT NULL WITH DEFAULT
option 115
NULL values returned by built-in
column functions 197
option in table definition 73

ordering of NULL values 160
test for 173
use for disconnecting validation
routines under DB2 116
use in built-in column functions 197
use in update 237
NULL keyword
inserting NULL values 226
Numeric values
use in WHERE clause 155

O

ON keyword
index creation 108, 136
Operating system
definition 7
OR keyword 170
ORDER BY clause
use within view under SQL/DS 92
Outer-level SELECT 183
OUTFILE keyword
of the UNLOAD DBSPACE
statement 102
of the UNLOAD TABLE statement
101

P

Padding of alphanumeric strings under
DB2 71
PAGE option
see LOCKSIZE keyword
Partitioned table space
table unload 140
PCTFREE keyword
acquiring DBSPACE 100
PCTFREE parameter
index creation under SQL/DS 108
PCTINDEX keyword
acquiring DBSPACE 100
Primary key
concept 40, 60
table creation 75
PRIQTY keyword
index creation under DB2 136
Projection
see relational operators

Q

QMF 108
Quotation mark

see apostrophe
QUIESCE point
see table space set

R

Recovery 52
REFERENCE keyword
see DB2 utility - RUNSTATS
REFERENCES keyword 79
Referential constraint 61
addition 78
deletion 80
Referential integrity 39, 60
Relational data model
characteristics 25
column value 24
definition 24
field value 24
foreign key 40
primary key 40
Referential integrity 39
relational operators see relational
operators
Relational operators
Cartesian product 33
Difference 25, 31
Intersection 25, 29
JOIN 25, 37
Projection 25, 34
SELECT 36
UNION 25, 28
RELOAD DBSPACE statement under
SQL/DS 102
RELOAD TABLE statement under
SQL/DS 101
REPAIR utility
see DB2 utilities
RESTART option of LOAD utility
under DB2 139
RESTRICT keyword
see delete rules 75, 79
Result table 177
combined 177
interim 177
Row 56
Row-id 136

S

SECOND function 210
SECOND(S) duration label 207
SECQTY keyword
  index creation under DB2 136
Security
  physical 10
Segment
  see segmented table space
Segment control block 121
Segmented table space
  advantages 123
  CREATE TABLESPACE
  statement 127
  segment 121
  Segment Control Block 121
  segment size 121
  Space Map Page 121
  table unload 140
SEGSIZE keyword 121
SELECT
  Eliminating duplicate rows 149
  FROM clause 150
  GROUP BY clause 214
  HAVING clause 216
  ORDER BY clause
    DESC keyword 158
    description 158
    ordering in ascending order 158
    ordering in descending order
    158
    ordering NULL values 160
  order of clauses 146
  Selecting all columns "*" 146
  UNION keyword 177
  WHERE clause
    AND keyword 170
    BETWEEN keyword 169
    Boolean operators 170
    comparison operators 157
    description 154
    IN keyword 164
    IS NULL keyword 173
    LIKE keyword 167
    NOT keyword 172
    OR keyword 170
    testing NULL values 173
SET clause 233
SET NULL keyword
  see delete rules 75, 79

SHRLEVEL keyword
  see DB2 utility - RUNSTATS
Simple table space
  table unload 140
Slots
  of storage pools 52
SOME keyword 185
SORT 166
Space map page 121
Special authorities
  DB2
    Data Base Administrator 242
    Data Base Controller 242
    Data Base Maintenance 242
    DBADM 242
    DBCTRL 242
    DBMAINT 242
    SYSADM 241
    SYSOPR 242
    System administrator 241
    System operator 242
  SQL/DS
    SQLDBA 241
Special characters
  apostrophe 155
  parenthesis 172
  percent sign 167
  underscore character 167
Special registers
  CURREN TIME 206
  CURRENT DATE 206
  CURRENT TIMESTAMP 206
SPUFI 138
SQL CONNECT statement 242
SQL/DS catalog tables
  SYSTEM.SYSCATALOG 77, 102,
  110
  SYSTEM.SYSCOLAUTH 249
  SYSTEM.SYSCOLUMNS 77
  SYSTEM.SYSDBSPACES 99, 110
  SYSTEM.SYSINDEXES 102, 106,
  108
  SYSTEM.SYSSYNONYMS 102
  SYSTEM.SYSTABAUTH 77, 102,
  249
  SYSTEM.SYSUSERAUTH 243
  SYSTEM.SYSVIEWS 102
SQL/DS data base machine 50

SQL/DS data type
    CHAR 68
    DATE 69, 205
    DECIMAL 68
    FLOAT 67
    GRAPHIC 69
    inserting data 226
    INTEGER 67
    LONG VARCHAR 69
    LONG VARGRAPHIC 69
    REAL 68
    SMALLINT 67
    TIME 70, 205
    TIMESTAMP 70, 205
    use in WHERE clause 157
    VARCHAR 68
        considerations on use 72
        index considerations 98
        use with index 73
    VARGRAPHIC 69
        index considerations 98
SQL/DS utilities
    DATALOAD 109
    RELOAD 109
    RELOAD DBSPACE 102
    RELOAD TABLE 101
    UNLOAD DBSPACE 102
    UNLOAD TABLE 101
    UPDATE STATISTICS
        use 110
SQLADBEX EXEC 103
SQLADBSP EXEC 95, 99
SQLDBA authority 241
STOGROUP keyword
    index creation under DB2 136
    use in database creation under DB2
    118
    use in STOSPACE DB2 utility 142
Storage group
    creation 117
    default 117
    general overview 55
    overview 116
Storage pool
    description 103
    general overview 52
    increasing storage allocation 103
    nonrecoverable 52
    recoverable 52
Storage techniques 6

STORPOOL keyword
    acquiring DBSPACE 101
STRIP function 201
Structured Query Language 145
SUBPAGES keyword
    index creation under DB2 136
Subquery
    correlated subquery - see correlated
    subquery
    description 182
    limitations of use 189
    use for view creation 87
Subselect
    use in the INSERT statement 230
SUBSTR function 201
SUM function 196
Synonym
    creation 90
    deleting 90
    establish new table names 151
SYSDEFLT
    see default storage group
SYSADM authority 241
SYSOPR authority 242

T
Table
    adding a new column 77
    alternate table name 152
    changing table structure under DB2
    116
    creation 114
    creation under SQL/DS 74
    data type
        see DB2 or SQL/DS data type
    determining number of tables 66
    drop table under SQL/DS 81
    dropping tables under DB2 121
    edit routines under DB2 115
    general overview 52, 56
    joining tables 158
    loading under DB2 138
    loading under SQL/DS 108
    monitoring tables under DB2 140
    size of rows 67
    table name 75, 114
    table shortname 152
    unload under DB2 140
    unload under SQL/DS 101
    validation routines under DB2 115

TABLE option
  see LOCKSIZE keyword
Table space
  disk space requirements 129
  general overview 55
  implicit table space creation under
  DB2 76, 115
  monitoring space utilization 141,
  143
  partitioned table space 124
  segmented table space - see
  segmented table space
  simple tablespaces 119
  size of partitions 126
Table space set
  concept 130
  QUIESCE point 131
  Recovery 131
Table under SQL/DS
  data type
    see SQL/DS data type
TABLESPACE keyword
  see DB2 utility - RUNSTATS
TABLESPACE option
  see LOCKSIZE keyword
Time 70, 205
Time arithmetics 212
TIME function 210
TIMESTAMP 70, 75, 79, 205
Timestamp arithmetics 213
TIMESTAMP function 210
TO keyword
  GRANT statement 242
TRANSLATE function 201
TSO LOGON-ID 150

U
UNION
  see relational operators
UNION keyword
  description 177
  difference between JOIN and
  UNION 179
  use within view 92
UNIQUE keyword
  index creation 108, 136
UNIQUE keyword
  index creation 108, 136
UPDATE statement
  general considerations 237

General format 236
Locking considerations 237
SET clause 233
updating a single row 233
updating multiple rows 233
UPDATE STATISTICS 110
User defined cluster 117, 129
USING keyword
  index creation under DB2 136

V
Validating data under DB2
  see validation routines
Validation routines under DB2 115
  changing routine 116
  deleting disconnecting existing
  routine 116
  disconnecting existing routine 116
VALIDPROC keyword 115
  changing validation routine 116
  table creation under DB2 114
VALUE function 201
VALUES keyword 226
VARCHAR
  disk space requirements for index
  under DB2 136
View
  altering views 92
  creating views 87
  definition 84
  deleting views 90
  establish new table names 151
  general overview 54, 56
  limitations of use 91, 232, 238
VIEW keyword 90
Views
  SQLDBA.SYSUSERLIST 243
VOLUMES keyword
  storage group creation 117
VSAM ESDS 117, 118

W
WHERE clause
  comparison operators 155
  description 154
WHERE keyword
  use in DELETE statement 239
  use in UPDATE statement 233

WITH CHECK OPTION clause
   limitations on Insert 232
   limitations on Update 238

Y

YEAR function 210
YEAR(S) duration label 207